DATE DUE

AP 27 '99			
OV 24 '99			
NO 2 '99			
MY 3 '00			
FE 14 '00			

DEMCO 38-296

Politics and Islam in Contemporary Sudan

R

Politics and Islam in Contemporary Sudan

Abdel Salam Sidahmed

St. Martin's Press
New York

St. Martin's Press, Scholarly and Reference Division,
175 Fifth Avenue, New York, N.Y. 10010

First published in the United States of America in 1996
Printed in Great Britain

ISBN 0–312–16144–1

Library of Congress Cataloging in Publication Data
Sidahmed, Abdel Salam.
Politics and Islam in Contemporary Sudan/Abdel Salam M.
Sidahmed
p. cm.
Includes bibliographical references (p.   ) and index.
ISBN 0–312–16144–1 (cloth)
1. Islam and politics – Sudan. 2. Sudan – Politics and government.
I. Title.
DT157.5.S53   1996
320.962′4 – dc21   96-48414
CIP

To Sahar, Asil and Mazin who bore the brunt of my solitude.

Contents

Contents

NOTE ON TRANSLITERATION

No specialised system of transliteration is being followed in this book. Place names follow the most common spellings. Arabic words and terms are normally italicised without diacritic marks except for the *'ayn* (') and the *hamza* (').

Preface

When Sudan appears in international media, it is mostly on account of its 13 year-long civil war and related disasters. Occasionally, reference is made to the ideological orientation of the present Sudanese regime and its "fundamentalist" leaning. Thus labelled, Sudan is viewed as one among few countries which are supposedly engaged in a process of radical Islamicisation of state and society.

The Sudanese case, however, is rather peculiar because neither its earlier history, nor the present composition of its society necessarily suggests its current image and actual state of affairs. In the first place Sudan was comparatively a late convert to Islam (later even than the Islamised West African societies), and as such had witnessed a different process through which Islam has become associated with its political and ideological discourses. Secondly, there are the reality and complexity of today's Sudan as a multi ethnic, and multi-cultural society with a sizable non-Muslim community. Yet, these historical and sociological considerations notwithstanding, the Sudanese politics (in the past as in the present) has been characterised by its curious fusion with Islamic religion.

The mainstream political parties – National Unionist Party (NUP) and *Umma* party – both of which appeared in the 1940s, were essentially founded on the basis of the influence of the major religious sects, the *Ansar* and *Khatmiyya*, who divide the loyalties of the majority of Sudanese Muslims. After Sudan's independence in 1956, and particularly in the mid-1960s the call and pressure for the adoption of an 'Islamic constitution' became an issue of central political controversy which dominated the politics of the period in question. In the early 1980s the regime of Ja'far Nimeiri (1969–1985) embarked on an Islamicisation experiment (of laws, whereby the Islamic *shari'a* sanctions became incorporated in the penal code), and

Nimeiri attempted to establish himself as a religious, as well as political leader. In 1989, yet another military coup brought an Islamist party, The National Islamic Front (NIF), to power a development that was designed to trigger a full swing of Islamicisation of politics, law and society.

This book approaches its subject through an assessment of the evolution of Sudanese contemporary politics in a chronological order. Due emphasis will be given to assessing the contextual framework of the formation and transformation of the socio-political forces which constitute the major contenders for political power in contemporary Sudan. The rise and development of Islamist politics and ideology, however, remain the central themes.

I am most grateful to the *Society for the Protection of Science and Learning* whose kind grant in 1994 enabled me to devote time and resources for research and writing of parts of this book. My thanks are due also to my friends and colleagues Khalid al-Mubarak and Muhammad Mahmoud who read and commented on some chapters of the manuscript, and to Yohannes Akol, Abdel Salam Hasan, and Ordesse al-Zubair who have kindly shared with me their time and information during my research into certain issues and periods.

Introduction

Throughout its contemporary history, the Sudan has experienced various regimes that have fluctuated between military dictatorial, totalitarian systems and civilian parliamentary ones. The period related to this study covers three parliamentary regimes (from 1953 to 1958, 1965 to 1969, and 1986 to 1989) and three military ones (from 1958 to 1964, 1969 to 1985, and 1989 to the present). In all these governmental systems the 'Islamic factor' figured significantly, either in a latent manner, as in the sectarian loyalties that lent the mainstream parties their power bases, or in an expressed manner as in the various experiments of Islamic constitutions and legislation. The experiments in drafting an 'Islamic constitution' in 1968, and enacting Islamic *shari'a* laws in 1983 and 1991; the execution of a religious reformist leader Mahmud Muhammad Taha in 1985 on charges of apostasy; and the rise of an Islamist party to power (the Islamic National Front) in 1989, are all but conspicuous cases in the above-mentioned process.

The underlining factor behind this process is the controversy surrounding the role of Islam in Sudanese politics and public affairs in general. The debate has been between Islamists who regard the role of Islam as extending beyond individual religious commitments in terms of human-God relationships to regulate and administer society's affairs (human-human relationship); and secularists who, in broad terms, call for a separation between religion and politics. On another level, the debate has also been between Islamists themselves who hold different, sometimes conflicting, views with regard to the nature of a projected Islamic state, and differ also as to the content of Islamic law and its applicability to modern conditions.

A comprehensive scheme of investigation in this debate has to look into the complex relationships among Islam as a religion, Islamism as

1

an ideology and Sudanese society and politics as the contextual framework.

I

In approaching the question of Islamic religion in general it may be useful to start by stating the obvious: Islam is *the* religion which historically appeared in 7th-century Arabia advocated by the Prophet Muhammad Ibn 'Abdallah (570–632/33 AD) and spread from there. Today it represents the religion of the majority in many countries in the Middle East, North Africa and Asia.

Essentially, the basic and most fundamental teachings of Islam are that God is one and there is no god save Him; that Muhammad Ibn 'Abdallah is His messenger; that every Muslim is required to perform five prayers a day and to fast during a particular month – *Ramadan*; to pay the annual *zakat* (alms-in-tax) out of his/her property or regular earnings; and to undertake *hajj* (pilgrimage) to Makka at least once in his/her life if he/she can afford it. These are called the five pillars of Islam. Furthermore, a Muslim is required to believe in God, His messengers, the Holy Scriptures, the Angels, Destiny, and the Day of judgement. As in other religions Islam requires that its adherents observe a strict code of ethics in their personal behaviour and in their conduct with their community, and co-religionists not to lie, steal, drink alcohol or fornicate, and to act kindly and considerately to other members of the community.

Apart from these 'fundamentals' Muslims as individuals, groups of individuals, or societies conceive of and approach Islam in various ways in accordance with differing interpretations, circumstances or times. Historically, basic differences existed between theologians who were more concerned with investigating questions relating to the essence of Islamic belief and faith; the jurists who emphasised the legal framework of the *shari'a* and worked out its detailed application, and philosophers who sought to reconcile the methods of logic and philosophy with the religious Revelation. Other important distinctions occurred between *orthodox* and *Sufist* (mystical) Islam. While the former emphasised the main tenets of Islamic law (the *shari'a*) on the basis of the *Qur'an* (the Holy Scripture), and *Sunnah* (the Tradition of Prophet Muhammad), the latter sought an inner interpretation of the faith and emphasised a mystical relation with God. Other divisions, such as the ones existing between the *Sunnah* and the *Shi'ah*, had their roots in political disputes but were transformed to the religious field. Even within the mainstream *Sunni* Islam there were divisions on the grounds of various interpretations of the *'Qur'an* and the Prophet's tradition, as could be seen in the vast works of jurists in their endeavour to formulate devices for the detailed application of the *shari'a* to daily life. Therefore, although the message of Islam is essentially a singular one, it assumes different forms and manifestations for different groups and societies and at different times and circumstances.

Such a variety of responses to the Islamic message and its different manifestations points to the essential distinction that exists between revelation and the human endeavour, or between the religious ideal and the religious ideology.

The religious ideal stems from the essential injunctions of Islam itself, its basic teachings, regulations and moral values which all aim at creating God abiding and righteous individuals and communities. While the religious ideology is conceived here as the manifestation of either the human interpretation and application of these teachings in worldly matters or the process of legitimising or enhancing human actions by giving them a religious zeal. Furthermore, depending on the spiritual strength of Islam, its ideal in socio-political terms is the belief of devout Muslims that God essentially intends a better and just world for the Islamic *umma*, and if reality is otherwise then reasons are to be sought in the deviation of Muslims from the righteous path.

It is this belief in the existence of a religious ideal and in the possibility of re-enacting it again on earth which constitutes the cornerstone of Islamic ideologies in the past and the present and which inspires the endeavour of various protagonists to achieve a unity between the religious ideal and the realities of human life. Throughout the centuries countless movements, groups and leaders arose with the projected blueprints of restoring the religious ideal. In some cases the undertaking took the form of advocating the necessity and/or the possibility of the appearance of a charismatic figure, such as the infallible *Imam* (leader or head of the community) of the *Shi'ah*, the mystical *mahdi* (righteous or well-guided) of *Sufism*, or the *mujadid* (renovator) of the *Sunnah*. All these charismatic figures were expected to set matters right after a period of decadence and initiate the Islamic community anew in the righteous path.

On another level, the majority of Muslims believe that the Islamic ideal *did* exist during the formative period of Islam, the era of the Prophet and his four 'righteous' successors (*al-khulafa' al-rashidun*). Accordingly if, as is commonly believed, such a unity of faith and reality had indeed existed during the Prophetic state of Medina, then Muslims have a duty to re-establish a similar state on the earth. This is the same view which informs and inspires Islamism as a 20th century Islamic ideology, variety of movements and manifestations notwithstanding.

Islamism as a movement of political activism may be traced to the foundation in 1928 of the Muslim Brotherhood organisation – *harakat al-ikhwan al-muslimun* – by Hasan al-Banna (1906–49) in Egypt. The movement soon grew into a multinational movement with branches or counterparts in many Arabic-speaking countries. Abu al-A'ala al-Maududi of Pakistan (d.1977) who initiated a similar movement in the Indian subcontinent, was one of the most influential articulators and ideologues of contemporary Islamism. Ayatollah al-Khumayni (d.1989), the leader of the Iranian revolution, endowed Islamism with charismatic leadership and an emphatic revolutionary zeal. The main objective of Islamism is primarily the establishment of an Islamic state or *order* along the lines of the prophetic model, that is, the re-enactment of the Islamic ideal. Islamism, however, operates in a completely different framework from the revivalist movements of Islamic history.

The prime connection in today's realities is the predominance of European civilisation and its associated systems. The rise of Europe confronted the Islamic world first as a challenge in the 18th and 19th centuries, then as outright colonial domination in the 19th and 20th centuries, and subsequently as the continued hegemony of the European/Western secular ideologies, and their economic and military powers. Within this framework the blueprints of contemporary Islamists vary between a rejectionist attitude, which holds that authentic Muslims must reject today's godless world and work for the establishment of a spiritually inspired and *shari'a* regulated one, and a realist school, which purports to strike a compromise between the injunctions of the Islamic faith and today's realities.

Variety of concepts and trends apart, the Islamist projects generally evolve around the centrality of the *shari'a* and the necessity of its enactment in the body of the laws of Muslim societies. For the Islamists the significance of the *shari'a* stems in the first place from the argument that Muslims have a *religious* duty to organise their life in accordance with the *shari'a*. Secondly, the enforcement of the *shari'a* is advanced as an act of liberation: by rejecting the 'colonially imposed' secular laws Muslims liberate themselves from the hegemony of Western culture and re-assert their own cultural authenticity.

4

Therefore, the controversy surrounding the interrelationship between Islam and politics has gradually come to focus on the centrality of the *shari'a* and its practical or symbolic implications. That said, the particularities of each society, its internal dynamics and external influences, and the respective inputs of the forces in action tend to shape the nature and form of the debate around Islam and politics.

II

The particularity of the Sudanese situation stems from two considerations: (a) in the Sudan the process through which Islam had become associated with its politics and ideology greatly differs from other countries in the Middle east and North Africa, (b) the reality and complexity of today's Sudan as a multi-ethnic, multi-cultural, and multi-religious society with a sizeable non-Muslim community.

The Sudan had not been part of the classical Islamic Order (*c.* 622–1258), or of the Ottoman Empire (*c.* 1400–1924). The Northern and Western parts of present-day Sudan became Arabised and Islamised through a lengthy process of missionary activities, commercial contacts, demographic movements and large-scale acculturation. During the 16th and 17th centuries certain political systems arose with nominal allegiance to Islam; such as the Funj Sultanate of Sinnar (*c.* 1500–1821 AD) which dominated much of the Sudanese Nile Valley, and the Fur Sultanate of Darfur (ca 1600–1916 AD.) which dominated much of today's Western Sudan. Although both structures were essentially based on pre-Islamic political and ideological institutions, their nominal allegiance to Islam together with a host of complex of socio-economic and political changes had led to an accelerated Islamisation and rapid acculturation (adoption of Arabic-Islamic culture) of Northern and Western Sudan. The process, which evolved over three centuries, reached maturity in the 18th and 19th centuries. Although both traditions of Islamic orthodoxy – *Sunni*, and mysticism – *Sufi* were introduced in the Sudan, the latter became predominant as it suited better the simple nature of Sudanese society. On another level, Islam gradually became integrated into the spheres of politics and ideology alongside other affinities such as kinship and tribalism.

In 1820/21 a 'Turko-Egyptian' army invaded the Sudan, supplanted the Sultanates and established a regime which dominated approximately the area of present-day Sudan.

Under the Turko-Egyptian regime (1821–85), Islamic laws and

5

orthodox education made substantial headway in Northern Sudan. Sufism, however, remained the vocal and predominant force in the country. Two developments in relation to Sufism, and with important future implications, occurred during this era; namely, the introduction of the *Khatmiyya tariqa* (Brotherhood or sect) in the Sudan, and the rise of *Mahdism*.

The *Khatmiyya tariqa* was introduced by its founder, Muhammad 'Uthman al-Mirghani, in 1818–20. It spread through the efforts of his descendants in Northern and Eastern Sudan and became a proto-national sect of considerable influence.

Likewise Mahdism arose out of the Sufi tradition. Muhammad Ahmad (1843–85), a disciple of the *Sammaniyya tariqa*, declared himself a *mahdi* (well-guided or righteous), staged an armed resistance against the Turko-Egyptian regime, ousted it and established a Mahdist state in the Sudan (1885–98). Despite its success in ousting a colonial power, the Mahdist coalition soon disintegrated after the victory of the revolution. Under al-Mahdi's successor Khalifa 'Abdallahi al-T'ayyshi, geo-political divisions, conflicting interests, and power struggles became the most conspicuous feature of the Mahdist state. Consequently, the latter became less a reflection of the Mahdist revolution than the outcome of the power struggle that ravaged the Mahdist coalition after the demise of its founder and charismatic leader Muhammad Ahmad al-Mahdi.

The legacy of Mahdism therefore is twofold: the legacy of revolutionary zeal and Islamic activism of the Mahdist revolution; and the legacy of the Mahdist state of divisions and bitter power struggles. While the former constituted a strong source of inspiration for contemporary Sudanese leaders (Islamists and non-Islamists alike), the latter has resulted in divided loyalties as manifested in 20th-century sectarianism which developed under the Anglo-Egyptian colonial regime (1898–1956).

The colonial administration introduced modern and secular systems in the fields of law, education and administration. However, for its sustained survival and continuity, the colonial regime found it expedient to seek the support of traditional leaders and structures, such as the tribal, but more crucially the religious leaders. Consequently, material and social benefits were extended to these leaders in return of their loyalty and that of their followers. This process, among other things, resulted in the rise of what came to be known as 'sectarianism'. Sectarianism arose on the foundations of established religious support on the one hand, and on the support and

6

encouragement of the colonial state on the other. Prominent among the sectarian leaders were the Mirghanists, descendants of Muhammad 'Uthman al-Mirghani who head the *Khatmiyya tariqa*, and the Mahdists, descendants of al-Mahdi's and leaders of his followers, the *Ansar*.

Thus, the particular version of 'Sudanese' Islam known widely as popular Islam, had, under certain circumstances, given birth to a Messianic movement: the *Mahdiyya*. In its turn the legacy of the Mahdist movement coupled with the tradition of popular Islam, was transformed into sectarianism under the colonial regime and in response to the policies of the latter. Sectarian loyalties then became the basis of political support for the mainstream political parties when these were founded during the 1940s.

Modern Islamism appeared in the Sudan with the rise of the Muslim Brotherhood in the 1950s – renamed the Islamic Charter Front in 1960s, and the National Islamic Front in the 1980s – and its projected vision of an Islamic state. Throughout Sudan's contemporary history, the Islamist movement has been at the centre of the Islamicisation controversy. Indeed, the debate itself was triggered in the first place by the Islamists' campaigns for the enforcement of an Islamic constitution and Islamic legislation.

III

The debate around Islam and politics in the Sudan involved three main realms: legal, political and ideological.

The legal aspect concerned *shari'a* law and its applicability to the Sudan. This involves two questions: a) the substance of *shari'a* law; and b) its practical implications. As far as the substance of the law is concerned there is a measure of vagueness in what exactly is meant by *shari'a* in practical terms since there is no codified law as such. The only certainty relates to criminal justices where there are specific penalties and regulations covering a number of offences and crimes. There are also provisions for the definition of these offences and the evidence for them.

In *shari'a* criminal justice there are three categories of penalties:

– *al-hudud* which cover the offences of *shurb al-khamr* (drinking of alcohol); *al-zinna* (fornication); *al-sariqah* (theft); *qazf* (false accusation/defamation); *al-haraba* (highway robbery and rebellion); *riddah* (apostasy).

7

- *al-qassas*, retribution, covering murder or bodily harm injuries;
- *al-ta'azir* which cover any offence that may not be classified under *hudud* or *qassas* either by its very nature or for lack of sufficient evidence. This area relates primarily to the discretional authority of the judge.

Once *shari'a* criminal justice has been proposed or enforced it raises questions on different levels, such as the controversy over the number of *hudud* penalties, the kind of *ijtihad* needed, the discretional authority of the judge, and crucially, who should be entrusted with the authoritative interpretation of *shari'a* sources. Another class of questions evolves around the timing of *hudud* enforcement and whether it should be applied in a society characterised by misery and social injustices or whether it is intended to lead to a prosperous society. A third class of questions raises the all-important issue of rights. What will be the situation of non-Muslims under a society regulated by *shari'a* law, or an Islamic constitution? Would they be relegated to a status of second class-citizens? If not, then what are the guarantees for the protection of their rights? Would a non-Muslim aspire to become a president under an Islamic constitution? Would a woman or a non-Muslim become a judge under *shari'a*? These questions are particularly relevant in the Sudanese situation where there are both Muslims and non-Muslims.

In the political sphere, as pointed out earlier, the introduction of Islamicisation has assumed centre-stage in Sudanese contemporary affairs and in the subject of debates around the role of the *shari'a* or the nature of the constitution. As such the Islamicisation issue has become the focus of alliances and polarisations at opposite extremes: Islamists and secularists. It was in this framework that the civil war in the Sudan, which broke between the north and the south on the eve of independence and continued for the best part of the country's independent history, came to assume its 'popular' image of a war between the Muslim north and Christian and animist south. The reality is far more complex.

Ideologically, the debate involved once again conflicting blueprints and visions for the future of the Sudan, focusing on Islamist or secular platforms. It is here that Islamist ideology and its projected blueprints become a focus of attention and controversy. The process involves questions relating to the projected Islamist visions of an Islamic state or order. It also involves conflicting visions regarding questions such as the Sudanese identity; that is, whether the Sudan is to be perceived in terms of an African, Arabic/Islamic, or Afro-Arab ientity. At the heart of the debate is again the question of citizens rights and whether an Islamic state could ensure the unity of a multi-religious society like the Sudanese one. On the other hand, the main contention of Islamist ideology is that Muslims have a duty to live in accordance with the requirements of their faith, and that as the country's *majority* they have the right to enforce the system that guarantees such harmony between faith and life.

The following chapters are not claiming to provide answers to these questions or their comprehensive investigation, but rather to map out the Sudanese context in which these and other related questions are raised and addressed by various forces. The level of assessment is primarily concerned with macro politics, that is, what happened or is happening at the centre of power and the input of the main actors in the scene. The study follows a chronological order that covers the entire post-independence period and includes a background to the colonial era.

Chapter 1

Background: The Impact of the Condominium

I. AN OVERVIEW

Towards the close of the nineteenth century an 'Anglo Egyptian' army overran and occupied the Sudan, which was then under the 'Mahdist state' (1885–98). The colonial rule that supplanted the latter came to be known as the 'Condominium regime' indicating that the Sudan was to be ruled jointly by both Britain and Egypt, and legalised as such by an Anglo-Egyptian Agreement which was signed on 19 January 1899.

Under the Condominium regime, which lasted from 1898 to 1956, the Sudan underwent a radical economic and socio-political transformation, the impact of which outlived the period in question. Indeed it was these transformations that formed the genesis and background of contemporary Sudanese politics and society, (that is post-colonial Sudan).

A significant determinant in these transformations was the mechanisms set in motion as a result of the colonial state's policies and ventures in the various administrative, economic, social and political spheres. In their turn these mechanisms created new social forces and transformed previous ones, both of which subsequently contributed to the shaping and reshaping of the contemporary Sudan.

The primacy of the colonial state in the transformation processes of 20th-century Sudan stemmed from its total destruction of the Mahdist state on the one hand, and its restructuring of Sudanese society under the auspices of the British imperial designs on the other. However, to appreciate the dynamics of the colonial state, a word on 'the condominium' and its nature is necessary.[1]

The condominium status of the colonial regime over the Sudan meant that the latter was neither a British colony nor an Egyptian one. It was supposedly a joint enterprise of both. Yet, the Anglo-Egyptian 'partnership' over the Sudan was mostly fictional as Egypt itself had been under British domination since 1882. In practice, the British retained effective control over the Sudan while Egypt paid the expenses and supplied occupants of junior administrative posts as well as some military detachments.

The Condominium Agreement had left out the all-important issue of the *de jure* sovereignty over the Sudan. Thus, when Egypt was granted her superficial independence in 1922 the Sudan question became the most contentious issue in Anglo-Egyptian relations.

The structure of the condominium administration in the Sudan was embodied in the 'Sudan Government' which was headed by a Governor-General, who was to be nominated by Britain and appointed by the Khedive of Egypt. All the Governors-General of the Sudan (1899–1956) were British, and so were all the senior officials of the Sudan Government. The Governor-General headed an administrative body known as the Sudan Political Service (SPS) which was charged with the entire affairs of the country. The SPS was a structure unique in the British colonies as it was composed of officials specifically recruited for service in the Sudan.[2]

For all practical purposes the Sudan government was meant to be an autonomous body, as may be discerned from the British government decision to place it under the jurisdiction of the Foreign and not the Colonial Office. This autonomy was further enhanced by a number of factors, chief among which was that neither of the condominion powers was in a position to exercise direct control over the Sudan. The growth of the legendary SPS has undoubtedly cemented that autonomy.

Thus the affairs of the colonial Sudan were virtually left to the discretion of the Sudan government which, in time, had effectively emerged as a separate centre of power on a par with both London and Cairo, curiously emulating the structure of an independent government administering the affairs of a colony.

None the less, the Sudan government did not enjoy unlimited freedom of action, as might be perceived from the above characterisation. In the first place, it had to look constantly over its shoulder for the reactions from Cairo and London. If the claims of the former to have its 'rightful' share in the colony's administration were to be deferred; the support and backing of the latter was needed more often than not. Secondly, there was the question of finances. The Sudan government's finances were as unique as the Condominium arrangement itself. Basically, it was the Egyptian government which was supplying the budget of the Sudan government in its entirety (including the British officials' salaries) until 1913. Subsequently, an annual Egyptian 'subvention' continued to support the Sudan budget until the1940s. On the other hand, the only contribution by the British government to Sudan finances was to guarantee one or two loans in connection with the implementation of the Gazira cotton plantation scheme.[3] Egypt's financial burden did not endow it with any control over the Sudan, but only helped to further the internationalisation of the latter's domestic affairs.

The Sudan government, nevertheless, was left with ample room for action; and, accordingly, remained the primary actor in the Sudan's affairs during the period in question. Yet, owing to the *de jure* Condominium status of the Sudan, its financial constraints, and a potentially rebellious society (the Mahdist legacy), the colonial state had to steer cautiously.

In consequence the overall policies of the Sudan government were a combination of innovation and conservation. Innovative measures, that is in administrative, economic and educational fields, as well as conservation of previous structures, frameworks, and modes of living and their integration into the colonial order.

The first innovation was the establishment of a 'modern' system of administration which, by the mid-1920s, has grown into a fully bureaucratised and professional civilian administration. These administrative structures were accompanied by a set of laws and legislation drawn mainly from European and Indian 'secular' traditions. Primarily, these laws provided for administrative establishments and regulations, economic measures and policies, education and security.

Requirement of effective administration and political security necessitated the development of a modern system of education with the aim of producing 'a class of clerks and artisans to man the junior levels of administration'. Thus, the Gordon Memorial College was opened in 1902 comprising of elementary, intermediate, industrial and vocational schools. In 1904 its curricula was extended to include an ordinary secondary school with a general education, and a small engineering school. Two primary schools were opened in Umdurman and Khartoum, as well as a primary teachers' training college, and a military school for training prospective Sudanese officers.[4]

Furthermore, for purposes of effective control of the country and better utilisation of its resources, the colonial state developed a network of transport and communication. Thus the railway line which was introduced first in the country during the conquest process to facilitate the invasion was extended to connect the various regions with the capital city and a sea port (a new port – Port Sudan – was built in 1906). This network facilitated import-export activities and enhanced domestic commerce and security.

An important area of the colonial state's innovation was in the economic field. Apart from the conventional colonial economic objectives of obtaining raw materials and securing an uncontested market for British manufactured goods, the Sudan government was also keen on expanding and maintaining a regular revenue for its budget.

As the country's potential was considered to lay primarily in agriculture on which the most of its population was dependent, the land question was to be addressed first. Hence between 1900 and 1925, the land tenure was tackled by a series of ordinances which vigorously revised the extant systems. The laws recognised three types of land holdings (government, tribal/village and private). Conspicuously, they prescribed that 'all waste, forest, unoccupied and unregistered land shall be deemed to be the property of the government until the contrary is proved'. Accordingly, out of a total of 596.5 million *feddans*, only 6 million were recognised as privately owned; the rest became government property.[5]

Other legislation in the economic field, required that private investors obtain licences for their activities in the fields of trade, agriculture and industry. Thus, by its monopoly of economic rights, the colonial state laid for itself the foundations of both initiative and tight control over this important field. Such a situation enabled the colonial state to reorient and restructure the economy in pursuit of its aforementioned goals. At this level of innovation a number of economic ventures geared towards market-oriented production, both exports and internal, were sponsored or encouraged.

The biggest and most important venture of the Sudan government was the Gazira scheme. On its inception in 1925, the scheme covered an initial area of 240,000 *feddans*. It was based on a system of crop sharing between the farmer, the government and the Sudan Plantation Syndicate – the company which implemented the scheme. The latter's share was bought in 1951 by the Sudan government.[6] Similar schemes, mostly modelled on the Gazira pattern, were also launched in other parts of the Sudan.

The government also introduced modern techniques in the field of irrigation and plantation to enhance private agricultural ventures. Significant among these was the introduction, of pump irrigation

13

along the Nile valley (Northern, Khartoum, and the Blue Nile provinces) for the growth of cotton and other crops. Later, during and after the Second World War, mechanised farming was introduced in the eastern and central rainlands.

Limited industry grew primarily in connection with the export commodities, such as ginning factories for processing of raw cotton and oil seed pressing.

It appears that all the innovative structures and techniques were dictated by necessity and utility. Moreover, progress depended on whether the Sudan government could raise the necessary funds or not. Other considerations related to the pursuit of complementary ventures, expansion, improvements, and repairs and on the impact of two world wars, and the servicing of a growing export-import sector.

The significance of these innovations – whether modern techniques or systems – was on the consequential impact on Sudan's economic and social structures. No matter how limited they were, once established, the innovative structures were bound to bring remarkable changes.

Yet, in considerations of political sensitivity or expediency, utility, economy, conservative outlook, or pragmatism, the Sudan government was by no means a radical innovator. As pointed out above, several structures, frameworks and activities were preserved intact or converted to form an integral part of the new colonial order.

By and large, the colonial state adopted a very cautious attitude towards Islamic religion (the religion of the majority in Northern Sudan). Thus in the field of education the traditional (religious) *khalwa* education continued throughout northern Sudan, and so did the Islamic *shari'a* law. The latter, however, was confined to the sphere of 'personal affairs' matters (such as marriages divorces and inheritance). To this effect special courts were allocated, and the training of orthodox *'ulama'*, *qadis* and *muftis* (jurists, judges and interpreters respectively) was pursued under the auspices of the state.[7]

In the administrative field, the colonial state sustained the authority of the tribal chieftains and eventually integrated it within a system of *indirect rule* known as the 'native administration'.[8]

Another area of the colonial state's conservatism was its attitude to slavery. The institution of slavery was widespread in the pre-colonial Sudan to the extent that slave labour formed an essential part of agricultural and household work in Northern Sudan. Despite the Sudan government's decision to outlaw slavery from the outset, it tolerated the institution for about three decades for fear of antagonising the slave masters and/or disrupting agricultural production. The implications of the continuity of slavery in 20th century Sudan were tremendous for both social and economic reasons. Slavery had helped to entrench imbalances and to sustain racial divisions and racism.

In the economic field, the Sudan government from the outset did not allow any European settlement or large-scale foreign purchase of land as was common in other colonies. Furthermore, the Sudan government adopted an unsympathetic attitude to private, particularly foreign, investment. Hence, any substantial economic development or ventures had to come from the colonial state. The latter, as can be seen was extremely utilitarian and conservative in its economic endeavours, and innovations in this field remained conspicuously limited. Few innovations in the economic field meant that the majority of the population continued to pursue their self same traditional, often subsistence activities, in agriculture and pastoralism.

On another level, however, the colonial state had, both by design and implication, set the pattern of integrating certain traditionally produced commodities in the international market. Products such as gum, livestock, and oil seeds entered the export market through a chain of brokers and traders who connected the producers with the export companies. These producers, however, entered the international market without altering their types of production or even patterns of living.[9]

One of the Sudan regions that was conspicuous by the lack of any significant colonial economic or social innovations was the South. Apart from establishing essential administration with emphasis on 'law and order' (which took some time to materialise), and opening the region to Christian missionary activities; the Sudan government was happy to 'preserve' the Southern Sudan almost intact in all aspects of life. Matters of education and health were left completely in the hands of the missionaries. The only substantial intervention by the colonial state was its policy of effectively separating the South from the North for fear of the latter influencing the former. That policy became official in 1930 when the Sudan government worked out a 'Southern policy' under which the South was declared a 'closed district' for Northerners. Southern Sudan was supposed to follow a separate course of development from the North. In reality, no development of whatever sort was followed in the region until late in the Condominium era.[10]

The dynamics by which the Sudan government opted for conservation rather than innovation varied with different fields and motivations. Yet, two patterns may be discerned both chronologically and organically.

During the first two decades of the colonial regime the Sudan government was primarily concerned with control, security and pacification. Accordingly, the administration was strongly militarised and centralised. Radical innovations were neither desirable for fear of the consequences, nor possible for lack of human and material resources.

The transition of the colonial administration into a more professional and civilian one after the First World War was to have been followed with greater involvement of the educated Sudanese in the administration in place of the 'Egyptians'. However, a rebellion in 1924, which had mainly involved and was led by the educated elements, cultivated extreme revulsion in the Sudan government. Thenceforth, and for a decade to follow, the colonial state acted on the premise that the new 'class' of educated Sudanese, the *'affendiyya* (affendi = government employee) were not to be trusted at all. Hence, expansion of modern education all but stopped, while religious (*khalwa*) education was encouraged. Native administration was feverishly pursued as a more prudent course of action, and so was the 'Southern policy'.[11]

The third pattern is to be found in the outlook of the long-serving and extremely powerful officials of the SPS. A romantic affection for the rural Sudan and the Sudanese matched only with an extremely disdainful attitude to the *'affendi* class and the urban Sudanese at large. This outlook, which came staunchly in favour of 'preserving' the *natural* Sudan, might partially explain the colonial state's extreme conservatism in the economic field. This, however, must be compounded by the more substantial factor of the colonial state's monopoly of economic initiative, a matter that had inadvertently left the question of economic development captive to fiscal considerations and the will of an often unimaginative, or reluctant, bureaucracy.[12]

The social order that evolved under the colonial regime, therefore, bore a cognitive combination of the latter's designs of innovation and preservation. The question that poses itself here is: how did the preserved structures interact with the innovative ones and vice versa? Essentially, the colonial order represented an important mark of discontinuity in Sudanese history. Its innovative measures and structures constituted important dynamics of change in the Sudanese economy and society with significant implications.

Through establishment of modern economic ventures, introduction of new techniques in irrigation and plantations, enhancement of its export-import sector and integration in the international market, introduction of modern education, new administrative methods and so forth, Sudanese society was subjected to lasting changes and transformations that were bound to affect its subsequent development.

New types of urban centres grew around administrative towns and economic schemes (such as Khartoum, Khartoum North, 'Atbra, Wad Madani, al-Ubeyyid), to become centres of commerce and manufacture (the latter quite limited), magnets of migrant labour, seats of education and culture, and centres of modernisation. Introduction of mechanised transport and farming and their related mechanical works had undoubtedly induced a qualitative growth of the craft industry which flourished in the new urban centres. Better communication and security enhanced internal trade and commerce, and so did the intensification of a cash economy. In a word, the innovative processes of the colonial state set the pattern of restructuring the Sudanese society on new lines and grounds.

Yet, the conservative and utilitarian approach of the colonial state had confined the process of innovation and change to few urban enclaves (the most outstanding of which being the Khartoum-Gazira triangle) a factor which curtailed a more radical transformation of society as a whole. Such a situation was manifested best in the continuity of most of the pre-colonial 'traditional' structures and systems in juxtaposition with the new 'modern' ones. Although the latter with its inherent dynamism was potentially capable of growing at the expense of the former, the formula had primarily produced a deficient structure.

The economy which emerged under the Condominium era was still dominated by traditional, subsistence, production with about 80% of the country's population enclosed in this sector as peasants and pastoralists. The country was dangerously dependent on foreign trade, a fact that made it extremely vulnerable to fluctuations of prices of the main exports such as cotton. Furthermore, as the colonial state was primarily interested in marketing British manufactured goods there was no domestic industrial development except in the limited fields of processing of certain export items.

The standard of living even in the 'modern' sector was very low, especially for unskilled and semi-skilled workers in government service or private business, and the average returns of the tenant farmers were mostly so low that the individuals concerned were barely living above subsistence levels.[13] Such a situation had literally put all the new techniques of production brought about by the colonial system beyond the reach of the majority of the population.

On the other hand, the colonial economic system opened chances for capital accumulation and reinvestment in such fields as agriculture (pump schemes and mechanised farming), trade (both internal and external), and industry (basically edible oïl and occasional manufactures during the Second World War).

Thus, as much as the colonial order preserved traditional economic and social structures and activities with almost the same modes of subsistence livelihood, it also created new chances of investment, new imbalances, and, partially, reproduced the pre-colonial social stratification in a new form. This brings us to a theme that might summarise the impact of the colonial order namely, the social forces that emerged under the Condominium.

When the Condominium regime was established there was neither an aristocracy nor a power elite, the Mahdist elite being effectively destroyed; nor was there another 'elite' that combined both political and economic power. However, there were a number of religious and tribal 'notables' with remarkable influence over substantial sectors of the society. Furthermore, in each and every sedentary area (a town, village or group of villages) there were some 'respectable merchants'. The rest of the population, the majority, were engaged in largely subsistence activities as farmers, pastoralists or craftsmen.

The aforementioned mechanisms of colonial innovation and conservation/integration and their related dynamics set the pattern for the emergence of new forces and the transformation of old ones.

Thus, new forces made their first ever appearance in connection with the colonial innovative structures like the intelligentsia (or *'affendiyya*) who appeared in connection with the colonial educational and administrative systems, and the tenant farmers and urban workers who appeared in association with the colonial agricultural and industrial ventures. The forces that existed prior to the Condominium era, such as the religious and tribal leaders, the merchants (traders), peasants and pastoralists, were subjected to significant influences and transformations.[14]

The patterns through which those forces coped with and reacted to their new positions and the circumstances surrounding them differed. The 'traditional elite' – religious and tribal leaders – were able both to retain the loyalty of their followers and benefit from the new opportunities of investment created by the colonial order. Thus, they were the pioneers in 'modern' agricultural, commercial and ultimately, industrial investment. Accordingly, they formed the core of the economic elite that emerged under the Condominium. Other groups that joined this emergent economic elite were the upper strata of the merchants who entered new fields of investment that fell outside traditional commercial activity such as pump schemes, mechanised farming and manufacturing.

On the other hand, the peasants and nomads who continued to pledge loyalty to their religious and/or tribal chieftains, were forced to fend for themselves in order to meet their new obligations of taxes, or to pay for some of the materials they desired. Accordingly they took part-time work as agricultural labourers in the new urban areas. The days in which the tribe or religious order could afford to run their own 'social security' system for their less fortunate members were gone.

The modern elite – the intelligentsia – occupied a highly respectable place as literate members in a virtually illiterate society. More specifically, some of their higher strata – the senior civil servants, army officers and professionals – were eventually able to join the economic elite mainly through utilisation of their prestigious and strategic positions. However, the majority of both tenant farmers and urban workers were not in a similar advantageous position. Their modest earnings were often strained by the additional demands imposed on them by government taxes and the growing requirements of a changing society. The urban workers were exposed to new experiences of socialisation in the new workers' towns and quarters in 'Atbara, Khartoum North and the Gazira. None the less, the majority of urban workers retained a vague loyalty to their home villages/or regions as well as their religious affinities. The tenant farmers, however, despite their increased contact with mechanised farming, more scientific methods of agriculture, and better social services, retained their self-same life-styles almost intact, retained as well as their religious (sometimes tribal) loyalties. Both workers and tenant farmers, however, eventually turned to collective bargaining as the only option available to them to improve their living conditions.

How did the emergent social forces react to the presence and continuity of the colonial rule? Again, responses differed with the different forces in question. At an impressionist level it may be observed that some forces assumed a collaborative attitude to the colonial state, while others adopted a rejectionist one. Certain groups took to collective and modern methods of organisation and mobilisation, others followed traditional and personified channels, and so forth.

This variety of actions and reactions was informed by several conditions and correlations, some of which were inherent in the socio-economic structure that grew under the colonial regime, while others related to the intrinsic characteristics of the respective social groups. Therefore, an analysis of each and every group to identify its input in the politics of the period is both problematic and unwarranted as far as this study is concerned.

Two forces, however, are to be singled out for closer examination, namely the intelligentsia, or *'affendiyya*, and the religious (sectarian) leaders, or sectarianism. Eventually, it was these two forces that figured prominently in the nationalist movement and political parties that led the Sudan to independence. To set the scene, however, a general outline of the nationalist movement is necessary.

II. THE NATIONALIST MOVEMENT

The term 'nationalist' is employed here rather conventionally for lack of a satisfactory alternative. It does not necessarily presuppose the existence of an adequate and articulated nationalist 'idea' or the prevalence of a cohesive Sudanese nation. Yet, rather than juggling with concepts and terminology, this study departs from the common understanding that nationalist ideas and ideals in Asia and Africa had primarily grown out of the anti-colonial domination in these regions.

The commonest pattern of anti-colonial struggle in these societies passed through three main phases: the first being the initial or primary resistance to the imperial subjugation either at the time of the conquest or in the course of the consolidation of the colonial authority, or both. This phase signifies the preliminary confrontation between the alien invaders and the natives wherein the former usually prevail, mostly, due to their superior military machine.

The second phase corresponds to the period in which the subjects of the colonies at large gradually come to terms with 'colonial order' and go on to pursue their day-to-day affairs within the boundaries set by colonial authorities, outbursts of resentment or rebellion notwithstanding. By then the changes and transformations brought about by the colonial domination would have taken hold.

The third phase signals the gradual development of a movement with articulated demands (self-determination, for example) which eventually succeeds in ending the colonial domination. Such movements were born, more often than not, from the very institutions and structures that the colonialists had established. It is with those movements that the term 'nationalism' is usually associated.

The Sudanese case followed more or less the same pattern. Yet, the Sudanese situation might have some particularity owing to the legacies and influences of the 19th-century Mahdism. The Mahdist legacy was a dual one: a revolution and liberation heritage embroiled in religious discourse and legitimation; and a state construction punctuated by sharp divisions, disputes and power struggles which cultivated historic enmities. This twofold legacy was bound to influence both the policies of the British administration and the politics of the nationalist movement.

The Anglo-Egyptian army conquered the country amidst bitter fighting, and spent another year before the remnants of the Mahdist armies were finally routed. The first two decades of the Condominium administration witnessed a number of petty revolts normally expressed in religious and/or tribal terms. Furthermore, it took the colonial state more then two decades to finally overcome the 'primary' resistance in the south and other remote areas.[15] However, from the 1920s onwards new and more sophisticated forms of resistance appeared with the intelligentsia as its focal point. The first occasion in this process was the 'Revolt' of 1924.[16]

The Revolt was preceded by the establishment, for the first time, of two non-religious non-tribal organisations, the Sudanese Union Society (SUS) and the White Flag League (WFL), in 1920 and 1924 respectively. The founding members of (SUS) were graduates of either Gordon Memorial College or the military school, and mostly employees in government service as junior administers or officers. The establishment of the WFL by breakaways from SUS signalled a process of more militancy as demonstrated by the events of 1924. Obviously, the leaders of the WFL were greatly influenced by the Egyptian nationalist Revolution of 1919. They called for British withdrawal from both Egypt and the Sudan and called for the *Unity of the Nile Valley.*

By virtue of its representation and demands, the WFL movement found itself at odds with the religious and tribal leaders. The latter favoured, instead of the 'hybrid' formula of condominium, an outright British rule until the Sudanese were in a position to govern themselves by themselves.

The year 1924 was dominated by the activities of the WFL in the form of demonstrations and other protest actions that engulfed most of the country's major towns and was even joined by the cadets of the military school. Consequently, the colonial authorities arrested and imprisoned all the prominent leaders of the League. Finally, on 27 November 1924, three 'platoons' of the 11th Sudanese Battalion rebelled and took to arms at the forced evacuation of the Egyptian troops and clashed with the British forces in a pitched battle near the Blue Nile bridge in Khartoum. However, the British forces easily put down the revolt. Whether the rebel officers and men of the 11th Battalion were acting as an integral part of the WFL is questionable. Yet, their actions were, directly or indirectly, inspired by the agitative activities of the league and its leaders with whom they had a lot in common. In any event, the violent confrontation of November between the Sudanese rebel forces and the British had brought the revolt of 1924 to an end. Its leaders either died in battle, were executed, or were imprisoned. Some were sent into exile.

The main cause of the revolt's failure was the lack of mass support. The membership and supporters of the WFL were confined only to some urban centres and a few groups of the intelligentsia. The religious leaders, who were from the outset opposed to the movement, 'succeeded in neutralising their followers and even in making them hostile to the League'.[17]

Following the fatal suppression of the 1924 Revolt a period of decadence and political stagnation ensued. The intelligentsia, who were the prime movers of the 1924 events, resigned in disappointment and apprehension and busied themselves with their 'graduates' clubs and literary activities (the first graduate club was founded in 1918 in Umdurman).

The 1930s, however, brought some changes to this gloomy atmosphere. In 1931 a reduction of salaries especially for the fresh graduates of the College was met by immediate rejection from the students who went on a strike. The significance of this event is that it had restated the confidence of the intelligentsia in themselves and their possibility of collective action.

In 1938 a 'Graduates General Congress' was established by the graduates of Gordon Memorial College and intermediate schools, most of which were in government service. The founding meeting was attended by about 1080 graduates out of a total of about 5000. In view of the 1936 Anglo-Egyptian Treaty, which ignored the Sudanese and their opinions, the Congress was looked upon by its founders as a forum through which they could represent the Sudanese at large.[18]

The congress received a conditional recognition from the authorities, and got an enthusiastic welcome from the enlightened sectors of the public as well. As long as the congress pursued social and educational matters it maintained its internal cohesion and remained on good terms with the colonial authorities. Yet in 1942, in view of the changing situations resulting from the Second World War, internal pressures and other considerations, the Congress executive took a clear political step and tabled a memorandum to the Sudan government demanding self-determination for the Sudan. This action, and the rebuff of the colonial authorities who questioned the right of the congress to speak on behalf of the Sudanese people, split the congress on the issue of the appropriate future action. This split actually spelled out the demise of the General Graduates' Congress which by 1945 had given way to the newly born political parties to take over the leadership of the nationalist movement each in its own conception.

Thus an *Umma* (nation or community) party appeared in 1945 under the slogan: 'Sudan for the Sudanese', backed by the *Ansar* sect and led by the Mahdi's family. On the other hand, an *'Ashiqqa'* (blood brothers) party had been organised in 1944 under the slogan: 'unity of the Nile Valley', and was backed by the *Khatmiyya* sect. Both parties eventually emerged as the mainstream parties of Sudanese politics. Both were – still are – organised and led by the intelligentsia, and supported by sectarian leaders and their following. It is to the examination of these two forces, sectarianism and the intelligentsia, that we now turn.

The Rise of Sectarianism

A sect is defined as 'a group of people that has separated from a larger group and has a particular set of religious or political beliefs, especially when these beliefs are strongly held or regarded by others as extreme'.[19] However, students of Sudanese history and politics often use the term 'sect' and sectarian to denote the involvement of those *sufi* orders of a proto-national character in Sudanese politics of the 20th century. The present study adopts the same understanding. Accordingly, emphasis is laid on the political rather than religious discourses of the sects in question. As for religious divisions between sufism and orthodoxy, and between the various *sufi* orders, this has always existed.

The rise of sectarian politics in 20th-century Sudan may be approached from three angles: the religious setting; the impact of the colonial regime and its policies; and the nationalist movement. As noted earlier, the Sudanese religious setting underwent dramatic transformations under the Turko-Egyptian and Mahdist systems. The Condominium era was bound to leave remarkable changes on at least two accounts: the political and socio-economic transformation; and the religious policy of the colonial state. These two processes were closely interlinked and may be analysed around the religious policy of the Sudan government.

Following the conquest, Lord Kitchener (leader of the conquest and first Governor General) sent a memo to his lieutenants asking them to adopt a very cautious attitude towards Islamic religion: 'Be careful to see that religious feelings are not in any way interfered with, and that the Mohammedan religion is respected.' At the same time he asked them to prevent the re-establishment of private mosques, 'takias', 'Zawiyas' and sheikhs tombs (i.e. centres of popular Islam), 'as they generally formed centres of fanaticism'.[20] In pursuit of its policy the government established a 'Board of 'Ulama' in June 1901 to advise on all questions regarding Islam. Naturally, the 'Board' was a representative of orthodox Islam as the policy was to encourage orthodoxy 'while striving to lessen the impact of *sufism*', which was regarded as a potential of Mahdist resurgence. The 'Board' played its advisory part to the government, but its chances of replacing popular Islam were indeed very narrow, and the latter continued to flourish. Indeed, the destruction of the Mahdist state had effectively lifted the ban on the multiplicity of religious orders and creeds and enhanced their positions. Lacking the necessary religious legitimacy, the British administration had to content itself with putting the centres of sufism under surveillance without much inference in their affairs or activities.

In any event the fears of a 'Mahdist resurgence' were not realised and the condominium administration was established with but a few locally motivated and scattered religious outbursts that could not gain countrywide support and were easily crushed. Yet, precaution against the potential of a Mahdist resurgence had its other side. In view of the obvious limited influence of the orthodox *ulama*, the colonial state sought the support of those religious orders and tribes who openly rejected the *Mahdiyya* or joined it reluctantly. In this regard the *Khatmiyya tariqa*, whose leaders returned from exile with the Condominium army, figured significantly in the collaborator's camp.

The outbreak of the First World War brought some changes. Turkey, who had until then held the seat of the Islamic caliphate, decided to join the war on the Central Powers camp, and called the Muslims to declare *jihad* against the Entente countries. Accordingly,

24

the British administration in the Sudan quickly changed its policy out of concern for the loyalty of its Muslim subjects. Hence, leaders of popular Islam were called upon to utilise their influence in pacifying the populace. Among those called to do the job was none other than Sayyid 'Abd al-Rahman al-Mahdi, the posthumous son of the Mahdi, who for many years was regarded with great suspicion by the authorities and kept under constant surveillance.

Subsequently, all the leaders of popular Islam who were regarded by the regime as actual or potential enemies, became recognised and gradually incorporated in the colonial 'Establishment', together with the other traditional collaborators. Thus in 1919, three of the most prominent sectarian leaders, Sayyid 'Ali al-Mirghani, Sayyid 'Abd al-Rahman al-Mahdi, and Sayyid al-Sharif Yusuf al Hindi, headed the delegation of Sudanese notables who went to London to congratulate the British Monarch on victory in the War.[21]

Official recognition of some of the leaders of popular Islam had undoubtedly opened for them chances of greater participation in public affairs and enhanced their access to the authorities. However, they knew quite well that such a privileged position was not awarded to them for the sake of forwarding the demands and grievances of their followers, but rather to ensure an orderly and stable situation for the colonial regime. Thus they defied Egyptian nationalism and Egyptian claims in the Sudan, and heeded a campaign of a separate Sudanese 'identity'. Later, they utilised their charisma, influence, and propaganda to counter the tide of Sudanese nationalism which culminated in the Revolt of 1924.[22]

In return of these services the British administration reciprocated by according the sectarian heads (especially the *Khatmiyya* and *Ansar*) with both material and moral awards that enhanced their social prestige, economic position, and, ultimately, their political influence. By the mid-1920s the leaders of the *Khatmiyya* and *Ansar* (the Mirghanists and Mahdists respectively) had accumulated enough prestige and influence to emerge as the most conspicuous contenders for political power among the forces of popular Islam. Thus the phenomena of *sectarianism* became exclusively associated with these two groups.[23]

The *Khatmiyya tariqa* was introduced during the early decades of the 19th century, and subsequently acquired strong footing in northern and eastern Sudan as well as in several urban centres. With the victory of the *Mahdiyya* the *Khatmiyya* was temporarily subdued and its leaders forced into exile, returning only after the Anglo-

Egyptian conquest. Under the condominium regime, the *Khatmiyya* leaders were able to revive rapidly the influence of the *tariqa* in its traditional strongholds.

With their social/religious basis revived, the *Khatmiyya* leaders (primarily Sayyid 'Ali al-Mirghani) managed to recover previous properties in land and estates which they had obtained and accumulated during the Turko-Egyptian period and to increase it further through purchases, donations and new grants. Moreover, Sayyid 'Ali received a regular salary from the Sudan government as well as loans and grants for his business. Furthermore, the *Khatmiyya* leader, who acted as an informal counsellor to the colonial state during its first quarter, received a series of honorific titles from the British government and was the first Sudanese on whom a knighthood was conferred. By the mid-1920s, however, Sayyid 'Ali's high position was shaken by the mounting influence of Sayyid 'Abd al-Rahman al-Mahdi, the leader of the *Ansar*.

Al-Mahdi's son made his first significant appearrance when he responded to the government's call to pacify his father's followers – the *Ansar* – during the First World War. Having accomplished the job satisfactorily he was included, as noted above, in the Sudanese delegation of notables to London in 1919. Significantly, during that occasion he offered his father's sword to the British Monarch, King George V, as a gesture of loyalty. Thenceforth, lines of collaboration between Sayyid 'Abd al-Rahman and the British administration remained open. The Sayyid kept his pledge of loyalty to the colonial state. Moreover, he rendered it very important services during crucial situations such as the events of 1924. Sayyid 'Abd al-Rahman was able to reverse the original tide of Mahdism from a rebellious, revivalist anti-colonial movement, into a collaborative one.

For its part the colonial state reciprocated first by recognising the Sayyid as the leader of his father's *Ansar*, who were thought to be transformed into a normal religious *tariqa* like the rest of the orders. Secondly, he was given a number of sizeable economic concessions in terms of, for example, land (property or usufruct) rights, leases of irrigation schemes, facilities of mechanised irrigation and farming, loans, grants and aid, and contract works. The Sayyid proved capable in business matters and was able to expand his business greatly. In 1926 he was also knighted.[24]

Thus by the beginning of the 1930s the leader of the *Ansar* had grown into an economic giant and a highly prestigious person. The movement he led was no longer the 'puritanical revolutionary [fanatic] movement', but 'a moderate political one' known as neo-Mahdism. Apart from its traditional *Ansar* following, neo-Mahdism was credited with the potential of having adherents from among tribal leaders, religious leaders, and even the intelligentsia.[25]

The British administration, who from the very beginning adopted an ambivalent attitude towards Sayyid 'Abd al-Rahman and his neo-Mahdism, was very alarmed at the latter's steady rise and vowed to check it. At first, native administration which was devised for other administrative and political considerations was also viewed as capable of undermining, or at least balancing the growing influence of neo-Mahdism. However, with his reputed astuteness, Sayyid 'Abd al-Rahman was able to manipulate the enhanced authority of tribal leaders, a substantial number of whom were in the Mahdist strongholds, to his own benefit. Eventually, the colonial officials fell back on Sayyid 'Ali al-Mirghani, their traditional ally and al-Mahdi's rival, and sought to encourage the *Khatmiyya* in order to counter the rising influence of neo-Mahdism. Yet, the definite reappearance of the *Khatmiyya* in the political scene owed more to the politics of the nationalist movement than the support of the colonial state.

The exclusive domination of the political scene by the *Ansar* and *Khatmiyya* – despite the existence of other orders, some of which had long roots and traditions – calls for attention. Essentially, the legacy of the 19th century accorded both orders with enough influence for them to become the major players in sectarian politics. Under, the Condominium, both leaders of *Ansar* and *Khatmiyya* were transformed into prominent capitalists and landowners while retaining the loyalty of their traditional followers. Being heads of proto-national and centralised orders, the Mirghanists and Mahdists were able to translate their charismatic influence among their substantial followers into material, and eventually political, gains and vice versa.

Thus by virtue of their economic might, their traditional authority, and the direct or indirect support of the colonial state, the leaders of *Khatmiyya* and *Ansar* emerged as most outstanding representatives of popular Islam in 20th-century Sudan. Furthermore, through, their wealth and prestige, they were able to extend their patronage to other influential social groups outside their traditional zones of influence, such as tribal chiefs, lesser local religious leaders, and eventually intelligentsia and political parties. Moreover, they came to champion media organs, as well as social, cultural and charity associations. Sudanese 'sectarianism' was born.

A word on the dynamics of sectarianism. As pointed out above, under the Condominium, the *Khatmiyya* regained its same constituencies in Northern and Eastern Sudan. As for the *Ansar*, or neo-Mahdism, there was no way for it to be revived as a *national* force. The bitter power struggle for control of the Mahdist state after the death of al-Mahdi, the atrocities of his successor al-Khalifa 'Abdullahi, and the defeat of the Ansar in 1898, had left no room for the revival of the nationwide Mahdist coalition which ousted the Turko-Egyptian rule. Thus, the Mahdist revival under 'Abd al-Rahman al-Mahdi, appeared basically among those tribes and groups who dominated the Mahdist *state*, namely the Western tribes (some of which had settled in central Sudan).[26] Naturally, most of the riverian tribes sided with the *Khatmiyya*.[27]

Due to the natural geographical differences between the zones of influence of the two sects, their economic patterns differed. A common denominator, however, is the willingness of the followers in both to contribute services and/or properties to the Sayyids. As the regions of the *Khatmiyya* constituted areas in which landed property and commercial capital was well-developed, the attitude of the adherents there was to donate presents in kind (either crop or cash or a plot of land). In the case of the Mahdist followers who flocked, sometimes *en masse*, to settle around the Sayyid 'Abd al-Rahman's schemes had only their labour force to give. Thus they provided the Sayyid with a secured source of labour for his schemes, in return he provided them with their basic necessities.

In the ideological field one should recall that both the *Khatmiyya* and *Ansar* had their roots in the reformist sufist movement of Arabia in the 18th and early 19th centuries, through the traditions of Ahmad Ibn Idris al-Fasi (master of the founder of the *Khatmiyya*, and that of the *sammaniyya tariqa* from which emerged Muhammad Ahmad al-Mahdi. Both sects therefore appeared in varying extents in the Sudanese scene as revivalist, puritanical movements. However, both were subjected to dramatic social and ideological transformations.

From the outset the *Khatmiyya* was forced to concede to the strong traditions of popular Islam in order to acquire a footing there. Accordingly, it was turned into a normal though distinguished *sufi tariqa* and has continued as such ever since. As the *Khatmiyya* posed essentially as a religious movement it did not develop an integrated political or religio-political ideology and its teachings remained virtually a kind of sober mysticism. Being generally on good terms with the Turko-Egyptian regime, and even on better terms with the Condominium, the *Khatmiyya* were content with their posture as *religious* leaders concerned mainly with the affairs of their order, and whenever possible, to act as intermediaries between the state and their followers.[28]

The appearance of Mahdism forced the *Khatmiyya* leaders to change their discourse. With the Mahdiyya the choices were only in pros and cons, and either way the *tariqa* was in danger of excommunication. Consequently, the *Khatmiyya* leaders were relentless in their rejection of Mahdism. They opposed it politically, campaigned against it ideologically, and even fought it militarily. Hence, the reappearance of Mahdism under Sayyid 'Abd al-Rahaman al-Mahdi, no matter how moderate the latter was, was bound to cultivate the hostility of the *Khatmiyya* leadership. Accordingly, it appears that Sayyid Ali's gradual involvement in sectarian politics owed more to his desire to check the overt political ambition of the Mahdist leader than to his own ambition.

In any event, neither in its conciliatory attitude to the colonial regimes, nor in its hostility to Mahdism and neo-Mahdism, had the *Khatmiyya* felt the need to provide a religio-political ideology of any sort. The *tariqa* leadership had developed early enough a strong sense of pragmatism in political matters while insisting on maintaining a religious posture. When Sayyid 'Ali felt the necessity of involving himself and his order in politics, he developed a *modus operandi* of tacit and indirect involvement.[29]

Unlike the *Khatmiyya*, the *Mahdiyya* was essentially a politico-religious movement which embarked on rigorous processes of revolution and state building. During the 19th century the movement – as personalised by Muhammad Ahmad al-Mahdi – had made the vital transition from a sub-*sufi tariqa* into the militant Mahdism which provided a rallying point for the revolt against the Turko-Egyptian regime. Under the Khalifa 'Abdullahi, al-Mahdi's heir, Mahdism was transformed into the legitimising ideology of the state.

The crushing defeat of the Mahdist state and the establishment of the Condominium regime necessitated a new structure and ideology. Thus when Sayyid 'Abd al-Rahman al-Mahdi revived regular contact with his father's *Ansar*, a new structure of the *Ansar* appeared quite similar to the other centralised *tariqas* in the country (a hierarchical organisation built around a holy man). None the less, the early 20th-century *Ansar* still continued the official Mahdist rejection of *sufism* and remained virtually a militant religio-political group with a goal of establishing once again the 'divinely guided' Mahdist state.

However, given the circumstances of the period, the best the *Ansar* movement could hope for was to obtain from the authorities official recognition first, and then perhaps develop into a *primes inter pares* among the other sects. Sayyid 'Abd al-Rahman al-Mahdi, who seemed well aware of the circumstances of his time, opted for a *modus vivendi* with the colonial regime. This in its turn entailed further ideological concessions and modifications. Accordingly, the 'eschatological' hope of the *Ansar* for a God-appointed leader who would appear and re-establish the 'divinely guided' Mahdist state was sophisticatedly transformed into a rather realistic expectation of a 'king' who would naturally be the leader of the *Ansar*. In due course the image of the king itself was changed into a modern vision of an elected head of the state who would also be the *Ansar* leader.[30] Here Mahdism took its second transition from Mahdism to *neo-Mahdism*.

Unlike the original Mahdism, neo-Mahdism appeared as a religious sect with political ambition but without a clearly defined blueprint. Thus despite its legacy of religio-political activism, neo-Mahdism ended up becoming a pragmatic movement, just like its rival the *Khatmiyya*. Yet, the Mahdist leaders differed from the latter in that they commanded the loyalty of militant grassroots who were still yearning for a Mahdist state of a sort. This, coupled with their own ambition and the legacy of the Mahdist movement, motivated the leaders to assume direct political control and leadership.

The Intelligentsia

The intelligentsia or *affendiyya* is the group which played a leading role in the formation and articulation of the Sudanese nationalist movement and political parties. Their role was not only an input of a social group in the political process, but also significantly that of potential catalysts, synthesisers or ideologues. Therefore, an investigation into the dynamics of their formation, development, and input as a group has to emphasise the intellectual/ideological influences to which they were subjected. Reference here is mainly to those generations of intelligentsia who emerged in different forms and associations during the 1920s and 1930s, who became the leaders of the nationalist movement, the mainstream political parties and ultimately became the successors of the colonial regime.

As noted above, the intelligentsia were a product of the educational system which grew under the Condominium regime. From the outset the colonial educational policy was guided by a very utilitarian principle which stipulated 'setting nothing on foot that has no real vital connection with economic needs of the country'.[31] Hence, the major objectives of colonial education were the creation of a 'competent artisan class', and a small 'native administrative class' to fill in the minor government posts. Those objectives continued to guide the educational policy for a long time. Furthermore, the educational development even stagnated from the early 1920s until the mid-1930s for political, administrative, and economic reasons. Chief among these were the colonial state's disappointment in the *affendiyya* following the events of 1924, its pursuit of a 'native administration' system based on tribal structures, and the economic depression of the 1930s. It was not until the 1940s that practical steps were undertaken to reform and expand the system significantly by transforming the Gordon Memorial College into a university College (it later became the University of Khartoum), expanding secondary and technical education and reforming the curriculum at all levels. The system, however, remained narrow in both institutional capacity and outlook until independence.[32]

In view of this the educated elite, the intelligentsia, were numerically a very small strata in the society (the overall rate of literacy stood at 14% in 1956, with 90.9% of the literate people having just elementary education).[33] Not only was it meagre, but the intelligentsia class was also not representative of the nation. As the educational, as well as the economic ventures were concentrated in the North, the educated elite was mainly located in the *urban* North with a majority coming from Khartoum, Northern, and Blue Nile provinces respectively. The other provinces were either poorly represented, like Kurdufan and Darfur in the west and Kasala in the East, or virtually not represented, like the three Southern provinces. In the latter, education was completely left in the hands of the missionary societies. The significance of this geographic composition of the intelligentsia is found less in the regional disparity than in its cross-cutting of racial and cultural disparities. The educated elite were essentially the sons (girls' education was rather insignificant for the best part of the Condominium era) of the Arabised and Islamised northern Sudanese, while the 'African' groups in the south and other areas emerged as the most disadvantaged people in literacy and educational training. Such a reality would have very serious repercussions in the future.

The majority of the intelligentsia were indeed graduates of

intermediate and secondary education, which was till the 1940s pursued at the Gordon Memorial College. Those who received post-intermediate education at the college were mainly drawn from middle-class origins, with a majority being the sons of government officials, merchants, army officers, and farmers. Most of the schools and College graduates found employment as *affendiyya* in government service, be it technical or administrative.[34]

These salient features of the intelligentsia composition were bound to affect their ideological and political responses and discourses. In general the intelligentsia may be regarded as a group who shared a common educational training, and common occupations and, as such, were distinguished as a particular social group. Consequently, as a group with multiple similarities common background and, proximity (in both work and residence) they had the potential of collective organisation and action. This was evident in the establishment of new organisations in the early 1920s (SUS and WFL), the literary and press activities of the late 1920s and 1930s, and the establishment of the Graduates' Congress in 1938. On the other hand, being employees of government service the *affendiyya* were quite vulnerable in their dependence on the state for a living. Apart from the possibility of losing their jobs at any sign of dissent, their position also allowed the intelligence authorities to keep a watchful eye on them. They were furthermore, divided by generation, position in the service, sectarian or racial background, and ideological orientation.

As noted above, this study is mostly concerned with the ideological orientation of the intelligentsia because of its significance to future political development in the Sudan. For an insight in the ideological discourses of the intelligentsia it is necessary to look at the potential sources of intellectual inspiration or influence at their disposal.

To start with, the system of education which produced the intelligentsia may be regarded also as a source of intellectual inspiration and knowledge, and, by extension, a source of ideological indoctrination. However, the colonial authorities were as conservative and cautious in their educational policy as they were in the economic field. Accordingly, the education system was structured just to produce the required *affendiyya*. Furthermore, they were explicitly opposed to the type of 'western' education that could only produce 'trouble makers' as in the cases of India and Egypt. Such an outlook was the main cause of the stagnation of education in the 1920s and 1930s and its poor quality.

Nevertheless, despite its limitations the modern educational training of the *affendiyya* was significant on at least two accounts. First, it provided them with literacy in Arabic and English – a window to further their intellectual and cultural knowledge. Secondly, as a 'secular' education it was a radical innovation from the traditional religious education which was the dominant form in pre-colonial Sudan. Consequently, it was the major factor behind the appearance of a 'secularised' intelligentsia.

In view of the poor and utilitarian nature of official education the vigilant members among the *affendiyya* had to educate themselves through group and individual reading of books and press materials. In this connection a number of literary societies and study groups emerged in the late 1920s and became the dominant feature of the *affendiyya* movement for the best part of the 1930s. The same period also witnessed the rise and flourishing of press forums and activities.

The press and study circles are usually sources of intellectual and ideological inspiration, as well as forums of articulation and dissemination of ideological formulations and discourses. The Sudanese press, however, appeared too late to influence those generations of the intelligentsia who assumed the leadership of the Nationalist movement, and, subsequently, that of the political parties. It was the other way round: the press was virtually founded, influenced, and indeed run by those very *affendiyya*. Consequently, the intellectual, literary and journalistic sources that contributed to the formation of the ideological roots of the *affendiyya* had to come from abroad, namely Egypt and Britain. This leads to the question of possible Egyptian and/or British influences over the intelligentsia.

This area involves two aspects: the first is associated with the *incidental* cultural influences of the Condominum powers; the second with the condominium status of the Sudan. In the first category Egypt appeared at a clear advantage since it was the gate through which Sudan used to receive most of its external influences. Added to this were the common language and religion which are particularly relevant as far as cultural influences are concerned. Thus the Egyptian press was widely read in the Sudan and so were the works authored by its renowned intellectuals, especially in the arts and literature. Moreover, the Egyptian nationalist struggle was indeed very inspiring to the Sudanese as, demonstrated by the events of 1924. Egypt's influences therefore involved both intellectual inspiration as well as political activism and agitation.

All the advantages of Egypt might be registered as disadvantages for the British. Yet, by virtue of having effective control of Sudanese affairs the British were well poised to influence the country's *affendiyya*. Thus, the higher educational institutions were modelled on British systems rather than the Egyptian. Proficiency in English among the educated elite enabled them to have an insight into Western intellectual traditions and culture. Moreover, being aware of the potential of Egyptian influence, the British were at pains to curtail it by whatever means. This brings us to the deliberate policies associated with the Condominium status of the Sudan.

The Anglo-Egyptian contention over the 'Sudan question', had occasionally manifested itself in their competition over the 'loyalty' of the Sudanese. Thus as early as 1920–24, there appeared two classes of opinions among the Sudanese intelligentsia and personalities: one calling for unity with Egypt 'Unity of the Nile Valley', and the other for 'Sudan for the Sudanese' under the British tutelage. These slogans and divisions were to shape the Nationalist movement for the remainder of the Condominium era.[35] Yet, what is emphasised here is not the pro-Egyptian or pro-British divisions and their causes, which has been the concern of most of the studies that dealt with this period, but rather the ideological influences incurred by such an association and the consequential impact of these influences on the ideological credentials of the intelligentsia.

It is rather difficult to consider the respective British and Egyptian ideological influences in isolation from the political considerations. The difficulty emanates from the fact that Egypt itself had come under profound European influence since the beginning of the nineteenth century, first via violent confrontation (the Napoleon campaign 1798–1801), and then through deliberate choice (Muhammad 'Ali and his dynasty, 1805–1952). To Muhammad 'Ali (1805–49) and his grandson Khedive Isma'il (1863–1879) is often attributed the 'modernisation' of Egypt on European lines. The ill-defined presence of Britain in Egypt (1882–1952) had undoubtedly accelerated and deepened that European influence. By the beginning of the 20th century, and particularly after the First World War, the dominant traditions among the Egyptian intellectuals and political elite were secular nationalism and liberalism. Inter-War Egypt's intelligentsia, which was contemporary to the Sudanese emergent intelligentsia, was living in the heyday of secular liberalism and not just in politics, and political philosophy, but also in culture, literary writings and criticism.[36]

In view of this situation, one can hardly distinguish what was 'Egyptian' from what was 'British' (or European by extension). As for the Sudanese intelligentsia a substantial part of the acculturation which they received through Egyptian organs was in itself 'borrowed' or at best 'synthesised' by the latter from Europe. Yet, those who chose a pro-Egyptian position were ready to accord Egypt with a particular, if vague, Arabic-Islamic identity, as opposed to the alien 'Western' Christian identity of the British. Those among the intelligentsia who were viewed as 'pro-British' did not have to rationalise such a leaning in ideological terms because its very existence had to be tacit and discreet. Yet, the group which was often 'accused' of pro-British sentiments appeared more explicitly associated with the Western ideas and ideologies of nationalism liberalism and secularism.

The best illustration of both currents is a brief examination of the literary and study circles of the intelligentsia that appeared in the late 1920s and continued through the 1930s. Significant among these were the 'Abu Ruf, and the Murada-Hashmab study groups. Both groups derived their names from certain quarters in the city of Umdurman in which most of their members were domicile.[37] Again in this study the emphasis will be on the intellectual basis of these groups and their ideological leaning, including information on their foundation, membership and subsequent political development.

The 'Abu Ruf group was founded or 'took a definite form' in 1928–29. Most of its members were post-1924 graduates of Gordon Memorial College, bound together by kinship, friendship and/or neighbourhood. They all belonged to the Arabised stock of the North and all shared a *Khatmiyya* background and anti-Mahdist attitudes. The group's readings were wide and diverse. It ranged from Arabic literature and history to the 'leftist Fabian Society literature and the publications of the Left Book Club'. Some members of the 'Abu Ruf school initiated another study group in the town of Wad Madani (provincial capital of the Blue Nile province) which later on proposed the idea of the 'Graduates' Congress'.[38]

In general the 'Abu Rufians were often regarded as pro-Egyptians and anti-British. They conceived of themselves as essentially Arabs and of Sudan as belonging to the Arabic and Islamic world. They were, however, emphatically opposed to sectarianism and tribalism. The group seemed to have cherished ideas of social reform and justice, but true to their social background and position, they had adopted a rather contemptuous attitude to the populace.

The al-Murada-Hashmab, or *al-Fajr*, group was founded around the same time as the 'Abu Ruf one, and its members belonged to the same generation of the post-1924 graduates. In terms of racial and social background the Murada-Hashmab group was more diversified than the 'Abu Ruf as it included some 'de-tribalised' elements in addition to the Arabised folks. The group also did not share a common sectarian background, although several of its members came from an *Ansar* background. In 1934, one of the group members, 'Arafat Muhammad 'Abdalla succeeded in establishing *al-Fajr* magazine which became closely associated with the group to the extent that the latter was renamed *al-Fajr* as well.

Like the 'Abu Rufians, members of *al-Fajr* group were passionate readers of various literary and intellectual material. The latter, however, appeared more influenced with Western ideas than their counterparts. *Al-Fajr* group were also opposed to sectarianism and tribalism and so their magazine was used as a forum of anti-sectarian ideas and enlightenment. Significantly, either because of its diversified racial background, Western influences, or both the group fostered and cherished the idea of 'Sudanese nationalism' (*al-qawmiyya al-Sudaniyya*). Prominent in the articulation of this idea were Muhammad 'Ashri al-Siddiq (a co-founder of the group, and believed to be the original articulator), and Muhammad Ahmad Mahjub (who later became Foreign and Prime Minister).

Both groups therefore were a collection of rather sophisticated *affendiyya* with common interests and/or backgrounds. Both groups more or less emphasised intellectual rather than political activism, and both were anti-sectarian, anti-tribal and patriotic in general. However, while *al-Fajr* group emphasised Sudanese nationalism and a particular Sudanese identity, the 'Abu Ruf group advocated the idea of a Sudan belonging to the Arabic-Islamic world.

In order to appreciate the ideological credentials of the two groups, their common denominators and major differences, the comparative analysis will be based on their attitude/conceptualisation *vis-à-vis* the dominant political philosophies and identifications, such as nationalism, Arabism, Islamism, liberalism, and secularism. Here, the necessary conceptualisation are given for the sake of clarity, although no vigorous set of definitions will be pursued.

Previously, it was stated that nationalism in a conventional sense is employed in connection with anti-colonial struggle. Yet, it is important to note that a more accurate concept of nationalism is closely associated with the idea of a 'nation', and the objective of establishment of a 'nation state'. If applied to the Sudanese context as such, then nationalism would have to be associated with the idea of a 'Sudanese nation' (*al-qawmiyya al-Sudaniyya*). There is no evidence whatsoever of the existence of such a politico-ideological concept, no matter how poorly articulated, either during the anti-colonial era, or today. The *al-Fajr* group actually came closer to such a concept when they espoused a separate Sudanese identity as distinct from Egypt and/or the Arabic Islamic world at large:

> The Sudanese identity is an ideal to which we should all work. It must be reflected in our politics, education, literature, and culture. It is the essential step which we should take before we can aspire to ally with some nation or make our way with other nations to approach internationalism.[39]

Their concept, however, was not fully articulated and remained tentative or rather a form of identification than an elaborate discourse.

The idea of a separate Sudanese nationalism was rejected by the 'Abu Rufians who called for a Sudan as part and parcel of the Arabic-Islamic world. This brings us to the concepts of Arabism and Islamism.

I would suggest here that whenever these concepts are used in a combination: Arabic/Islamic, Arabo-Islamic, etc. they, more often than not, indicate a rather vague identification emphasising the adoption of Arabic/Islamic culture or tradition. Such an association might entail certain racial or historical connotations but falls short of clear-cut ideological discourse. On the other hand, when employed separately – Arabism, Islamism – these concepts are definitely associated with particular ideological discourses and expositions. Arabism may be regarded as a derivative of Arab Nationalism, while Islamism may refer to the ideologies of political Islam, or the movements that seek to establish an Islamic state or order.

There is nothing in the extant literature and studies of the period in question to suggest that the 'Abu Rufians were Arabist or Islamist ideologues. Their scheme, just like the nationalism of the *al-Fajr* group, was a vague identification with the Arabic Islamic world (sometimes symbolised by Egypt). The 'Abu Rufians saw in the Arabic Islamic civilisations strong roots of their identity as belonging to the Sudanese Arabised folks. 'Non-Arab' Sudanese are better off being assimilated into this wider world with its glorious heritage than in seeking a precarious 'Sudanese' or 'African' identity.

Moreover, unlike the 19th-century leaders of liberation movements, these intelligentsia did not conceive their political roles in terms of a *jihad* against the alien infidels or crusaders, but rather in

37

terms of their leadership of a *nationalist* movement. Nor did they regard their objective as the establishment of an Islamic state or order, identification of an Arabic Islamic heritage among the majority of them notwithstanding. In searching for models of anti-colonial resistance and inspiration, even the Arabo-Islamic 'Abu Rufians did not look, say, to the Libyan 'Umar al-Mukhtar (who was a contemporary), still less to Muhammad Ahmad al-Mahdi, who liberated the Sudan less than half a century ago, but to secular figures such as Ghandi, Nehru, and Sa'ad Zaghlul.[40]

There is, however, another aspect of Islamism – a conspicuous feature of the Condominium (and today's) Sudan – namely,: sectarianism. As alluded to above, both 'Abu Ruf and *al-Fajr* had rejected sectarianism and vowed to fight against it and to unify the intelligentsia away from sectarian influences.

To what extent would the rejection of sectarianism brand the intelligentsia of both schools with the label of 'secular liberalism'? The significance of this question is with regard to the fact that during its self-rule and immediate post-independence periods the Sudan was governed by secular liberal institutions. Let us have a closer look at both these categories of secularism and liberalism.

By virtue of their anti-sectarianism, and the absence of an overt *religious* discourse both schools may be regarded as being virtually *secular*. Yet, one can hardly say that it was a secularism by design. In the first place, rejection of sectarianism did not necessarily involve rejection of the religious, or religio-political foundations that substantiate it. Rather, it was a protest against the 'unjustified' privileged position of the religious leaders and their pro-establishment postures, as well as a rejection of the sectarian loyalties and rivalries as they 'divide the people'.

Furthermore, there was no attempt whatsoever from either of the two schools to labour the themes of secularism, modernity, and/or the place of religion in the future Sudanese society. If one is to compare the Sudanese intelligentsia with their Egyptian counterparts and contemporaries, such questions, which fed lively debates and controversies among the latter, were not even posed in the Sudanese context.

Hence, the 'secularism' of both schools and by extension the Sudanese intelligentsia of the time, may be defined as the absence of an overt religious discourse or project. One may say that the secularism of the Sudanese intelligentsia was an attitude rather than a state of mind.

As for liberalism, some sectors professed an *explicit* adherence to it like the *al-Fajr* group, and later the appearance of a *liberal* party in the 1940s. The majority of the intelligentsia, however, had *implicitly* accepted and adopted the tenets of liberalism in its institutional form. Yet, as in the case of secularism, the concept of liberalism not only lacked any serious articulation, but was virtually absent from the discourses of both schools despite their 'Western' education and secular acculturation. Here, it may be relevant to appreciate the wider crisis of liberalism in the colonial setting at large.

As a product of modern European political thought and philosophy, secularism is often regarded as a twin of liberalism. Yet, in the colonial world which was supposedly created after Europe's image, a divorce between the secular and the liberal traditions was inevitable. The European 'masters' who had, by implication or design, triggered a vigorous process of secularisation in the colonies, had readily disposed of the liberal ideals, that underlay secularism, as antithetical to the autocratic essence of imperial domination. None the less, some stirrings of liberalism were *allowed* to operate within strict limits as in the case of constitutional experiments in the European protectorates or dominated areas (such as Egypt, Iraq and Syria). Precarious as they were, such experiments provided room for the rise of some liberal attitudes and orientations (particularly in inter-War Egypt).

In Condominium Sudan, the hostile attitude of the colonial state towards the intelligentsia apart, no such experiment had taken place until the late 1940s. By then the country was already heading towards independence. Hence, as in the case of secularism, any ostensible manifestations of liberalism among the Sudanese intelligentsia remained inarticulate and rather accidental. In retrospect, their liberalism was even more precarious and superficial than their secular stirrings.

Thus, the contributions of both schools are characterised by the absence of a comprehensive ideological theorisation or discourse. In general, their undertones and orientations remained largely formative and rather tentative. Conspicuously, there was lack of articulation of the basic ideas (such as nationalism, Sudanism, Arabism, Islamism) that normally inspires and perpetuates the anti-colonial struggle. These were little more than vague notions, and/or categories of identification. As to the ostensible secular and liberal attitudes, one is increasingly led to believe that these traditions emerged as by-products of the colonial order, its culture and innovations, and were adopted by the intelligentsia in the absence of other fully articulated alternatives.

Reasons for these impoverished ideological schemes of even the most 'intellectual' sectors of the *affendiyya* may be found in a multiplicity of factors. The simple nature of the Sudanese society at the time, the dominance of traditional structures and informal institutions, the conservative and utilitarian policies of the colonial state which produced limited transformation, the poor calibre of education, and the very limited exposure of the intelligentsia to the outside world, may all account for this poor ideological discourse. It was in general a reflection of the structural weakness of the Sudanese intelligentsia.

Such a weakness was later demonstrated by the rapid decline of the Graduates' general Congress and its disintegration into various factions that sought the support and patronage of sectarian heads. In social terms, this intelligentsia-sectarian alliance summarised the peculiar and hazardous evolution of the socio-political and economic structures of Sudanese society under the colonial rule. Politically, it was closely associated with the Graduates movement and the emergence of the political parties in the 1940s.

III. THE SUDANESE POLITICAL PARTIES

The formation of a 'Graduates' Congress' was meant to provide a forum for the further ideological articulation of the various ideological currents and orientations, fostering the unity of the intelligentsia, and strengthening its ability to create and lead an independent constituency *vis-à-vis* the colonial state. However, despite the attempts to sustain different factions and generations within a carefully formulated congress' constitution, the organisation was soon ravaged by factionalism and contradicting tendencies.

Disputes came to a head after the congress's memorandum of 1942 demanding self-determination.[41] The action in itself represented a clear politicisation of the congress, while the negative response of the Sudan government it precipitated consolidated the congress's factionalism. Eventually, those congress factions emerged into various political parties.[42]

The first parties to be formed were the Unionists-*itihadiyyun*, and Nationalists – *qawmiyyun*, both in 1944. The former was formed by a nucleus of the 'Abu Ruf study group and led by 'Abdalla Mirghani, Khider Hamad, Ahmad Khair, among others; the latter by *al-Fajr* group and was led by Muhammad Ahmad Mahjub and Ahmad Yusuf Hashim. Both parties called for the abrogation of the Condominium and the establishment of 'a free democratic government' in the Sudan. However, while the unionists pledged the necessity of a close association with Egypt in a form of 'a dominion', the nationalists called for Sudan's complete independence from Egypt.[43]

The same year (1944) witnessed the foundation of the *'Ashiqqa'* party. A year later, 1945, the Umma party was established. Other smaller parties also appeared, mostly as splinter groups from the above mentioned, but under either of the two main slogans: 'unity of the Nile Valley', and 'Sudan for the Sudanese'.

Among all those parties only the 'sophisticated' Unionists and Nationalists had clear-cut programmes and constitutions. Both parties, moreover, retained their non-sectarian posture and liberal undertones, but not for long. Being minority parties, both the *itihadiyyun* and *qawmiyyun* were eventually absorbed in the mainstream *'Ashiqqa'* and Umma respectively. Both of the latter were associated from the outset with sectarianism.[44]

The merger of the *itihadiyyun* and *qawmiyyun*, the very anti-sectarian 'Abu Ruf and *al-Fajr* schools, with sectarianism marked the limits of the 'solo-action' of those generations of intelligentsia. Consequently, the political parties that emerged as a result of this sectarian-intelligentsia alliance appeared more often than not as organised expressions of sectarian interests and rivalries rather than organs for the advancement of nationalist struggle. In this category are the mainstream or 'traditionalist' parties: the Umma party and the National Unionist Party (NUP) (the amalgamation of the various unionist parties around the *'Ashiqqa'* core).

On the other hand, the impact of the Second World War and its experiences (as reflected in stronger contacts with the outside world), the intensification of the nationalist movement, increase in influence of the press, and the introduction of radio broadcast, have all influenced the minds of the younger generations of the intelligentsia, and motivated them to seek new ideas and approaches beyond the achievements of the liberal/nationalistic intelligentsia of the older generations. Subsequently, Marxism and Islamism appeared in the Sudanese political scene and with it appeared the doctrinaire (radical and Islamist) parties. Unlike the traditionalist parties the doctrinaire parties had clearer conceptions for the future of the Sudan as well as clearly defined and organised party structures and membership.

a) The Traditionalist Parties

The formation of the mainstream political parties (the Umma and 'Ashiqqa' parties) reflected the divergent opinions among the *affendiyya* on the future political course of the congress after the memorandum of 1942. It also reflected the divergent attitudes with regard to co-operation with the Sudan government on the grounds of a gradual process that would eventually lead to self-rule, or choosing an alliance with Egypt as a catalyst in defying the British domination. Those who chose the former emerged in alliance with Sayyid 'Abd al-Rahman and later on formed with him the Umma party; whereas those who adopted the pro-Egyptian stand emerged under the banner of the 'Ashiqqa' party which had enjoyed the tacit support of Sayyid 'Ali al-Mirghani.

The nucleus of the 'Ashiqqa' in fact dates back to the early 1930s, the era of literary societies, when a group of graduates from the mid-Umdurman area formed a society on a par with the 'Abu Ruf and *al-Fajr* groups. However, unlike the latter the 'Ashiqqa' group emphasised political activism and agitation more than intellectual matters. Consequently, after their graduation this group was immediately 'plunged' in the factional politics of the Umdurman graduates' club, which were drawn along the lines of 'Mahdists' and 'Mirghanists' graduates. Throughout, the 1930s and early 1940s, they rallied around Isma'il al-Azhari (then a teacher at Gordon Memorial College) and supported the Mahdist faction in both the politics of the graduates' club and the Graduates' Congress and formed an important part of Sayyid 'Abd al-Rahman al Mahdi's 'council of intelligentsia'. However, following the Congress memorandum of 1942 a friction soon occurred between the Sayyid and the 'Ashiqqa' who favoured throwing their lot in with Egypt and the unionist call, and eventually emerged as a pro-Egyptian party under the leadership of Isma'il al-Azhari, who was to become the first Prime Minister of the Sudan. Utilising this friction that occurred between Sayyid 'Abd al-Rahman and an important sector of the intelligentsia (the 'Ashiqqa' had the upper hand in the congress), Sayyid 'Ali al-Mirghani, who had hitherto stayed at a distance from the graduates movement, gave his cautious support to the 'Ashiqqa' party.[45]

Sayyid 'Abd al-Rahman al-Mahdi, on the other hand, fell back on the moderate, senior graduates who could easily co-operate with him in pursuing a policy of 'constitutional development' under the tutelage of the colonial state. Together with this group and a number of tribal leaders the Umma party was established in 1945. The Umma party was headed by al-Siddiq 'Abd al-Rahman al-Mahdi, as its president, and 'Abdalla Khalil, as secretary.[46] As noted earlier the *'Ashiqqa'* party advocated the slogan 'Unity of the Nile Valley', that is, unity between Egypt and the Sudan under the Egyptian Crown, whereas the Umma party raised the slogan: 'Sudan for the Sudanese'.

In the early 1950s, and through the efforts of the Egyptian government (after the Revolution of July 1952), the Unionist parties came together under the name National Unionist Party (NUP), likewise the smaller partisan groups which were advocating the 'Sudan for the Sudanese' came under the umbrella of the Umma party. An attempt to form a party of tribal leaders – the Socialist Republican party – by some breakaways from the Umma did not last long.[47]

Characteristic of the Umma/NUP parties is their lack of any comprehensive programmes for the post-independence period and that even for the nationalist movement there was nothing more than the loose slogans of 'unity of the Nile Valley', and 'the Sudan for the Sudanese'. This indeed had to do with the above-mentioned pragmatic ideology of sectarianism and the equally pragmatic intelligentsia (such as the *'Ashiqqa'* group).

Furthermore, the sectarian heads who did not have a blueprint of any kind, had naturally left the task of organisation of these parties to the intelligentsia. The latter, by virtue of their modern education, 'liberal' and 'secular' attitudes, organised these parties on modern forms and structures (e.g. executive bodies, councils, regional committees), with a clear hint of a parliamentary model.[48] For their part, both the *Ansar* and *Khatmiyya* leaders reviewed their sectarian organisations and added specialised youth structures (*shabab al-'Ansar* and *shabab al-Khatmiyya*) as 'religious' structures, which were politically (not organically) affiliated to the Umma and NUP respectively. What should be noted further about these sectarian youth structures is that they were organised (especially in the case of the *Ansar*) in a quasi-military manner implying the possibility of usage of violence against enemies and rivals.

The traditional parties thus emerged with a combination of secular, quasi-liberal party structures and a religio-political hierarchical sectarian structures. This formula, strange as it was, gave the intelligentsia as the formal leaders and spokesmen of the parties, room for manoeuvre within the limits of sectarian control. Divergent patterns, however, existed between the two parties. While the Mahdists assumed full control over the Umma party (the president of the party has always been from the Mahdi's family), the Mirghanists gave 'behind the scenes' support first to the 'Ashiqqa', and then to the NUP. This factor coupled with the presence of rather vigorous personalities among the 'Ashiqqa' leaders had enabled them to enlist substantial support apart from that of the *Khatmiyya*, among the graduates, the urban population and the traditionally anti-Mahdist tribal and religious groups (which were not affiliated to the *Khatmiyya*). Accordingly, unlike the Umma party the NUP was not merely a manifestation of the *Khatmiyya*'s influence, though the latter's support was historically crucial to the party especially in its formative years and later during the first elections.

b) Radicalism

Radicalism refers here strictly to Marxist or other left-wing movements. In the absence of another radical or leftist party with similar or greater influence than the Communist Party of Sudan (CPS), radical politics in the Sudan were closely associated with the latter. The emergence of the CPS took place when a faction of the intelligentsia who studied in Egypt and were introduced to the Marxist literature there, came back to the Sudan after the Second World War) and organised Marxist cells among the students of Gordon Memorial College and at the town of 'Atbra among the railway workers. After a short while, the Sudanese communists formed their own organisation, under the name of the Sudanese Movement for National Liberation (SMNL) in 1946. As the SMNL continued underground, a legal umbrella organisation was formed under the banner 'Anti-Imperialist Front' in 1952 composed of both communists and their adherents.[49]

The communist activities coincided with the emergence of the working-class movement in the 1940s and its attempt to found the trade union organisation. The communists lost no chance to recruit some of the leading figures of the working class, a number of whom later assumed leading positions in the Communist Party. Hence, the development and activities of the Labour movement were closely attached to and affected by the CPS and vice versa. The experience gained in the organisation of the labour movement enabled the CPS as well to influence the organisation of the tenant farmers in the Gazira and similar schemes along 'semi-proletarian lines' in the early 1950s.[50] Furthermore, the CPS managed to establish a footing among the student movement wherein an organisation called the 'student congress' appeared in 1949 in both college and secondary schools (later it was renamed the Democratic Front of the Students, 1954). Other mass organisations inspired by the communists were the women and youth unions. Accordingly, despite its small membership and underground activities, the CPS was able to influence the course of political events through a network of professional and/or mass organisations, first in the last decade of anti-colonial struggle, but more conspicuously in the post-independence era.

As a communist party its ideology and organisations are clear and indeed typical of all such parties; the Marxist-Leninist ideology, and the disciplined Leninist type of structure based on the principle of 'democratic centralism'.[51]

c) Islamism

In 1945, a delegation from the general centre of the Muslim Brothers Society in Egypt (founded in 1928) visited the Sudan and held various meetings in the three-town capital (Khartoum, Umdurman and Khartoum North) advocating and explaining their ideas. However, the first unit of a Sudanese Muslim Brotherhood Organisation appeared in April 1949 and one of the pioneers was appointed as 'director general' from Egypt. The Sudanese Muslim Brotherhood was considered an organic extension of the Egyptian Muslim Brotherhood.

Simultaneously, a faction of the Sudanese students was introduced to the Brotherhood's doctrine while studying in Egypt. As militants of the 'Islamic Direction' (the student wing of the Muslim Brotherhood; these Sudanese Students formed the 'Association of the Sudanese Students' in contrast to the 'Union of Sudanese Students in Egypt', which was then controlled by the communists).

At another level a spontaneous Islamic-oriented group appeared in secondary schools and later among the students of the Gordon Memorial College, apparently with no connections with either of the two groups mentioned above. This indigenous group, which started to operate under the name 'Islamic liberation movement', must have been an outright reaction to the communist monopoly of the student activities, as demonstrated by their control of the student union of the college and their establishment of the 'Student Congress' referred to above.

In August 1954, a conference was conducted and attended by representatives from the three groups to assess possibilities of unification. The conference voted for the establishment of a Unified Sudanese Muslim Brotherhood Organisation[52] (*al-Ikhwan al-musli-*

mun, or Ikhwan) based on the teachings of Hasan al Banna, the founder of the original movement in Egypt. Some of the leaders of the Islamic Liberation Movement who perhaps did not wholly share these principles broke out and formed their own organisation *al-Jamma'a al-Islamiyya* that continued thenceforth under different names but without much influence.[53]

Another Islamist group was the Republican party (which later became the Republican Brothers), led by Mahmud Muhammad Taha which was established as an ordinary party in 1945, but appeared with a peculiar Islamist programme in 1951. However, this party also remained insignificant until the 1970s when its activities witnessed a noticeable increase.[54] Indeed, the only Islamist party that achieved an established place in Sudanese politics was the *Ikhwan*. Unlike the CPS the *Ikhwan* were not to advance their influence on class basis, but sought instead to address their message to the entire Muslim society in the Sudan (and elsewhere). Yet, due to the strong hold of the sects and other centres of popular Islam, they had only a limited success with some sectors of the urban middle class. Their visible mounting influence, however, appeared among the students in the post-independence era when the student movement became polarised between the *Ikhwan* and CPS. Ideological implications apart, the nature of the forces among which the *Ikhwan* primarily operated, brought them in sharp hostility to the communists whom they sought to supplant.

To sum up, it may be argued that the formation of the Traditionalist parties (Umma, NUP) which came as a result of a convergence between 'nationalist elite' (the first generations of intelligentsia) and the traditional elite (sectarian leaders) did not signal any blueprints in either secular or Islamic terms. Sectarianism was more inclined to maintain its pragmatic approach, which it had developed during the process of its collaboration with the colonial regime, in order to sustain its hegemony over these parties. Thus, the latter became, increasingly, representative of sectarian interests in spite of their secular forms and structures.

In response to this intelligentsia-sectarianist alliance coupled with the absence of clear blueprints for the future Sudan there appeared the radical groups such as the Communist Party in close association with a number of trade unionist and other mass organisations. Furthermore, in response to the increased communist activities and in defiance of the sectarianist type of Islam, there appeared a number of Islamist groups the most important among which has been the Ikhwan organisation.

In general terms the Traditionalist parties, although broadly based and loosely organised structures with no clear programmes or blueprints, were mostly controlled and directed by the upper classes of landowners, businessmen, merchants and upper strata of the intelligentsia groups, who were able to manipulate the religious and tribal loyalties to their own interest. On the other hand, both of the doctrinaire parties were based on ideologically defined and tightly organised structures. However, whereas the CPS was clearly operating among the forces of the modern sector (such as workers, tenant farmers, students and intelligentsia), the Ikhwan were calculating to supplant both radical and Traditionalist parties. Their real influence, however, remained confined to the student politics for a long period to come. Such were the major trends of the Sudanese political map on the eve of independence; and it remained virtually so despite splits, alliances and new forces until the present day, but naturally with considerable modifications adaptations and shifting balances.

Chapter 2

The Secular Face of Sectarianism

During the 1950s, the Sudan attained its independence from colonial rule, the Condominium. The decolonisation process took the form of a 'constitutional developments' that gradually ushered the country through limited participation by the Sudanese into decision-making bodies, self-government and eventually independence. Both the form of this process of decolonisation and the way through which it evolved had largely shaped the subsequent political system and influenced the evolution of the political forces in question.

The political parties that had emerged during the 1940s and early 1950s continued, with varying degrees, to be the driving force of Sudanese politics during the decolonisation process and after.

During this period, the Traditionalist parties enjoyed an almost unchallenged monopoly of power and politics as both the Radicals and Islamists were not yet major political forces. At best, the Radicals were becoming a noticeable pressure group, due to their influence among workers, students and tenant farmers. The Islamists, who barely existed on the eve of independence, appeared on the political scene only during the controversy over the Constitution (1956–57), as we shall see below.

As long as the Traditionalist parties felt no serious challenge from these forces they were not inclined either to concede to the demands of the Radicals for equity and social justice or to the Islamists' for Islamic legislation. Their politics remained virtually secular on the surface.

I. THE DECOLONISATION PROCESS: ISSUES, FORCES AND PROBLEMS

The Politics of Constitutional Developments

The last decade of colonial history in the Sudan coincided with what was known as the era of constitutional developments. It refers to the

British colonial policy of establishing a number of constitutional institutions with the expressed aim of training the Sudanese for self-rule and ultimately independence (in the distant future).[1]

An Advisory Council for the Northern Sudan (i.e. excluding the Southern provinces) was formed in 1944, and, as indicated by its name, with advisory powers only. In April 1947 the colonial government organised an Administration Conference to investigate the possibilities of developing structures through which Sudanese participation in government could be introduced. The conference recommended the establishment of a 'Legislative Assembly' and an 'Executive Council' for the whole of Sudan including the Southern provinces. This Assembly was formed during the Autumn of 1948 from directly elected members, indirectly elected members and appointed members. Its legislation was subject to the endorsement and/or veto of the Governor-General, and some issues remained completely outside its jurisdiction.

In early 1953 an agreement was concluded between the new government of Egypt (that had assumed power after the military revolution of 1952) and the leading Sudanese political parties on a scheme of 'self-rule' for the Sudan. This was soon followed by an Anglo-Egyptian agreement on the same issue in February 1953. This agreement stipulated the election of an all-Sudanese Parliament with full legislative powers, which in turn would elect a government responsible for implementing the stages leading to independence in addition to routine government. The agreement also recommended the appointment of one multinational committee (including two Sudanese) to assist the Governor-General in his responsibilities as head of state, another multinational committee to oversee the conduct of general elections, and a third committee headed by a Sudanese – for the Sudanisation of civil and military posts.

Accordingly, elections for Parliament were held in November 1953. It met at the beginning of January 1954 and elected the first government which was headed by Isma'il al-Azhari, the leader of the NUP. In August, 1955 the Sudanisation committee accomplished its work and the armies of the two Condominium governments withdrew accordingly in November 1955. In December 1955, the Parliament declared independence and on 1 January 1956 the new 'Republic of the Sudan' officially celebrated its Independence.

Behind this seemingly organised process and these calculated stages towards independence lay a complex web of political issues and events which together combined to produce this process. The two main mechanisms that brought about the process were the Anglo-Egyptian relations and the drive of the Sudanese Nationalist Movement.

In the 1940s the Anglo-Egyptian negotiations had been beset by one difficulty after another, the end result of which had been a total failure to reach a common agreement as far as the future of the Sudan was concerned. At the same time, Egypt's insistence on its over-lordship over the Sudan made it impossible for her to reach an agreement with the Sudanese political parties, especially the 'independence' camp. It was only after the change of government in Egypt in 1952 that such an agreement became possible as the new rulers had apparently different views on the Sudanese question.

For Britain, however, the issue was different. The failure of her negotiations with the Egyptian government prior to the Egyptian Revolution of 1952 had encouraged her to carry on with the schemes of self-rule in the Sudan, despite Egyptian protests. These schemes, with their proposed Sudanese participation of moderates and collaborators would be antithetical to the Egyptian claims of sovereignty over the Sudan. Furthermore, the proposed constitutional developments would create an additional source of divisions and disagreements within the Sudanese Nationalist movement, between those who would agree to collaborate with the British administration and its proposed institutions and those who would reject it.

Indeed, the Graduates' Congress which was still active in 1943–44 rejected the idea of the Advisory Council and turned down the offer of two seats in it. So did the 'Ashiqqa and other Unionist parties. The Umma party, however, opted for co-operation and joined the Advisory Council which emerged as a collection of tribal leaders, British officials and the few Sudanese civil servants who defied the Congress's boycott. Likewise the Administration Conference was boycotted and joined by the same groups respectively. When the Legislative Assembly was proposed it was found to be 'too little too late' by the Unionists and other 'new groups' in the nationalist movement – the radical elements. It was perhaps due to the influence of the latter that the Nationalist movement of the time became characterised by 'radicalism and militancy' in its opposition to the scheme of the Legislative Assembly.

Consequently, as a result of the mass boycott of its creation and by virtue of its poor representativity and sanctioned statutes, the Legislative Assembly could not undertake any serious legislation.

Significantly, the campaign against the Legislative Assembly coincided with important socio-economic developments that paved the way for the political activation of some social forces which would play important roles in Sudanese politics. Two of these forces were indigenous capitalist and merchant classes who benefited from the commercial and industrial boom during the Second World War.[2] Their growth in economic strength increased their political importance. Documented evidence of the political affiliations of these classes during the 1950s is at present not at hand; however, if one can judge by the tendencies of the first elections, the merchant class in general must have shared the sentiments of the unionists.

On the other hand, the lower classes were deeply hit by the economic hardships of the war period: the sharp rise of prices, the scarcity of necessities and the subsequent unemployment. This situation contributed to the growth of socio-political consciousness among these groups, as demonstrated by the workers' and tenants' strikes and their efforts to form trade union organisations.[3]

As mentioned earlier, the 1940s also witnessed the founding of the CPS, which was active among these groups as well as among students and other sectors of the urban population. It is to the combined efforts of these new forces that the radical politics of the anti-Assembly campaign were attributed.

After the establishment of the Legislative Assembly the *Khatmiyya* who founded their own party, the Nationalist Front in 1949 tried unsuccessfully to negotiate an 'honourable' participation in the said institution. The Umma party, with its strong pressure for self-rule, was at pains to prove that its participation in the Assembly was not without good reason after all. However, their attempts in this field were soon foiled by the British.[4]

The failure of the Legislative Assembly to present itself as a legislative body capable of leading the country along the path of self-rule encouraged its opponents, who had temporarily relapsed into obscurity, to resume anti-colonial activities under the umbrella of the 'United Front for the Liberation of the Sudan' which was established at the initiative of the newly formed Sudanese Workers Federation of Trade Unions.

It was the widespread nature of the efforts of the various elements of the Nationalist movement and their united action at the end that finally compelled the Condominium powers to relinquish their hold over the Sudan when they signed the Self-Rule Agreement on the 12 February 1953.

The significance of the politics of the self-rule period lies not only in the fact that this period set in motion the effective mechanisms of decolonisation and finally independence, but also in its role as a formative period during which the forces in action were tested, political and administrative precedents were established and, not least, problems of complex dimensions and prolonged repercussions appeared. Of the latter class is the problem of the Southern Sudan.

The Southern Question

In August 1955, soon after Parliament's decision on self-determination, a mutiny arose by a regiment in the Torit district of Equatoria Province. This soon spread throughout the province and became a general uprising in which more than two hundred Northerners were killed. The direct cause of this mutiny, as stated by Muhammad Omer Beshir 'lay in the mistakes and faults of the Northern political parties which were exploited and fanned by those administrators and missionaries who had always objected to the new, [Southern] policy [i.e. of integrating the South in the North]'.[5] Another writer, Francis Deng, stated:

With the unrelenting development towards an independent united Sudan, one incident after another intensified Southern fear of domination by the North. The attitude of the Northern officials towards the Southerners, the discrediting propaganda of Northern political parties against one another in their scramble for Southern votes, the alienating strategies by which the Government sought to intimidate Southerners into passivity, and above all, the announcement of the results of the Sudanisation of 800 posts previously held by the colonial powers, out of which the South received only four minor posts, fanned Southern opposition into the violent revolt of August 1955.[6]

Other incidents of socio-economic significance that contributed to the factors which triggered the mutiny were also related by yet another writer:

An event which had occurred in the Azande scheme, however, was itself one of the factors which triggered the mutiny. Following the strike and demonstration by workers in the cotton mill, calling for higher pay, tough police action led to the death of a number of strikers. The soldiers of the southern corps reacted sharply to this incident seeing in it an example of how Southern Sudanese could expect to be treated by Northerners after independence.[7]

Substantially, however, the unique position of the Southern Sudan, which had virtually produced the North–South disparities and consequently the Southern problem, had its genesis in the colonial Southern policy of 1930. As we have seen, the ultimate objective of this policy was the separation of the South from the North.

By 1946, however, the British colonials, both for reasons of policy and because of mounting pressure from the Nationalist movement, had adopted a new policy which aimed at the gradual integration of the South with the North. This new policy coincided with their plans for constitutional development and consequently, the Administration Conference (April 1947) recommended that 'the South should be integrated with the North and represented in the proposed Legislative Assembly'.[8] A specialised conference at Juba in June 1947 also ratified the issue of unity, but some reservations were voiced as far as the immediate representation in the nationwide Legislative Assembly was concerned. Nevertheless, the Southerners finally occupied their seats in the Legislative Assembly alongside their fellow Northerners.[9]

Thus both the North and South were introduced to the system of self-rule despite the disparities between them and the Southerners' suspicions of the Northerners which had been nourished by isolation and the colonials and missionaries' policies. The North was far more developed economically, and more sophisticated politically than the South, which suffered from sustained backwardness as a result of its isolation and absence of any economic ventures for most of the colonial regime.[10]

Apart from the question of uneven development which also applies to other regions, the question of the South was further complicated by racism and religion. Rampant racism demonstrated itself in the attitude of most of the Northerners to the Southerners. This was rooted in the history of slave trade and slave institutions that continued throughout the 19th century and the first quarter of the 20th century. In addition, religion had and has a strong impact on the problem of the South. To be sure it is not a question of Islam versus Christianity but is rather the religious factor in Sudanese politics. The educated Southerners, who eventually led the political activity of the South, were products of the Christian missionary acculturation and were essentially secular in their political outlook, unlike the educated Northerners who were essentially conformist to their Muslim tradition.

What should be emphasised, however, is not the 'inherent' implications of Islam and Christianity as political and apolitical religions respectively, but rather the particular experiences of both religions in the Sudanese context. From the eighteenth century onwards, Islam gradually became associated with politics and ideology in Northern Sudan. This association was boosted by the vigorous Mahdist movement in the nineteenth century, and the rise of sectarianism in the early twentieth century.

In contrast Christianity in the Sudan, which was the product of missionary activities (of various churches but notably the Roman Catholic), was kept outside the sphere of politics. Although the missionary educational activities were at the heart of the Southern policy of 1930 and, for that reason, received grants from the colonial administration, Christianity was never presented as an integral part of the religious policy of the colonial state.

The leaders of the Traditionalist parties who were either greatly preoccupied by the issue of independence, or who did not realise the complexity of the Southern question had acted in a way that only helped to deepen the suspicion of the Southerners. First, they did not invite representatives from the South to their Cairo talks in January 1953 which paved the way to the Anglo-Egyptian Agreement of Self-Rule. Secondly, during elections the Northern politicians gave the Southerners too many promises which they must have known that they could not fulfill. Indeed, as pointed out above it was the very actions and policies of those who assumed power after the Self-Rule elections that contributed to the outbreak of the 1955 mutiny.[11]

With concerted efforts the mutiny was suppressed and confined to some few 'outlaws' who disappeared in the bush. The Sudan was declared an independent unitary state on 1 January 1956, on the strength of a promise that 'the requests by the southern members of Parliament for a federal status for the South will be given due consideration by the Constituent Assembly'.[12] That promise was never honoured by the Northern leaders who led the country after independence, and, as we shall see later the problem was to linger and then escalate into a protracted civil war.

Parties and Politics

The self-rule period was, as we have said, a formative era that left lasting imprints on both parties and politics. The most significant event during this time was the first general election (in November 1953) to elect the self-rule Parliament.

In this election the NUP polled the majority of votes and won 51 out of 97 seats in the Lower Chamber. The Umma party won 22 seats, the Southern Liberal Party nine, the Socialist Republican Party three and the Anti-Imperialist Front (AIF) one. The rest of the seats were occupied by neutrals, who nevertheless sided with this or that party. Consequently, the NUP was able to form the government alone and its leader, Isma'il al-Azhari became the first Sudanese Prime Minister.[13]

The Umma party claimed that the victory of the NUP was attributable to Egyptian financial assistance and propaganda.[14] Indeed, the Egyptians preferred, and perhaps assisted the party which then called for the 'Unity of the Nile Valley'. Objectively, however, the NUP was rather more popular than the Umma party due to the former's relentless campaign against the colonial institutions and its refusal to collaborate with the colonial state, a stance that won it the support of the urban population. This sector of the population, which later became the stronghold of the NUP, was particularly active during the anti-Assembly campaigns mentioned earlier. Also the rising commercial bourgeoisie played a part in the NUP's victory mostly through financial and material support during the election campaign. Furthermore, the NUP was preferred over the Umma Party, particularly in Northern and central Sudan, out of fear that if the latter won power it might attempt to crown its patron Sayyid 'Abd al-Rahman al-Mahdi king of the Sudan, thus re-establishing, the Mahdist state. To all this may be added the sectarian influence of the *Khatmiyya*.[15]

For the Umma Party, the results were extremely disappointing. Unlike the NUP, the Umma Party had neither an impressive record of anti-colonial militancy or resistance, nor could it associate itself with the history of the Graduates' Congress. Its record of collaboration with the colonial state did not enable it to refute successfully accusations of being a British protégé. Consequently, the Umma Party won mostly in those constituencies where the *Ansar* had sustained sectarian influence. Again in contrast to the NUP, the Umma Party's character and policies were influenced by its rural roots and support.

In spite of its definite victory the NUP assumed office during the self-rule period with only the vague slogan of the 'Unity of the Nile Valley'. Controversial as it was, the slogan did not indicate either a mechanism or a form through which this unity was to be achieved, something that was to become a source of fresh disagreements and disputes among the various factions of the hastily amalgamated party. Indeed, the NUP leadership and its slogan came under fire from external as well as internal sources. Disappointed by the election results the Umma party was determined to demonstrate its strength to its rivals in power and to their Egyptian 'backers'. Thus on 1 March 1954, the day of the official inauguration of Parliament, the Umma Party gathered together several thousands of its militant *Ansar* youth with their weapons and marched in a paramilitary parade to Khartoum Airport so that General Nagib (the President of Egypt) 'can hear the voice of Independence'. As it was, the move inevitably resulted in street rioting and collision with the police and several deaths occurred on both sides.[16] Those in the Umma Party who recorded the event claimed that the march was organised with peaceful and good intentions. This claim, however, is contradicted by the conclusions of the same writers:

> It became clear that if the government tried, depending on its parliamentary majority, to isolate the opposition from decisions of crucial national importance, the opposition would resort to extra parliamentary means in order to make its voice heard, . . . nobody then could guarantee the consequences . . .[17]

Clearly it was a calculated move aimed at showing the NUP government and its Egyptian allies that they could not get away with such a controversial issue of unity. This show of force by the UP was not to be the last.

Pressures from the Umma apart, the NUP was having difficulty in convincing its adherents and constituencies, particularly the more politicised urban population, of the validity of unity with Egypt when there was a possibility of choosing complete independence. Indeed, other forces like the AIF were actively working with the same urban population for the purpose of complete independence and even joined the 'Independence Front' together with the Umma Party. Due mostly to the AIF's influence the Independence Front was soon joined by the student and workers' organisations and the pressure for independence acquired a 'popular' character.[18]

As mentioned above, the NUP was a hastily arranged amalgamation of the various unionist groups which had different interests and orientations. The most significant among these were the *'Ashiqqa* (al-Azhari's old party), the *Khatmiyya* faction (that founded its own 'Nationalist Front' party in 1949), and a small, but prominent, number of extreme unionists. When the NUP assumed power its Council of Ministers was composed in a way that would satisfy all the factions. Yet, in less than a year, the *Khatmiyya* faction felt marginalised by a strong hegemony of the *'Ashiqqa* group. Three

Khatmiyya ministers made their grievances public and were sacked accordingly. Later the *Khatmiyya* ministers founded another party called the Independence Republican Party (in January 1955) which was apparently blessed by Sayyid 'Ali al-Mirghani. Although some *Khatmiyya* elements still supported the Prime Minister, al-Azhari, the position of his government became increasingly precarious. As he tried to make an about- turn in favour of complete independence, he faced opposition from the extreme unionists.[19]

With all these problems, it was only natural that the NUP government lost a vote of confidence in Parliament in November 1955. However, al-Azhari was able to manoeuvre his way back into office by regaining the premiership with a slight majority four days later. Irremediable cracks, however, continued in the NUP, and eventually al-Azhari had to yield to pressure and form a 'national' (all parties) government in February 1956.[20] This government, which was nothing but a motley collection of differing powers, lasted for just five months, and by mid-1956 al-Azhari had lost the premiership once and for all. By then the various *Khatmiyya* groups had established their own party, the People's Democratic Party (PDP) with the publicly declared support of Sayyid 'Ali al-Mirghani.[21] The next government was a coalition between the Umma Party and the newly formed PDP.

II. SECTARIAN RULE

Reconciliation of Rivals

Surprisingly, after about three decades of bitter rivalry the two prominent religious sects of Northern Sudan, the *Ansar* and *Khatmiyya* came together and formed a coalition government. A summit of the two Sayyids which was made public on 3 December 1955, signalled the possibility of co-operation. However, nothing in their joint declaration indicated an adoption of a joint strategy or a particular programme except general references to their determination 'to co-operate on what is bound to bring happiness, welfare, freedom and complete sovereignty to the Sudanese people'; they also emphasised the necessity to form a 'national government'.[22] This rather ambiguous declaration formed the basis of the government that took over the difficult task of conducting the affairs of a newly independent state.

This sectarian alliance is indeed a phenomenon of great curiosity to students of the period in question. For some, nothing brought the two particular sectarian heads together except 'greed, scramble for power, vanity and personal interests'; or, 'their common rejection of Azhari and their ambition for office'. Others see in it an attempt by the two Sayyids to protect 'their class interests as landlords'.[23]

All of these explanations may be regarded as plausible in general and complementary. The NUP government had sought to reward some middle class sectors (mainly civil servants, merchants and businessmen) for their support at the elections with jobs through the Sudanisation process, loans and other economic facilities.[24] This only helped to antagonise the powerful capitalists of the two sects, who must have felt excluded and who began to co-operate to oust the NUP government and replace it with their own. Viewed from the politico-ideological level, the sectarian alliance was a natural product of the politics of the self-rule period, in particular the departure of the *Khatmiyya* from the NUP and the minority position of the Umma party in the Parliament. On the other hand, the alliance was a legitimate child of the pragmatism of the two Sayyids.

Although the two parties had no significant ideological differences, they definitely had different views on foreign policy reminiscent of their strategies during the latter decades of the colonial period. Consequently, the Umma party was in favour of Sudan throwing in its lot with Britain and the West in general, whereas the PDP still looked towards Egypt (even as the latter was showing signs of moving to the left after the Suez War of 1956). Furthermore, their long history of rivalry left no room for the mutual confidence and trust needed between partners.

There was at least one area in which the two partners could agree, and that was how to expand their particular class interests as landlords and businessmen. For that purpose state power and public resources were flagrantly manipulated for the service of private sector. This manipulation took the form of various economic facilities for the private sector such as commercial and agricultural loans, exemption of customs duties on imports for businessmen, light and fixed taxation for the propertied and high income groups (i.e. income tax was not progressive and there was more reliance on indirect taxation), and significantly, an unprecedented expansion of private pump schemes for cotton plantation.[25]

As the enrichment of one is the poverty of another, the sectarian government denied similar economic concessions to other groups, especially the subsistence nomads and peasants who continued to pay the colonial poll tax, as well as agricultural and livestock taxes. To the dismay of the urban low-income groups, indirect taxation was increased and a social security bill for workers was rejected by Parliament. Loans, agricultural and otherwise, were restricted to those with capital or other guarantees of repayment. In conformity with such a policy the sectarian government maintained the structure of the colonial state apparatus and its repressive laws as a buffer against any actual or potential unrest from the lower classes.

At another level the sectarian coalition sought to engineer a return to office through an electoral law that regulated the division of the country into constituencies on the basis of population density. Consequently, as the constituencies of the capital and other towns remained the same, those of the rural areas (the stronghold of sectarianism) doubled. The new electoral law also abolished the specialised graduates' constituencies because it would unlikely return 'sectarian' candidates.[26]

In the 1958 elections the sectarian alliance gained a majority of seats (63 for the Umma, 26 for the PDP out of a total of 173). The NUP, in spite of the fact that it polled the highest number of votes, won only 44 seats. The remaining 40 seats were won by the new Federal Party of the South. Accordingly, the Umma–PDP coalition was once again restored.[27]

A Difficult Power Share

For the sectarian coalition, the second term of office was a nightmare. One problem after another exploded through the papered-over alliance of the two Sayyids. The irrational and hurried expansion of private pump schemes for cotton plantation, embarked on by the government and agricultural capitalists resulted in serious problems.

First, in their preoccupation the government and beneficiaries (the pump schemers) seemed to have ignored the Nile Waters Agreement with Egypt (1929) that restricted the Sudan's share in the Nile Waters to a certain limit. The agreement was due for re- negotiation in 1959 and while Egypt was drawing up its plans for the construction of the High Dam at Aswan (in Southern Egypt), the Umma party, the senior partner in Sudanese government, was considering negotiating a better share of Nile Waters. Accordingly, the two partners entered into complicated and prolonged negotiations. Yet the rapid expansion of irrigated cotton cultivation in the Sudan must have greatly alarmed the Egyptian government.[28]

It was perhaps in connection with this state of affairs that Egypt suddenly staged a border quarrel with the Sudan in what was known as the Halayib Dispute.[29] Significantly, it was this dispute that clearly revealed the latent differences of the two ruling parties. The Umma party was not pleased with the PDP's silence during the crisis, whereas the latter was equally not happy with its partner's over hostility to Egypt.

Secondly, the extensive expansion of cotton plantation meant that there was plenty of cotton for sale at a time when there was no markets for it because of low prices, the temporary closure of the Suez Canal and the refusal of Britain to buy Sudanese cotton (because of the latter's position during the Suez war). Consequently, the Gazira and other public schemes' cotton remained unsold for two successive seasons (1956–58). As cotton was the main export crop, the Sudan's balance of payments reserves dropped to just half a million pounds. An economic crisis began to loom. The government responded by taxing most consumer goods, and consequently, unrest grew in the urban areas where anti-government demonstrations and strikes were organised by workers and students.

The PDP became increasingly alarmed by the growing unpopularity of a government in which it was a junior partner. Furthermore, the PDP's rival, the NUP was gaining too much political capital from the economic crisis and was becoming more popular. The Umma Party did recognise the gravity of the situation, but as the major party in the coalition (the Prime Minister as well as Finance and Foreign Ministers were members of the Umma) was trying to find a solution. The latter seemingly presented itself in an offer of 'American Aid'. The Umma clung strongly to this as the only possible way out of the ailing economic situation.[30]

Thus an agreement for economic and technical aid was negotiated and eventually signed by the Sudan and the United States in April 1958. This agreement was met by strong opposition from different quarters and popular unrest spread. Consequently, the government's position became worse, especially when both the radical and NUP opposition rallied together under the banner of a 'Nationalist Front'. When the issue of American Aid was brought before the Assembly, the PDP leader saw no reason for siding with its partner in yet another unpopular step. Nevertheless, some of the PDP deputies voted with their government and the bill was passed by a majority.[31]

Although the will of the government prevailed in the Assembly, it became quite clear that the coalition had collapsed. Other issues, such as lapses in co-ordination during elections, differing views on the draft constitution, especially on whether the Sudan should become a parliamentary or presidential republic, had aggravated the coalition's cohesion. Therefore, during the few months that followed the heated debate of the American Aid issue in the Assembly the two coalition parties became almost totally estranged from each other. By November 1958 there were conflicting reports to the effect that each of the two ruling parties was separately negotiating a possible coalition government with the opposition NUP to replace their own.[32]

III. THE SECULAR FACE OF SECTARIANISM

We have seen above how the Traditionalist parties which incorporated the mainstream of the Nationalist Movement had assumed power during the decolonisation process and after independence. Although their influence had primarily rested on sectarian affinities, the conduct of their politics and government was virtually secular. This was indeed the work of the 'liberal' intelligentsia who were the reputed leaders and career politicians of these parties. It has to do also with the character of the post-colonial Sudanese political system which followed the Westminster Parliamentary model in its forms and procedures. The content of its politics, however, was entirely different. The liberal politicians knew only too well that they owed their positions of power to the sectarian influences in the countryside and for that reason they could not oppose any policy upheld by their patrons no matter how strange or controversial it may have been.

At first sight it appears that the developments of 1953–56 had regrouped the forces in question between purely sectarian ones (the Umma party and the PDP), and secular ones (NUP). The former's influence rested on that of the *Ansar* and *Khatmiyya* sects respectively; the latter rested on the gradually consolidating commercial class, most of the middle class (but significantly the civil servants), and other sectors of the urban population. Most of these forces are considered virtually secular. However, on closer examination the situation becomes more complex. The politicians of the two sectarian parties were neither fanatics nor advocators of vigorous Islamicisation of Sudanese politics. They belonged to the same generation and school of thought as the NUP leaders, and when they supplanted the latter in government they maintained its secular form.

On the other hand, 'despite his call for *secular* politics Azhari [the NUP leader] behaved as though he were promoting a third neo-*tariqa* with himself as leader and patron and his followers as the faithful believers in his mission.'[33] This is indeed the *modus operandi* of al-Azhari who was perhaps more pragmatic than the sectarian leaders. However, to his credit, his outstanding history in the nationalist movement accorded him with sufficient charisma to pose as a third force in the politics of the time.

The first test of the practical orientations of these parties came in a matter of particular importance, namely the issue of the constitution. Significantly, on this subject sectarianism, in spite of all its religious connotations, had virtually preserved its secular face. Surprisingly, as we shall see, the NUP's declared position on the issue did not reflect that of a secular force.

In September 1956 a National Committee for drafting the Permanent Constitution was established by the Council of Ministers. It was composed of 44 members who represented all the political trends in the country and was presided over by the Speaker of the House of Representatives – Babiker 'Awadallah. The committee spent some time organising its work and divided itself into sub-committees. By January 1957 the technical sub-committee tabled its report to the attention of the National Committee. The latter continued its deliberations throughout 1957 and in April 1958 it presented its draft constitution to the Constituent Assembly which, however, was not able to discuss it due to the political controversy around the American Aid and other issues, and ultimately the abrupt termination of the Parliament by the military takeover of November 1958.[34]

All the same, the issue of the constitution itself, the committee's deliberations and the wider discussions generated by the whole process were very revealing. The issue of the permanent constitution for the newly independent Sudan was a matter of great importance to its various political forces which naturally had varying interests. The Southern political forces were interested in a federal system of government, some sectors of the Traditionalist parties wanted a presidential government, the radical forces demanded a 'national democratic' constitution, and so on. Of particular significance, in this context, was the call for an Islamic constitution by the Islamist forces who were then slowly emerging onto the political scene.

As soon as the National Committee was established it received a memorandum from the Grand *qadi* (the Chief Judge of the Islamic courts) Hasan Muddathir, urging the Committee to adopt a constitution based on the principles of Islamic *shari'a*:

> In an Islamic country like the Sudan, the social organization of which has been built upon Arab customs and Islamic ways and of which the majority are Muslims, it is essential that the general principles of the Constitution of such a country should be derived from the principles of Islam; and, consequently, the laws governing its people should be enacted from the principles of an Islamic Constitution and in accordance with Islamic ideals out of which such a community has been shaped.[35]

When the National Committee began its deliberations on the draft constitution, the representatives of the "Islamist Forces' in the Committee (i.e. the Muslim Brothers and *al-jama'a al-islamiyya* proposed to qualify the nature of the Sudanese Republic by calling it an *Islamic* Republic.[36] The motion was argued as follows:

> That the Islamic idea [sic] had a positive role in the liberation of 'our' people, it contains the concept of *shura* (council) which vests power in the people, and that Islam integrates Sudanese society with a larger entity (the World of Islam). Furthermore, Islam guarantees justice and equity in the distribution of wealth by abolishing *ribba* [usury].

> In addition, an Islamic constitution links the Sudanese with their Arabic-Islamic tradition, protects minorities' rights and preserves national unity. Moreover, calling the state 'Islamic' would indicate its orientation and give the constitution a 'sacred' image. And, the call for an Islamic constitution had become a popular drive and a rallying point of the major parties. Finally, it says in the Qur'an: 'Whoso judgeth not that which Allah hath Revealed: such are evil-livers. (V: 47); But Nay by they Lord, they will not believe (in truth) until they make thee Judge of what is in dispute between them and find within themselves no dislike of that which thou Decideth and submit with full submission' (IV: 65).[37]

More ideological, however, were the arguments that Islam is essentially a state and a religion, and that true faith cannot be without an Islamic constitution, and that the door is open for *'ijtihad* (creative or independent formulation of laws and judgement) within the context of present-day problems.

Those who opposed the motion, on the other hand, advanced the following arguments:

People may differ in their religious beliefs but agree on other matters, and the Sudan is composed of various beliefs and religions, a matter that necessitates a search for broader identities transcending Islam. That citizens' loyalty should be to the state as such and not to a state with a particular religion; and in this sense the phrase 'Islamic' Republic does not add anything beyond identification of the state's official religion, a matter which may be specified in the particular section of the constitution. As well, equality before the law necessitates a secular state, because in an Islamic state a non-Muslim can never aspire to become a head of state no matter how talented he or she may be. Furthermore, all civilisations have contributed to the democratic ideas and systems, 'until it became universal so that we need not necessarily refer to Islam in order to attain democracy. Finally, there were the fears of the Southerners, foreigners and our relations with other countries. Religion is for God, but the nation is for everybody.[38]

When the motion was put to the vote, the Islamist forces lost by 21 to 8. However, a decision was passed in favour of specifying Islam as the official religion of the state and the Islamic *shari'a* as a basic source of legislation.[39] Those who voted for an Islamic constitution were naturally the representatives of the Islamist groups, and the NUP, whereas the rest of the Committee including those representing the PDP and Umma, voted against (the latter called for gradual application of Islamic *shari'a*).[40]

When the result of the vote was announced the representatives of the Islamist groups walked out of the Committee and resorted to tactics of popular pressure and agitation. Under the umbrella of *al-jabha al-Islamiyya l'l-dastur* (the Islamic Front of the Constitution) which undertook various activities advocating the notion of an – Islamic Constitution.[41] Later, they brought the issue once again to the attention of the National Committee on the grounds that there were new circumstances, because:

After the rejection of the proposal of the *Islamic* Republic, the Islamic groups have waged vigorous campaigns and have been able to assemble the support of many members [of the Committee] and the activity has been crowned by the joint declaration of the two honourable Sayyids (i.e. al-Mahdi, and al-Mirghani) in this regard.[42]

However, when the issue was voted on again in the Committee, the result was the same; the majority opposed the proposal of an 'Islamic constitution'.[43] Therefore, what was finally drafted by the National Committee was primarily a secular constitution with Islam as the official religion of the state, and the *shari'a* law as a source of legislation.

The above-mentioned polemics show that the issue of Islam in politics had been revealed and highlighted over the question of the Constitution. The content of the polemics, however, reveals a rather poor political and ideological literature. The nature of the Islamists' arguments for example reflects a rather simplified outlook that presents Islam and the thesis of an 'Islamic Constitution' as something to be taken for granted rather than a comprehensive new view of politics and society.

Nevertheless, there were some arguments that tried to present the issue more vigorously as in the series of articles written by an Islamist intellectual 'Ahmad Safy al-Din 'Awad. The essence of this writer's argument is that by the very nature of Islam Muslims cannot observe and abide by any legislation unless under the rule of Islam due to the comprehensive nature of Islamic *shari'a* which covers all aspects of life. Accordingly, the issue of an Islamic Constitution for Muslims is part and parcel of their basic human rights. A non-Islamic (i.e. secular) constitution would amount to an encroachment on Muslims' religious freedoms, whereas for non-Muslims whose religions do not stipulate comprehensive legislation of society and are confined to spiritual matters, they can enjoy full religious rights under an Islamic constitution.[44]

It is interesting to note how the writer borrowed the *alien* concept of human rights, rather mischievously, to make a point. However, the overriding simplicity of his logic hardly needs emphasising. Why should non-Muslims be happy with a constitution that denies them their political rights on the grounds that it offers them freedom of worship? Furthermore, the writer did not indicate how such issues of justice and *shura*, the cornerstone of the projected Islamic constitution, would be tackled in a practical way. Neither did he specify a particular type of political system indicating that Islam does not prejudice a particular type of government and it would be up to Muslims to choose a suitable one.

These were perhaps some of the most *advanced* views as far as the advocators of an Islamic constitution were concerned. As can be seen, they are not heavily ridden with ideology or comprehensive reasoning, something that may be linked to the nature of the politics of the time which were not yet characterised by strong ideological discourses.

The 'secularists', on the other hand, *did not* advocate complete separation between Islam and the state. Aware of the sensitivity of the issue for Muslims they argued that the issue was surrounded with multiple complexities of which rights for non-Muslims was the most prominent one. Posing as conformists in general, and akin to the mass base of the sectarian political parties, with its Muslim majority, the secularists were at pains to specify Islam as the official state religion and the *shari‘a* as a basic source of legislation.[45]

The controversy over the constitution revealed interesting positions among the major parties. Neither of the sectarian parties the Umma and the PDP showed particular enthusiasm for the notion of an Islamic constitution, whereas – the 'secular' NUP supported the idea and even included it in its campaign for the 1958 election.[46]

The fact that the two Sayyids expressed sympathy for the idea does not alter this statement as it had not altered the expressed positions of their parties' representatives in the National Committee when the issue was voted on once again. The position of the Sayyids should be regarded as an ideological gesture from religious personalities on an issue of particular relevance to their constituencies and the sentiments of the mass of their followers. Yet they knew perfectly well that an Islamic constitution would not add anything to their established influence in the countryside, their sustained base of power. On the contrary, such a constitution might jeopardise the already strained relations with the Southerners. Therefore, without revealing their hand the champions of popular Islam left it to their 'liberal' politicians to work out a secular constitution.

As for the NUP its position was basically informed by politcal expediency. With its attention focused on power, the NUP's preoccupation was how to supplant the ruling sectarian parties and guarantee re-election. Hence their curious formula of Islamic socialism – through which the NUP leaders aimed to appeal both to traditional and modern sectors.[47] Their strong campaign for an Islamic constitution, although in line with this formula, may be regarded as part of their opposition to the ruling parties.

Indeed, judging by the politics of al-Azhari one cannot believe that the NUP had a programme of comprehensive Islamicisation awaiting implementation. But then neither had the Islamist groups who were vehemently leading the campaign for an Islamic constitution, and the slogan of an 'Islamic Republic' remained as vague as the slogan of the 'Unity of the Nile Valley'.

Having examined, and tried to explain the positions of the parties over the constitution, it is important to emphasise that at the time the issue of an Islamic constitution was not a central theme in the body politic as it turned out to be later on. Issues of a more practical nature such as federation and whether the political system was to be presidential or parliamentary were of more concern to the ruling parties and other forces with vested interests. The issue of an Islamic constitution was rather an attempt by the Islamist groups, who had not yet constituted a strong pressure group, to find a place in the Sudanese political scene.

To sum up, following the self-rule period the political discourse of the ruling parties took on a secular form in spite of the sectarian bases of their power. Such a character dates back to the politics of the nationalist movement and the liberal orientation of the first generations of intelligentsia who became the leaders of both the nationalist movement and the political parties that assumed power after independence. In the absence of any comprehensive programmes or alternative ideologies from the sectarian-nationalist parties they adopted the Western parliamentary system with its strong secularism.

Experience has shown, however, that the Traditionalist parties were unable to continue with this sort of secular modern politics with its strong overtones of civil and political rights and its emphasis on democracy and participation. Judging by the very composition of the socio-economic structure of Sudanese society, which was characterised by the dominance of subsistence economy and general backwardness, a parliamentary democracy in the circumstances was bound to be deficient.

Indeed, most of the rural population of the Sudan did not take part in the nationalist movement which remained confined to the urban areas. Consequently, at elections the rural population chose their immediate tribal and religious leaders which led to the ascendancy of the Traditionalist parties.

These parties that assumed power after independence had no clear vision of the magnitude of the problems of the new state. Even if they had they lacked the imagination of how to solve them (as in their treatment of the Southern Question and their many economic mistakes). Blinded by their own interests the leaders of the ruling parties did not listen to the complaints of the lower classes which surfaced as a result of the growing economic crisis and a system of unjust taxation. The result was increasing unrest and civil strife to which the government responded negatively by a clamp down on protest activities.[48]

The coalition governments which resulted from regional and sectarian divisions or party splits became full of tension. The preoccupation of the parties was either to assume power, or to preserve it. In the process every possible means of intrigue and manoeuvre were used, including buying the loyalty of MPs. The Parliament had become everything else but the chamber for responsible legislation.

Failing either to contain the crisis or to provide solutions for it, the sectarian government with its ailing coalition found its back against the wall. The Prime Minister 'Abdalla Bey Khalil, with or without the consent of his party, sought the 'solution' of handing over power to the military. Thus the Commander of the Sudanese army, Lt. General Ibrahim 'Abbud assumed power through a military *coup d'état* on 17 November 1958.

The military takeover was a clear indication of the failure of the politics of the period. In essence it was a failure of the parliamentary system, as practised, to become a genuine platform for representation of society, and power succession; the failure of the ruling parties to live up to the expectation of their supporters and the high hopes of independence, as well as their failure to contain or satisfy the demands of the population at large for a more equitable distribution of wealth and power.

Chapter 3
Generals, Militants and Politicians

I. THE RULE OF THE GENERALS

Intervention of armies in the politics of the Third World or underdeveloped countries has become as common as the regular parliamentary elections in Western Europe and no longer raises curiosity among researchers or observers as it used to some decades ago. Yet, in 1958 Sudan the phenomenon, though by no means an innovation, had not yet become widespread. What was peculiar about the Sudanese military takeover of 17 November, 1958, was that it was more of a hand-over of power or a *'coup by courtesy'* than a classic military *coup d'etat*.

Various studies emphasised the role of 'Abdalla Khalil, the Prime Minister in 1958, in the perpetration of the *coup*. Others drew attention to the army's increased politicisation as an inevitable product of the manner in which Sudanese politics had developed.[1] The present writer is more concerned with the nature of the military regime and the impact of its policies on Sudanese society and politics.

From the outset the Generals displayed an extremely authoritarian and despotic attitude. As usual in military takeovers, the regime's first action was to ascertain its authority through a series of decrees and regulations. Thus the first Decree declared a state of emergency throughout the Sudan 'in accordance with section 2 of the Defence of Sudan Ordinance'. The second Decree was 'for the suspension of the Sudanese Transitional Constitution, 1956'; the dissolution of the Sudanese Parliament as from 17 November 1958 and the dissolution of all political parties and associations. Whereas the 'Third Order' was for the suspension of all party and independent media organs, until further orders (later on independent papers were allowed to operate but with many restrictions).[2]

By the same token three 'constitutional orders' were issued by way of legalising the new regime. The first established a 'Supreme Council of the armed forces' to be the highest legislative, executive and judicial authority in the land. The same order announced the delegation by the Supreme Council of its entire powers to its president Lt General Ibrahim 'Abbud who was also the commander-in-chief of the armed forces. Under these provisions a Supreme military council composed of twelve high ranking military officers; and a council of ministers composed of eight military officers and five civilians were formed. The second 'constitutional order' stipulated that the president of the Supreme Council of the armed forces would also be the Prime Minister. The third 'constitutional order' legalised the suspension of the transitional constitution, and the parliament and the banning of all political parties.[3]

After less than a week in power the military regime issued the Sudan Defence Ordinance 1958, and the Sudan Defence Regulation, 1958. The first document decreed that 'whoever acted for the formation of parties or called for a strike or acted to overthrow the government or spread hatred against it be either sentenced to death or long imprisonment". The second gave the Minister of the Interior access to private mail, press censorship, and the authority to compel citizens to give any information requested by the police. He could also restrict the movement of any citizen within any territory, control exit out of the Sudan and stop the importation of any publications, and so on.[4]

At first the new leaders resolved to rule without political and legislative institutions apart from the two councils. Later on, however, and in response to the increasing protests from the old politicians and other sectors of the society the Generals, as did the Colonial state twenty years ago, introduced certain measures of gradual constitutional developments that came into effect by 1962/63 and culminated in the establishment of a central Council to share in the Legislative authority of the Supreme Council of the armed forces.[5]

In no way did these constitutional reforms enhance the legitimacy of the military regime or expand the base of its decision-making mechanisms, and the regime remained as authoritarian as ever. The rule of the Generals had undoubtedly represented a continuity of the tradition of an authoritarian administration which was embodied, in different forms, in the Condominium government, the Mahdist state, and the Turko-Egyptian regime.

In the economic field the military regime showed some initial success as in its selling of the accumulated cotton and the restoration of a surplus (of about LS 20m on average) in the country's balance of payments. A pragmatic foreign policy adopted by the regime resulted in the expansion of Sudan's relations and the flow of funds from different quarters of the world. Secondly, a number of projects were started or implemented mostly with foreign loans and/or technical assistance. A ten-year Economic and Social Development (1961/62–1970/71) Plan was launched with the expressed objectives of increasing the national and per capita incomes, broadening the economic base of the country, increasing export production and intensification of import substitution industries, improvement of social services, and comparative standardisation of market prices.[6]

Conspicuously, the regime's economic policies had greatly benefited the indigenous capital, which resulted in a notable rise of private sector investments, in the shadow of foreign capital, especially in the fields of light industry, real estate, mechanised farming and pump schemes. The activity also attracted a number of top civil and professional officials who utilised their high posts for private economic purposes whether technical know-how or corruption. All in all, the implemented public and private projects created a sort of a boom in jobs, industry and commerce and the result was a modest economic growth compared with the previous years.

However, by 1964 the picture had changed and signs of recession appeared once again. Budget reserves naturally fell shorter than the requirements of the Ten Year Plan (with estimated total cost of LS 565m). The accumulated foreign debt was hitting alarming figures and the repayment of loans and interest became an increasing burden on a budget with a very ambitious development plan. The plan itself was poorly designed and conservative in outlook. Apart from being extremely urban biased, it 'did not invariably include projects adequately studied worked out and of real utility'.[7] At the same time, the growing cost of military operations in the south, as the scale of the war there widened dashed any hopes of a definite economic takeoff.

In his first policy statement 'Abboud made no reference to the Southern problem, despite the mutiny of 1955, the call for federalism and the growing disappointment of the Southerners with the post-independence governments. Failure to refer to the South, however, should be measured by the overall substance of the statement which was characterised by its lack of vision or comprehensive policy.

However, when the Generals set to govern the country, they sensed that something had to be done with regard to the South. Responding to the Southerners demands of federalism was, of course, out of the question by the very authoritarian nature of the military regime and its centralised administration. Rather, they fell back on the thesis which held that a definite 'solution' to the southern problem was to reverse the British policy (i.e., national integration of the South through Arabisation and Islamisation to replace the British policy of segregation). Such a policy was elaborated and advocated by the sectarian government, but was not implemented due to partisan squabbles which engulfed the conduct of that government.[8]

Freed from the constraints of parliamentary politics the military regime set to eradicate the Southern 'particulism' with great zeal. Their method was one of forced Arabisation and Islamisation of the South. Thus they established Qur'anic schools in different parts of the South. Intermediate Islamic institutes were established in six southern towns, and a secondary Islamic institute was set up in Juba.[9] In 1960, a decree was issued replacing Sunday by Friday as the weekly day of rest. In 1962 a 'Missionary Societies Act' was promulgated wherein the missionaries were asked to obtain licences from the government to operate lest they would be liable to expulsion. The Act furthermore prohibited the societies from carrying out any missionary activities towards any person or persons professing any religion or sect or beliefs. Between 1962–63 some 243, mainly Roman Catholic, missionaries were expelled. In February 1964 the remaining 300 missionaries were expelled.[10]

When the Southerners protested or even expressed the slightest dissatisfaction with these policies they were met with severe and violent repression. Preoccupied with 'law and order', the Junta set at once to eradicate Southern opposition by force. Such a measure was, of course, akin to the oppressive and authoritarian nature of the regime. Yet, in the south the magnitude of the army's violence was abhorrent.[11]

The result of the regime's policies in the south was both catastrophic and far-reaching. Panic spread in the Southern provinces driving huge numbers of refugees to neighbouring countries (mostly Uganda, Kenya and Zaire). New political organisations, mostly with blueprints of separation appeared among the Southerners in exile, such as the Sudan African Closed Districts National Union (SACDNU – later renamed the Sudan African Union-SANU), and led by William Deng and Joseph Oduhu; and the Sudan Christian Association led by Father Saturnino Lahure. In 1963 a military organisation sprang out of this overwhelming dismay under the name Anya nya. With its nucleus consisting of some of the veterans of the 1955 mutiny, Anya

nya sought to lead an armed resistance to the government precipitating civil war.

Coupled with violent repression, the regime's 'Southern policy' had resulted in bitter hostility by the Southerners not only to the regime but to the North in general, which became an almost uniting factor for the southern politicians and intellectuals. Furthermore, the expulsion of the European missionaries had led to the latter's mobilisation of the Western public opinion against the Northern Sudan as prosecuting a war against 'Christians, and Christian faith'. Missionaries retaliation apart, it seemed as if the indiscriminate treatment by the military regime of the Southerners as potential rebels had cultivated a counter response from the latter who came to regard the entire north as bent on destroying them.

At last when the situation in the South became intractable, the military government sensed that its policy in that region was cultivating just the opposite effect and a commission was appointed to assess the roots of the Southern problem. By then, however, it was too late. Opposition to the military regime had been gathering momentum during its six-year-long rule, increasingly and to varying degrees drawing in different sectors of the population until the break-even point was reached in October, 1964 when opposition exploded with unprecedented unanimity.

In the beginning the regime was able to enlist the support of two important forces in the society, namely the two prominent sectarian leaders of the *Ansar* and *Khatmiyya* on the one hand, and the bureaucracy on the other.[12] The support of the former meant also the support of their parties (Umma – PDP) and followers at large, whereas the latter 'by their uninterrupted working of the administrative machine, put the zeal of authority on the coup'.[13] During that early period opposition came solely from the left to which the regime responded by oppression and several communist and labour leaders were arrested and/or imprisoned after court-martial trials. In 1959 the regime was able to foil a *coup* attempt led by junior officers. Meanwhile, the *Khatmiyya* support continued to the regime while tension grew between it and the Umma party as well as the NUP.

By 1960, it seemed that most of the political parties had become impatient with the rule of the Generals (who had initially promised to relinquish power as soon as possible). A Front of opposition political parties was formed under the leadership of Sayyid al-Siddiq 'Abd al-Rahman al-Mahdi (who succeeded his father in the leadership of the *Ansar* while retaining the presidency of the Umma party after the latter's death in 1959). The Opposition Front sent a Memorandum to General 'Abbud demanding that the army should refrain from politics, the state of emergency to be lifted, and a national government to be set up to draw a constitution and hold general elections. As long as the opposition parties followed their 'war' of memoranda and petitions the Generals turned a deaf ear, and ultimately imprisoned most of the leaders of political parties. The Opposition Front of the politicians, however, proved ineffective and with the death of al-Siddiq al-Mahdi (1961) nothing more was heard about it.[14]

Other forces, however, took matters into their own hands and started to voice their grievances *vis-à-vis* the regime. Conspicuous among which were the urban workers, tenant farmers and students. Every group had its separate collision with the regime, but in general their methods were similar: strikes, demonstrations and other forms of civic protest. It was perhaps the scattered conflicts of these forces and their accumulated experiences in opposition to the regime that ensured the success of the general political strike which eventually toppled the regime in October 1964.[15]

A word on ideology. The Generals were not in the least concerned with matters of ideology. As pointed out earlier they did not approach power with a blueprint of any sort; neither were they bothered with legitimacy of their rule. The 'constitutional reforms' introduced by the regime in 1962–64 took too long to mature and were a little more than a token gesture of popular representation. The regime continued to govern without a constitution until its last hour.

As for the opposition matters were different. The aforementioned memorandum of the Opposition Front called for the reinstatement of parliamentary democracy. The significance of this call was twofold. First, it set the pattern for future change, as happened in 1964; and later in 1985, it established the principle that military regimes must be replaced by parliamentary ones. Secondly, it reflected a commitment by the Traditionalist parties to parliamentary democracy. In its turn this commitment may be viewed from two angles. An ideological one, reminiscent of the commitment, and indoctrination of the 'nationalist' intelligentsia to *institutional* liberalism; and/or a cynical one – parliamentary democracy as the surest way for these parties to attain power.

On the other hand, the CPS, which represented the hard core of the radical forces, had opposed the regime from the outset and mounted resistance to the regime through mobilisation of 'modern sector' forces (workers, tenant farmers, intelligentsia, students). Basically, the process

74

involved articulation of grievances of these forces (whether economic or political) *vis-à-vis* the regime and its oppressive policies. Particular attention was paid to freedom of organisation and trade union rights. Later on (1961) the CPS elaborated the theme of the 'general political strike' as the most effective way of overthrowing the military regime.

However, the CPS did not develop a clear vision with regard to an alternative political system to replace the military regime. At one point the CPS seemed to have endorsed the parliamentary alternative of the Opposition Front of which the CPS was a member. The CPS, however, pulled out from the opposition Front (1963) in protest of the latter's incompetence.

More elaborate answers pertaining to questions of politics and society were worked out later when the CPS conducted its fourth Congress (1967). What should be underlined here is that during the military regime the CPS became more associated with the 'modern forces' more through the championship of their grievances, than the tenets of a 'Marxist ideology'. This *discourse of agitation* was to be the brand of the CPS thenceforth.

II. OCTOBER 1964 AND AFTERMATH

In October 1964 the regime of the Generals was overthrown by a popular uprising (better known as 'October Revolution'). By its mass character, leadership, and objectives the October Revolution represented not just a change of regimes, but a wider range of outspoken demands of radical political, economic and social change that were heeded, for the first time, at the highest levels of the government.

The initial response of the Traditionalist parties (who were the power holders before the *coup*) to this new situation was a mixture of cautious and rather cosmetic concessions on the one hand, and, a firm and an unequivocal determination to contain the radical forces unleashed by the revolution, on the other. The success of the conservative forces in this endeavour had virtually spelt out the failure of the revolution as conceived by its populist leadership and the majority of masses who chanted slogans such as *'la za'ama lil qudamah'* (no leadership for the antiquated).[16]

Chronology of Events

The culmination of the 'Southern problem' combined with the oppressive policies of the military junta and its mounting economic failures brought the crisis of the regime to climax. As demonstrated later by events, by October 1964 time was ripe for change, and the process took the following course:

On 21 October1964, the police attacked a students' rally in the University of Khartoum and two students were shot down.

On 22 October a mass protestation against the regime was manifest in the funeral procession of the first student killed, Ahmad al-Ghurashi Taha.

Demonstrations continued until the beginning of strikes on 24 October and the declaration of a general political strike on 26 October under the leadership of the newly formed National Front of the Professional organisations (hereafter, the Front of the Professionals).

On the same day (26 October), Lt. General Ibrahim 'Abbud declared the dissolution of both the Supreme Council and the Council of Ministers.

On 28 October the Front of the Professionals united with the Nationalist Front (a composition of the main political parties in the North: the Umma party, National Unionist Party (NUP), Peoples Democratic Party (PDP), Sudanese Communist Party (CPS), and the Muslim Brothers, (the latter had reorganised themselves under the banner of the Islamic Charter Front (ICF)) in the United Nationalist Front.

On 30 October, a Caretaker government was formed with Sir al-Khatim al-Khalifa (an educationalist non-partisan personality) as Prime Minister; and a fifteen-member cabinet that included eight ministers from the Front of the Professionals, five ministers representing the above-mentioned political parties, and two from the Southern Front (a newly formed organisation of Southerners in the north). However, Lt General 'Abbud remained head of state though under the auspices of the National Charter of October, and the provisions of the transitional constitution of 1956 (amended 1964).

On 15 November General 'Abbud resigned and handed over his powers as head of state to the civilian Cabinet under Premier al-Khalifa.

On 3 December a five-man council was appointed to act as Sudan's head of state.[17]

The newly composed government was to continue in office as a Caretaker government until the holding of general elections, under the supervision of an independent Elections' Committee, by March 1965, for a Constituent Assembly that would approve a permanent constitution. Meanwhile, the Caretaker government would exercise both executive and legislative powers.

The success of the Uprising in ousting the rule of the Generals was widely attributed to the effective implementation of the general political strike that paralysed the country (particularly the capital). At the same time, divergent opinions within the ruling 'Supreme council' that represented a wider split in the army, and in particular the role of the junior officers who eventually sided with the uprising, played no smaller part in its victory.[18]

The resignation of General 'Abbud as head of state meant finally the victory of the uprising and civilian rule; yet it also focused attention on the political composition of the victorious coalition: the United Nationalist Front.

On the one hand, there was the Front of the Professionals (broadly representing modern sector forces: organised labour, tenant farmers' unions, white collar and professional organisations) backed and led by the radicals; and, on the other hand, there were the Traditionalist parties and the ICF. With the definite victory of the uprising divergent opinions on the next course of action soon appeared among the components of the United Nationalist Front. The camp of the Front of the Professionals and radicals advocated the necessity of vigorous socio-political reforms in order to create better conditions for genuine democratic practice. Whereas the other camp, the Traditionalists regarded 'October' as the long awaited opportunity to regain office. With such divergent opinions the United Nationalist Front, once a symbol of united action against the military regime, quickly disintegrated and was deserted by the CPS, the Front of the Professionals and the PDP. The other parties (Umma, NUP, ICF), however, maintained the Front's name not only as an alliance body between them, but also with an expressed gesture that this was the *sole and legitimate* organ of the uprising.

Yet by virtue of its prominent role in the uprising the Front of the Professionals obtained a majority in the cabinet. Furthermore, due to their presence in the leadership of a majority of trade unions and, consequently, the Front of the Professionals the CPS emerged as the strongest party in the government (with at least three members in the cabinet and other sympathisers or allies). For the first time in the history of civilian rule the Traditionalist parties found themselves in a minority position.

Due to the 'revolutionary' circumstances of its formation and the prevailing leftist domination, the caretaker government had, unsurprisingly, embarked on a number of radical measures and policies such as: women were given universal suffrage right (lowered to 18 years); a committee was established for the purpose of purge of corrupt officials from the civil and military services and many steps were taken in that direction; freedom of the press was restored and the state of emergency lifted; a project was drafted for the liquidation of the Native administration (*al-idara al-ahliyya*); an Act of Unlawful Enrichment was issued; some plans were set for a process of 'agrarian reform'; certain items that used to restrict fundamental rights in the penal code were repealed; and so on. Furthermore, with regard to the 'Southern question', the Caretaker government issued a general amnesty to all Southerners who had carried arms; all political detainees in the South were released; and a decision was taken to hold a conference with the objective of solving the problem on 18 February 1965.[19]

Such policies were regarded by the radicals as important steps towards socio-political and economic reforms in the country. A given set of these policies aimed at liquidating the vestigial traces of the military and colonial regimes such as the measures of law reforms, purge, restoration of public freedoms, and so on. The other declared measures; such as agrarian reform, native administration, aimed at removing the social and economic constraints that retarded the politico-economic activity of the majority of the populace especially in the rural sector.

On the other hand, these very policies greatly alarmed the right-wing parties who saw in them direct threats to their vital interests. Native administration with its tribal base represented a stronghold for the Traditionalist parties (especially the Umma party). Purge of the civil and military services threatened the positions of many top officials loyal to or having vested interests with the Traditionalist parties (particularly the NUP), and so would the Unlawful Enrichment Act. Consequently, the right-wing parties voiced their opposition to these policies on two levels: first, opposing it in the cabinet, or campaigning against it publicly; and, secondly, denouncing the totality of the government policies as irrelevant since its major, if not sole task, was to hold elections by 31 March as stipulated by the 'National Charter'.

Indeed, the proposed general election had itself become another bone of contention. The dispute was triggered by the government's decision of a possible postponement of elections because of the unstable conditions in the South. In response to that declaration the 'Nationalist Front' immediately sent a memorandum to the government requesting it either to hold elections as scheduled or resign. This was the beginning of a series of declarations, memoranda and accusations between the parties of the Nationalist Front on the one hand, and the caretaker government, the CPS, PDP, and the Front of the Professionals on the other – the former pressing for elections, the latter for postponement.[20]

Although the situation in the south was indeed grave and would have not allowed the holding of elections there, the call for postponement involved other considerations as well. For the CPS and other leftist forces, the transitional period of six months was 'too short for a government with a radical programme'.[21]

On the other hand, the traditionalist parties – who insisted upon holding the general elections on the old basis of one man – one vote, were confident that they could gain an absolute majority that would enable them to form a government either separately or in a coalition (e.g. Umma-NUP). Thus calculated, elections for the right-wing parties also meant an end to the 'troublesome' caretaker government and its radical policies.

As the dispute over elections lingered the Umma party, an important element in the conservative alliance, brought its para-military militia of the *Ansar* youth (about 30,000 of them) in a clear show of power. Under this threat the compromise, non-partisan Prime Minister Sir al Khatim al-Khalifa resigned on 18 February 1965, and consequently the caretaker government was dissolved. Following a week of difficult negotiations, a second caretaker government was formed, but this time with a conservative majority (three ministers each for the NUP, Umma, PDP, and the Southern Front; and one minister each for the CPS and the ICF).[22]

With the formation of the second caretaker government the revolutionary zeal of the October uprising had practically come to an end as far as the conduct of government was concerned.

Genesis of Failure

Why did the radicals fail to carry the day in spite of their having an upper hand in a cabinet with both executive and legislative powers? Several responses might, and were indeed, given to this question. The thesis forwarded here is that the leadership of the October coalition, formed by the radicals, was not able to design a workable mechanism for the establishment of a new political order. To grasp the full dimension of this state of affairs one needs to look at the structural arrangements that resulted from the October Uprising.

These were the October National Charter that set the objectives and statutory principles of the political change brought about by the revolution; the caretaker government which was entrusted with the leadership of the country at that critical period; and the Front of the Professionals that led the political strike and was in effect, the leadership of the revolution and its government as demonstrated by its majority position in the cabinet.

The National Charter that was adopted during the lengthy negotiations between the leaders of the 'United Nationalist Front' and representatives of the armed forces, called for:

> liquidation of the present military rule, release of all public freedoms (of the press, expression, and organisation); ending of the emergency situation and cancellation of all emergency laws in areas where security was not threatened; ensuring the independence of the judiciary and university; releasing of all political detainees and prisoners; formation of a Court of Appeal from a panel of not less than five judges to exercise the powers of the head of the judiciary; and formation of a committee to draw up new laws reflecting the country's traditions.[23]

In effect, the October Charter meant nothing more than a return to the pre-November *modus vivendi*, which, arguably, was not what the leadership of the Professionals' Front had wanted and worked for. Yet they did not see to it that their considerations and vision of change were clearly specified in the charter. Worse still, by agreeing to a provision that terminated the transitional period by March 1965, they had played into the hands of the conservative forces who clung to that clause alone in the charter and demanded its implementation. For all consequential considerations, fixing a date for a general election before finding a solution to the southern question which had reached unprecedented complications under the military regime, and before working out a formula for a more sustainable democratic framework, had been a gross mistake that was discovered only too late.

None the less, once in office the radicals, who formed a majority in the caretaker government embarked on a series of radical policies in the manner described above. No matter how noble this endeavour could have been it was not backed by any provision in the National Charter or the amended transitional constitution. Its pursuit therefore only helped to cultivate the dire hostility of the right-wing parties and their clients in the top brass of the civil and military services, and accelerated their assault on the caretaker government. As demonstrated by events the latter proved as unprepared for such a challenge as its radical leaders.

As pointed out earlier, the caretaker cabinet – which was composed of members from the Front of the Professionals, the main five political parties in the North and the Southern Front – had enjoyed both executive and legislative authorities. So formed, and with such powers, it was not an ordinary cabinet accountable to an elected legislative body or an executive president. Yet, there is every indication that this unusual cabinet acted and was treated by the political parties like a parliamentary cabinet without a Parliament – that is to say the Prime Minister represented the ultimate authority in the government. Hence, the cabinet was automatically dissolved when the Prime Minister, Sir al-Khatim al-Khalifa resigned. In his letter of resignation al-Khalifa pointed out this dilemma when he said that he had 'failed to run the cabinet because of inharmonious ministers in whose selection he had had no hand.[24] None the less, the Prime Minister went ahead and dismissed a cabinet that he had not appointed.

As far as the knowledge of the present writer goes there is no record of a challenge to this trend of events on the ground that the Prime Minister did not have an explicit (*de jure*) right to dissolve the cabinet. On the other hand, however, there was no provision – in the Charter or constitution – that impedes the Prime Minister from such an act. In retrospect, one would say that the unprecedented composition and powers of the caretaker government and its crucial role in those particular circumstances, should have called for an innovative constitutional and/or statutory arrangements. In the absence of such arrangements the course of events that ensued was almost inevitable, and could have been reversed only through a successful fight back by the radical forces – primarily, the Front of the Professionals.

Yet, however crucial the role of the Front in the uprising, it was by no means a militant and cohesive body. Rather it was a collection of all shades of opinions and ideologies that included liberals, independent radicals, communists, Muslim Brothers, Arab Nationalists, and so on. Despite this heterogeneity the main force behind the Front appeared to be the Communists who prevailed over a majority of the Front's organisations. Hence the strife which was inherent in the very composition of the Front crystallised around the communist majority in its leadership, a matter that stimulated the hostility of the

Muslim Brothers within the organisation. Other factions, who were equally annoyed by the increasing influence of the Communists, had either sided with the Muslim Brothers or assumed independent actions.[25]

Consequently, the offensive pursued by the parties of the Nationalist Front in early 1965 on the leadership of the Front of the Professionals was bound to leave lasting cracks on its heterogeneous body. Thus, its first conference, which was held in January 1965 was the last. The conference only demonstrated the acute power struggle within the Front. For example, a suggestion by the leadership to invest the civil servants with the right to political activity provoked a strong opposition. Some Islamic-oriented organisations called for a purge of communists from the Front. Furthermore, many committees and general assemblies did not consider the resolutions of the Front's conference obligatory, though these were passed by an absolute majority.[26]

The resignation of the first caretaker government was indeed a hard blow to the Front of the Professionals which constituted a majority in that government. The second and final blow came two days later when fifteen member organisations broke away from the Front, following which its demise was only a matter of time. The disintegration of the Front not only facilitated the conservative takeover, but also frustrated a successful fight back by the radicals. Accordingly, the former prevailed on the Prime Minister until he formed a second caretaker government in which they enjoyed a majority. The party was over.

III. CHANGING POLITICAL SITUATIONS

As has been alluded to earlier, one of the issues that triggered the demise of the military regime was its drastic attitude to the Southern problem. By 1965, a decade after the Torit mutiny of 1955, the entire South was on the brink of open rebellion against the North.

By 1958, the call for federalism had stricken roots among the Southern politicians and intelligentsia, and was gradually becoming a rallying point between them. 'Abbud's military *coup d'état*, therefore, was regarded by the majority of the southerners as a conspiracy by the northern politicians against the South.[27]

The military regime was to realise the Southerners worst fears. Not only did the regime use systematic and unprecedented force to 'eradicate' Southern opposition but, significantly, it pursued a policy of forced Arabisation and Islamisation of the South. Increasingly, the

Southerners came to regard the Northerners more as 'colonisers' than fellow countrymen. The situation was not at all helped by the presence of a 'Northern' *national* army, a 'Northern' police and prison corps, a 'Northern' administrative staff, 'Northern' schools, and indeed Northern merchants.

Under the 'Abbud regime, the North–South relations had taken a dramatic twist. The accumulated mistrust resulting from successive disappointments during the 1950s was transformed into open and bitter hostility under 'Abbud. The birth of the Anya Nya movement represented a graphic symbol of such a situation.[28]

The outbreak of October Revolution was significant in many ways. As far as the Southern enlightened opinion was concerned, the October government represented the first 'true national' government since independence. Significantly, it was headed by a Prime Minister who was highly regarded in the Southern circles. Likewise the Southerners occupied senior ministerial posts; as Ministers of Interior and Communication. Furthermore, Southern representatives in Khartoum were able to persuade the Prime Minister to replace one of their representatives by another of their choice and, ultimately to increase their representation in the Cabinet from two to three. The event helped to build the Southerners confidence both in themselves as well as the new government.[29]

This October 'honeymoon', however, did not last long. As early as December 1964 some violent clashes occurred between Southerners and Northerners in Khartoum and resulted in casualties on both sides. The event, known by local press as 'bloody Sunday', laid bare the fragility of the situation and the magnitude of mutual mistrust that existed between the North and South.[30]

None the less, the October government was able to contain the outcome of bloody Sunday, and to initiate a process of negotiations with the Southern leaders in exile. Consequently, a decision was taken by the government to convene a roundtable conference for all political forces to discuss the Southern question with the aim of reaching a democratic settlement.

The political scene in the South had of course remarkably changed owing to the above-mentioned transformation during the military regime. Towards the end of that era, SANU emerged as the most significant force among the Southerners in exile. Yet, a serious rift was building among the leaders of SANU. In November 1964, a SANU conference brought the dispute into the open as a faction led by Joseph Oduhu, Agrey Gaden and Saturnino Lubhoro vowed to oust

William Deng who was hitherto the party's secretary general. The latter refused to accept the Congress resolution and a split occurred between a SANU headed by William Deng and another headed by Agrey Gaden. Subsequently, Deng returned from exile to head a legally recognised SANU which became a party within the 'national' political process. Agrey Gaden and Joseph Oduhu, however, continued to lead the exiled SANU.[31]

Meanwhile, a new organisation – the Southern Front – appeared in Khartoum during the wake of the October Revolution. The Southern Front had been active underground during the military regime and surfaced during the events of October 1964. Indeed, the Southern Front played an important role in expressing a 'Southern view' during the formation of the October government. Its role in the negotiations with the Southerners in exile that followed was crucial in convincing some of them to take part in the projected roundtable conference.

The conference was finally convened in Khartoum on 16 March 1965. From the South it was attended by the Southern Front, both SANU factions, and 'other shades of opinion' who were represented on individual capacity. From the North there were the five main political parties, Umma – NUP, PDP, CPS, and ICF – as well as the Front of the Professionals. The Southern Front demanded the right for self-determination for the South and a plebiscite to give the South the opportunity to decide the nature of its relationship with the North. Leaders of the exiled SANU called for outright separation, while the internal SANU (Deng's faction) called for federation.

The Northern political leaders appeared willing to reach a settlement 'which would allow social and economic development for the South, equality of citizenship, and establishment of a system of local government'. Though, the formula went some way to recognising the dimensions of the Southern problem it fell short of Southern demands, particularly as it projected a solution within an indisputable concept of a united Sudan.

After about ten days of deliberation the conference resolved to adjourn for a period of three months, and to set-up a twelve, man committee to study and 'recommend constitutional, administrative and financial relations between the South and the central government.' A 'crash programme' was also recommended for the South consisting, among other things, of resettlement of southern returnees, southernisation of administration, equalisation of salaries between North and South, and so on.[32]

All these resolutions were regarded favourably by both participants

and observers. Yet, the conference did not achieve its main objective
of a political solution acceptable to all concerned parties and capable
of ending the war. Essentially, the Northern and Southern views were
miles apart. While the former operated on the premises that 'unity'
was to be taken for granted, separatism to be condemned, as was the
rebels' violence; the Southern view was preoccupied by its distrust of
the North per se and its grievances because of the atrocities of the
'Northern' army. Accordingly it espoused demands for separation,
self-determination and a loose federation.

The failure of the conference was compounded by the fact that
none of the Southern parties and politicians who took part in it
appeared to have commanded sufficient influence on the Anya Nya
fighters, who continued their attacks despite the negotiations.[33]

The immediate consequence of the failure of the roundtable
conference to achieve a settlement was the decision of the Supreme
Council to postpone the general elections (scheduled for 12 April
1965) in the three southern provinces. Consequently, the South was
relegated to a peripheral position in the country's national politics.
Worse still, due to the fact that the Supreme Council's decision was
not promulgated into a law, some Northern merchants (who were
candidates before the council's decision) were elected to the
parliament as 'unopposed' candidates. That event alone had inflicted
irreparable damage to the North–South relations.

Later on supplementary elections were held in the remaining southern
constituencies. They were contested and won mostly by SANU, NUP, and
other southern parties within the Establishment (the Southern Front had
boycotted because of the continuation of the state of emergency in the
south). The twelve-man committee held several meetings throughout
1965/66 with some progress but without a real breakthrough. The
situation remained tense and strained because of the continued civil war.[34]

Continuation of the war in the south was the second and far
reaching repercussion of the failure of the roundtable conference. The
Anya Nya, which adopted the line of violent resistance, became the
rallying point for all the disgruntled southerners whether those who
from the very beginning maintained their hostility to the North
despite the change of government in October, 1964; or those who
were disappointed by the outcome of the conference. The decision to
hold partial elections in the country, and the 'election' of *Northern*
merchants to represent the *South*, must have convinced many,
particularly the educated Southerners, that force was their only voice.

Ironically, the all good-intentioned October government, had indirectly contributed to the escalation of the war. The radically dominated Cabinet of the first caretaker government had allowed an arms shipment from the 'Eastern Bloc' destined to the Simba fighters in Zaire to be transferred through Sudan. Ultimately, most of these weapons found their way back to southern Sudan, and into the hands of the Anya Nya insurgents. From then onwards the civil war took a definite turn and the second parliamentary experiment had to operate under its shadow.[35]

With the holding of the general elections the 'euphoria' brought about by the October Revolution came to a close and again the political process seemed to have relapsed back to the pre-November 1958 era. Yet, the political situation of the post-October era was never the same. The situation in the South apart, there were important changes among the socio-political forces in the North. Forces like the communists and leftists in general, hitherto of negligible presence, appeared with considerable influence as was demonstrated by their high positions within the Front of the Professionals and the first caretaker government. The period also witnessed rising fortunes of the Muslim Brothers, the hard core of the Islamists especially in the student politics and within a limited sector of the middle class. Immediately after the October uprising the MBs established the Islamic Charter Front (ICF) as an umbrella organisation for Islamic-oriented groups and individuals with the MBs as its nucleus, with the declared objectives of establishing an 'Islamic State'; and reorganisation of the economy on 'Islamic basis' such as the state collection of Zakah (the Islamic alms-in-tax) and abolishment of interest rates from the banking system.[36]

Other leftist forces appeared, with no significant influence but rather as a reflection of the changing political situation, such as the Democratic Socialist Congress and loosely organised groups of Arab Nationalists and Arab Socialists.

Old-guard politicians, on the other hand, tried to cope with the new situation at least formally. This was more apparent, however, in the two sectarian parties, the Umma and PDP. The Umma party emerged under a new generation of leaders represented by the new party chairman, Sayyid al-Sadiq al-Mahdi (son of the deceased leader of Umma and *Ansar* Sayyid al-Sadiq al-Mahdi), who tried to restructure the party on new lines that would make it more attractive to the intelligentsia and the ever-active forces of the modern sector. In this context slogans of socialism, modernity and development found a place in the new programme of the Umma party.[37]

Apart from the general impact of the new political situation brought about by the October uprising, the revitalisation of the Umma party may also be attributed to certain socio-economic considerations. The growth of capitalist elements in its ranks due to the favourite conditions of private investment that prevailed under the military regime have necessitated restructuring of the party on a new basis. Hence came the attempts of liberalisation of the party structures, loosening the yoke of the sectarianist grip and the adoption of a 'national' outlook that would in its turn attract other forces outside the traditional sphere of the *Ansar* sect.

In its turn, the PDP had adopted a constitution for the first time. This constitution affirmed the party's commitment to socialism 'as long as it doesn't contradict the spirit of Islam and its *shari'a*, Arab Nationalism, Islam, and a parliamentary system. As such the PDP's constitution did not differ greatly from the other Traditionalist parties but its practical policies showed a vehement leftist orientation, as demonstrated by its alliances with the CPS during the period in question. In retrospect, this PDP's leftist tendency might be assessed as a tactical move in order to cover up the party's support to the 'Abbud regime. Yet, one must not overlook the Egyptian – *Nasserite* – impact on the PDP and the prevalence of a faction of Arab Nationalists within its leadership, including the party chairman himself Shaykh 'Ali 'Abd al-Rahman al-'Amin.

By contrast to the PDP, the NUP was moving consistently to the right as demonstrated by its position during the aftermath of the uprising (its opposition to the caretaker government, its alliance with the Umma and ICF, and the feverish anti-communist zeal which this alliance had assumed). As in the case of the Umma, the changing positions of the NUP could be also attributable to the upward social mobility within its ranks. 'The party of small traders, villagers, shopkeepers and young nationalists had become the party of an expanding commercial group. This group had been fertilised by the military regime and was growing in the shadow of foreign investment.'[38] Unlike the Umma, the NUP did not undertake any radical restructuring of its organs neither had it elaborated a comprehensive programme beyond the vague pronouncements of Islam and socialism (the currency of the day).

Such were some of the measures undertaken by the traditionalist parties either as an outcome of the objective transformations that reshaped their social basis during the period of the military regime, or as a response to the changing political situations caused by the October uprising and its aftermath. It was against this background that the general elections of 1965 took place. Judging by the polarised atmosphere between left and right, elections, especially in the urban areas, were contested under the slogans of 'anti-communism' by the right-wing parties on the one hand, and the 'achievements of October revolutionary objectives', raised by the left on the other. Yet, as the left with its various tributaries was by no means a major rival to the rightists (especially Umma and NUP), the latter had no need to run a co-ordinated contest. Consequently, the door was open for the traditional Umma–NUP rivalries to surface as each of them aimed at polling a convenient majority with the prospect of securing an upper hand in government formation. The result of elections returned the old brokers of the Traditionalist parties to power in yet another coalition government from Umma and NUP (92 seats for Umma, and 73 NUP). Significantly, however, the special graduates constituencies were dominated by communists and their allies (returned 11 out of 15). The ICF returned five seats (two in the graduates constituencies and three in the geographic ones). For the first time, certain regional groupings appeared in the legislative body such as the Beja Congress, the Nuba Mountains Union, and later on the Darfur Front.[39]

By then, coalition phenomena had become an established factor of Sudanese politics owing to the objective regional and sectarian divisions of the country. As for the Umma and NUP they had tested possibilities of co-operation within the opposition front to the 'Abbud regime, and actively collaborated during their painstaking campaign against the 'communist threat' in the aftermath of the October Uprising.

What was new in this coalition was that for the first time it was based on a 'charter', a matter which must be attributed to the changing political situations of the post-October era. If the Umma–PDP coalition in the 1950s was based on nothing more than the summit of the two Sayyids, in the post-October period the Traditionalist parties felt the need to express their commitment to a written programme.

The 'national charter of the coalition', which was signed on 24 June 1965 elaborated the policies of the coalition parties in four areas: democracy, economy, foreign affairs and the Southern question. In the Chapter on 'Democracy' the charter emphasised: 'Securing the public and fundamental freedoms, e.g. freedom of the press, organization and expression', (point a), 'developing local government by liquidation of the native administration in the developed areas and its democratisation in the backward ones' (point d), 'safeguarding the independence of the judiciary, the civil service and the university' (point g). In the economic field, the charter spoke about 'the creation of a public-sector under the direction and supervision of the State embracing public services, strategic industrial and agricultural schemes'; and, encouragement of private and co-operative sectors. Moreover, the charter promised to 'review the laws that determine production relations so as to be more socialist'. In foreign policy commitment to non-alignment, détente and international peace was underlined.[40]

Clearly the charter had virtually echoed the most popular slogans of the October uprising whether raised by mass organisations, embodied in the National Charter of the uprising, or the programme of the first caretaker government. Yet, as was to be proven by the actual policies of the coalition government, the charter far from being a solid commitment to the objective of the uprising, was in fact a series of promises meant to placate, at least temporarily, the forces activated by the uprising.

Significantly, the document said nothing about Islam which had been the battle cry of both parties *vis-à-vis* the communists during elections. Failure of the charter to refer to Islam in whatever context questions the seriousness of the coalition parties' pronounced attachment to Islam. Accordingly, one is increasingly led to believe that the role of Islam had in effect been utilised by these parties as an ideological tool of mobilisation more than a blueprint of government. Otherwise their politics remained secular as it used to be in the 1950s. As we shall see, however, this picture was to change. In view of the roaming spectre of communism the old-guard politicians were increasingly posing in religious robes.

IV. DEMOCRACY FOR THE FAITHFUL!

On the evening of Monday 8 November 1965, the students of the High Teachers' Training Institute had a rally where a student named Shawqi Muhammad 'Ali spoke insolently about Islam, the prophet Muhammad and his dependants. The students' organisation of the Institute condemned the 'blasphemous' student and requested that the administration take measures against him. The 'Islamic Direction', student wing of ICF, of the Institute took responsibility of considering it an individual incident to be dealt with at the level of the institute.[41]

The leaders of the CPS held a press conference at which they drew attention to what they labelled as a conspiracy against democracy.

They also showed that the named student had no relation whatsoever with the CPS. The party also circulated a statement in which it attacked the MBs.

On the morning of Thursday 11 November 1965, the Islamic Direction of the HTTI issued a statement claiming that the student Shawqi was indeed a member of the CPS. Together with the students of some religious institutes and supporters of the ICF, organised a demonstration against the CPS, and a group of them marched to the Council of Ministers premises where they handed the Prime Minister, Muhammad Ahmad Mahjub, a petition that demanded the dissolution of the CPS.

On the afternoon of Friday 12 November 1965 the Minister of Interior, Ahmad al-Mahdi, broadcast a statement disapproving the contents of the notorious speech delivered by student Shawqi and especially his attack on Islam 'the most important value embraced by the Sudanese society'. He went on to affirm that the government would take measures to stop this misbehaviour.

The central committee of the CPS issued a reply to the Minister's statement, which was handed to him. They affirmed that student Shawqi was not member of the Communist Party, showed their disapproval of what came in his speech, and confirmed the respect which the party had for all the beliefs of the Sudanese people, especially the Islamic religion.

Other events succeeded, al-Sadiq al-Mahdi gave a public speech at the mosque of al 'Imam 'Abd al-Rahman al-Mahdi. Isma'il al-Azhari, Chairman of the Supreme Council, spoke to demonstrators and expressed his discontent of that attack against Islam. The masses marched to *Bayt al-Mal* in Umdurman and attacked the headquarters of the CPS branch there, demolished the walls, burned all papers, damaged the furniture and engaged in fights with members of the party.

The drama reached its peak when six deputies proposed that

it is the opinion of this Constituent Assembly, regarding the events that happened recently in the capital and provinces, and regarding the experience of democratic rule in this country and its lack of protection necessary for its growth and development, that the government be assigned to present a preamble in conformity to which the Communist Party of Sudan should be dissolved and the establishment of any communist parties or organisations, the principles of which incorporate atheism, disrespect of beliefs or the practice of dictatorial methods, be banned.[42]

On Monday morning, 15 November 1965, the Constituent Assembly commenced its session. A number of members spoke, defending the motion demanding the dissolution of the CPS. From time to time some deputies walked out to address the supporters who had been brought outside the assembly building. They were shouting 'no Communism inside the assembly'. Some 151 deputies voted for the amendment, 12 against it and 9 abstained. This action necessitated another amendment in the constitution to enable the Assembly to expel the Communist Party deputies. Thus, one amendment followed another till the Communist Party deputies were finally dismissed from the Constituent Assembly.[43]

The leftist camp for its part gathered its forces in order to fight back. On 16 November 1965 a conference was conducted in the headquarters of the Peoples' Democratic Party and attended by the parties of the PDP, CPS, Arab Socialist Front, Republican Party, Democratic Socialist Congress in addition to some thirty-one trades unions and other mass organisations representing labour, civil service, professionals, tenants, students and youth. The Conference naturally condemned the recent resolutions of the Constituent Assembly and called for its dissolution. Among the resolutions adopted by the Conference were:

- Division of electoral constituencies proportional to political consciousness (i.e. to give more weight to the urban rather than the rural areas in the constituencies' division);
- Formation of a national committee to draft the permanent constitution wherein there should be a special guarantee of freedom of expression and organisation;
- Formation of an all national committee to hold general elections on the above-mentioned basis of the constituencies division.
- To hold a march comprising of all the associations represented in the conference to protect democracy. The march should hand a protest petition to the Supreme Council. In addition to that the Conference decided to form a permanent association for the defence of democracy and public freedoms.[44]

Consequently, on 21 November some 30,000 people demonstrated in the capital against the dissolution of the CPS and 'in defence of democracy, the Constitution and public freedoms'. The demonstration – an initiative of the National Conference noted above – clashed with a counter demonstration and consequently 88 persons were wounded and 32 arrested.[45]

While similar protest demonstrations broke out in other cities (such as 'Atbra, Madani, Kosti), other parties like SANU and Southern Front, as well as many individuals and independent press papers also denounced the Assembly's decision. All in all, the measure had turned substantial parts of the intelligentsia and urban population against the coalition government. They all fought under the banner of democracy, and, although the battle did not yield its fruits it still indicated the widening gap between the coalition government and the 'modern forces', particularly in view of the fact the communist candidates were virtually the representatives of the intellegentsia in the assembly.[46]

On another level, the measures taken by the leftist forces against the dissolution of the CPS invoked yet another reaction from the rightists' camp. The Umma, NUP and ICF parties quickly held a conference which announced the setting up of the Islamic Conference for the Defence of Religious Beliefs on 28 November 1965 and adopted the following resolutions:

– The formation of a permanent association to protect Islamic beliefs and take measures against any possible conspiracy to repeal the decision taken by the Constituent Assembly;
– The formation of a committee responsible for the organisation of demonstrations, marches, rallies and conferences as well as to train and mobilise youth for *jihad*;
– In the process of atheism abolishment the Conference took the following decisions:

   a) modification of educational curricula to include more Islamic teachings, to enable the youth to grow in a religious atmosphere,
   b) formation of a press house to spread Islamic thought and Islamic publications,
   c) confiscation of communist publications,
   d) drafting of an Islamic Constitution and submitting it to the Constituent Assembly as soon as possible.[47]

Apparently the 'Islamic Conference' bore a very polemical tone to the 'National Conference for the Defence of Democracy'.

By then the affair of the 'blasphemous' student of the HTTI had become irrelevant. The right-wing forces advanced the reasoning that the very existence of a communist party in the Sudanese society should not be tolerated because, as in al-Turabi's words, of its 'voidence to the principles of faith, ethics, sincerity to the homeland, and national unity';[48] or, as in al-Sadiq's words, 'its contradiction of the belief in existence of God, its binding Sudan's sovereignty with an international creed [and its call for] class dictatorship'.[49]

Yet, from the preceding account of the dramatic events that accompanied the dissolution of the CPS it must be realised that the decision was taken for more structural considerations than just the communists' 'voidence to principles of faith, ethics' and patriotism. The active role played by the communists during the October Uprising, their comparatively efficient organisational capacities that enabled them to ascend to the leadership of the Front of the Professionals and consequently to dominate the first caretaker Government, their majority position in the graduates constituencies and their mounting influence in the modern sector as demonstrated by elections results, had all alarmed the right-wing parties and provided the real motives for the dissolution of the CPS.

Remarkably, Islam figured very high, as an ideological weapon, in this campaign. The Minister of Interior broadcast his above-mentioned statement pointedly on Friday (Muslim religious holiday) drawing, as he did, analogies between the religious ritual of the day and the blasphemous practices of the communists. The most advanced arguments, just quoted from al-Turabi and al-Sadiq al-Mahdi, such as those dwelt on the idea that communism by nature is antithetical to the Sudanese Muslim society. Mosques and Friday sermons were extensively utilised to stimulate the religious sentiments of the populace and to mobilise them in what was called *thawrat Rajab* (Rajab Revolution). A *fatwa* was announced by the Sudanese *ulama'* against the Communist Party and eventually, as pointed out above, a decision was taken by the Islamic Conference to adopt an Islamic Constitution.

To sum up, the dissolution of the CPS had culminated in a crisis of parliamentary politics. The inconsistency of the parliamentary system in the Sudan was recognised not only by the leftists and their liberal allies, but by the rightists as well who argued that a system which admits communism was not a proper system 'for the nation's progress'. The alternative of the latter, as we shall see later, was a Presidential republic based on an Islamic Constitution.

This perhaps signalled the end of the liberalist tendency which appeared in the 1930s and was significant through the era of the nationalist Movement and the 1950s. Yet, in reality, it had never taken root in the society and remained an exotic cult confined to the first and second generations of the intelligentsia. Unfortunately, the latter, blinded by their ruthless pursuit of power, had not taken the trouble either to substantiate their association with liberalism or to adapt it to Sudanese circumstances. On the contrary, as we have just seen, they had easily repudiated it and took complete refuge in an inarticulate and poorly defined Islamic ideology. With this, secularism also lost its position as an acceptable form of Sudanese politics. Henceforth, although some segments of the Traditionalist parties continued to adhere to secularism, it became increasingly associated with the leftist forces.

Chapter 4

The Making of an Islamic Constitution

With the banning of the Communist Party in December 1965, the feverish left–right confrontation that had dominated the scene immediately after the October Uprising came to a temporary halt. However, the controversy surfaced once again when, a year later, the High Court ruled in favour of the Communist Party, stating that the decision of the Constituent Assembly was not constitutional.[1] Yet the government of the day, led by al-Sadiq al-Mahdi, was in no mood to abide by the Court's decision and neither was the Supreme Council. Such an attitude led to a constitutional crisis and the Chief of Justice, Babiker 'Awadallah, resigned in protest.

Thus, if the dissolution of the CPS had signalled a crisis in the Sudanese parliamentary system, the government's violation of the judiciary's authority had rendered the system practically unworkable.

In January 1967, a committee which had been appointed to draft the long awaited permanent constitution opted for an 'Islamic' constitution. In view of the above-mentioned circumstances, such a move might be regarded as an attempt by the government both to overcome the embarrassment caused by its failure to abide by a decision of the judiciary (the authority entrusted to interpret the constitution), and to legitimise in unequivocal constitutional terms the illegality of the CPS. These political motives notwithstanding, the issue of an Islamic constitution needs more thorough investigation.

I. GENERAL CONSIDERATIONS

The demise of the liberal element within the Sudanese political movement, caused partly by its intrinsic weakness, and partly by the alliance of the first generations of the intelligentsia with sectarianism, was bound to leave a vacuum in Sudanese political thought. As we have seen earlier, two new forces attempted to fill this vacuum, namely the radicals and the Islamists.

Assessing the respective achievements of these new forces we have already pointed out that the leadership of the modern sector forces (such as the workers, tenant farmers, students and professionals) had eventually passed to the radicals, namely the Communist Party. Yet as the nature of the latters' leadership had been essentially associated with trade unionism rather than ideological indoctrination, its politics became rather characterised by agitation and unrest. This gained it the violent hostility of the Traditionalist parties that came to power at Independence. As we have seen in the previous chapter, this hostility reached its climax during the October Uprising and its aftermath when the Communists ostensibly emerged as the strongest party in the 'October Coalition'.

On the other hand, the Islamists, who emerged basically in response to the Communists had succeeded, by the 1960s, in building up some influence on student politics and sought to compete with the Communists over the leadership of the intelligentsia and other forces of the modern sector.

Accordingly, the ideological scene during the 1960s became mostly dominated by the conflicting blueprints of the Communists and Muslim Brothers with other rallying forces at both poles. The controversy, however, was not between Islam and secularism as it was between socialism – as conceived by a Communist Party, and Islam – as conceived by a *neo-salafiyya* movement.[2] In spite of the strict ideological concepts of the adversaries, however, the slogans of 'socialism' and 'Islam' were capable of attracting other forces with differing interpretations of these.

Judging by the wider regional situation of the time, the slogan of socialism was more in circulation. The 1950s and 1960s had been momentous decades in the Middle East and Africa, characterised by the explosive emergence of independent states in Africa, the strong tides of Nasserism, Arab nationalism, Arab socialism, Pan-Africanism, African socialism, the birth of the Non-aligned Movement and the OAU. It was a period full of hopes, optimism and great expectations. Leaders such as Nasser, N'Krumah, Sukarnu and Nehru became symbols of patriotism, social justice and anti-imperialism. A prominent feature of this radical wave was its *populist* ideology, which developed mostly at the expense of liberalism and in association with militarism and charismatic figures.[3]

Under the hegemony of this populism both Communist and

Islamist movements were suppressed. Yet while the Communist parties were banned and their leaders jailed, the populist regimes emphasised socialist, or 'non-capitalist' ways of development, adhered to a socialist philosophy of a sort (including 'scientific socialism') and contracted alliances with the Eastern bloc of the time.

As for Islamism, the most outspoken representative of which since the Second World War has been the Muslim Brotherhood, it was not only suppressed as a political movement but banned rather strongly as a 'reactionary' ideology. The reason for this may be sought in the nature of the movement itself, which emphasised political activism and vowed to establish an Islamic state or order. Such a pledge entailed the *illegitimacy* of all political systems, and invariably embroiled the movement in violent confrontation with the populist regimes in the region, especially the Nasserite.

Naturally the Sudan was influenced by these developments in neighbouring states, particularly Egypt, which remained the gate through which the Sudan received external influences. Nevertheless, due to the internal dynamism of Sudanese society and its particularities the situation in the Sudan was not simply a reflection of what was happening elsewhere. The Sudanese cannot identify easily with either Arabism or Africanism and the synthesis of Afro-Arabism which was worked out as a reflection of the 'double identity' of the Sudan has, as in the words of one scholar, cultivated a 'multiple marginality'.[4] The point of emphasis here is not the external image of the Sudan, but rather its complicated political map. For, instead of either Arab or African nationalism there was not much of a 'Sudanese nationalism'. As we have seen, the so-called 'nationalist movement' was anti-colonial, full of sectarian, regional, tribal and partisan divisions, rather than a reflection of a Sudanese nationalism per se. This situation continued after independence and intensified because of the failure to tackle the Southern question with its direct implications for national identity and unity.

This complex reality made politics an equally complex affair. Any polarisation, such as the left–right confrontation of the post-October era, meant conflicting coalitions of various and broader forces.

The majority of the Sudanese intelligentsia, having just participated in a victorious popular uprising, were indeed more inclined to be influenced by the strong tides of socialism, nationalism and freedom than with Islamic 'fundamentalism', whose tide was rather ebbing during the 1960s.

Consequently, a broad coalition of the left came into existence with the Communist Party as its nucleus. It made itself visible on many political occasions, such as the Front of the Professional Organisations during the October Uprising, the 'Democratic Socialist Ensemble' during the aftermath of the uprising, and the Conference for the Defence of Democracy during the crisis of the CPS. At odds with this leftist coalition stood the rightist camp under the banner of Islam. At its core was the ICF, sometimes alone, but at crucial times such as during the 'Communist threat', in alliance with the Traditionalist parties.

In ideological terms the two camps sought to convey new messages in terms of Islam and socialism. Because of its relative strength among the intelligentsia the leftist contributors were more outspoken, especially in the fields of culture, literature and art. The Muslim Brothers were not able to score similar successes, as demonstrated by their poor performance during the 1965 elections, especially in the Graduates' Constituencies. Even their initial advance into student politics during the early 1960s were halted in the post-October eras by the leftist coalition.[5]

With influential parts of the intelligentsia, professional and other modern sector forces virtually turning left and/or secular, the influence of the ICF became increasingly confined to the traditionally educated sectors. These included groups as *shari'a* judges, lawyers, and *muftis* – that is, the Islamic orthodox *'ulama'* – and a rather insignificant sector of the middle class, such as teachers, shopkeepers, mosque *'Imams* and, of course, students (who later became their stronghold). Due to such a narrow and traditionally-oriented constituency, the ICF did not develop a clearly defined Islamic blueprint in a sophisticated way, either in apologetic or in 'fundamentalist' terms. Its formulations on its central theme of an 'Islamic state' remained as vague and generalised as they had been in the 1950s, and most of the ICF propaganda energies were devoted to attacking their most hated enemies, the Communists.[6]

This position of the ICF in relation to the CPS had induced the former to form alliances with the Traditionalist parties in an attempt to eradicate the Communists as we have seen earlier. Needless to say, the Traditionalist parties were more than ready to utilise the comparatively better organisational and ideological capacities of the Muslim Brothers in mobilising the populace against the increasingly troublesome Communists. The impact of this Islamist-traditionalist alliance was twofold: on the one hand it somehow deterred the ICF from waging an orthodox campaign against sectarianism and *Sufism*, the practices of which were dismissed by the ICF as overloaded with many pre-Islamic traditions and other non-Islamic innovations. On the other hand, the traditionalist parties had become more inclined to concede to the call for an 'Islamic constitution' as it coincided with their feverish campaign against the 'blasphemous' Communist Party. Furthermore, the intelligentsia of the traditionalist parties who had sacrificed their liberalism, first on the *altar* of sectarianism, and then defied it completely in the face of the rapidly maturing radicalism, sought to protect themselves behind fences of an Islamist ideology of a sort.

The choice of the Traditionalist parties of Islam as a more feasible ideological forum reflected Islam's strength at the social level. Indeed, the influence of popular Islam in the rural areas remained as strong as ever, and substantial sections of the urban and suburban population retained their traditional loyalties to their respective popular Islamic *tariqas*. The social structure that had come into existence in eighteenth- and nineteenth-century northern Sudan, and in which Islam played a profound role, continued virtually intact during the first half of the twentieth century. This social structure, as we know from previous chapters, was predominantly characterised by kinship and tribal loyalties which became integrated within the framework of popular Islamic loyalties, first through the efforts of the autonomous *sufi tariqas* during the period of Sinnar, and then more vehemently during the *Mahdiyya*. It was on these bases that the prominent sects of the twentieth century, the *Ansar* and *Khatmiyya* divided the loyalty of the majority of Sudanese Muslims.

As for the 'modernity' that accompanied the colonial administration in economics and education it proved to have been little more than a series of enclaves in an overwhelmingly traditional society. Furthermore, due to the conservative and utilitarian character of the colonial development ventures, these enclaves retained many of the traditional loyalties. Therefore, the change brought about by the colonial administration did not represent a break with past traditions nor did it initiate a new era in which the values of Western liberalism and democracy were completely assimilated. As was pointed out earlier, liberalism remained a rather exotic creed confined to sectors within the intelligentsia. Yet even the attachment of the latter to liberalism had been more of an adherence to a political system than to the totality of values and traditions that underlines and inspires that very system. In view of this, it is not surprising that Islam maintained, with varying degrees of success, its command over the modern sector of the population.

Thus the Gazira region, which became the homeland of the largest irrigated scheme of cotton plantation in tropical Africa, continued to be the stronghold of popular Islam. Similarly, the majority of industrial workers retained their sectarian affinities in spite of their radical trade unionist activism. The intelligentsia, predominantly the product of modern secular education, retained a clear attachment to Islam either as a religion, a culture, an ideology or a social tradition. Therefore, if due to political and economic considerations tribal or kinship loyalties were altered or weakened, the religious (Islamic) bond continued pretty much intact, sometimes in the traditional form as in the case of the popular Islam of the rural population, or in the modified forms of the intelligentsia in the urban areas.

It was against this background that a 'marriage of convenience' had taken place between the first generation of the intelligentsia and sectarianism, and which, as we have seen, was underpinned by mutual pragmatism. The failure of the Traditionalist parties, the offspring of this sectarian intelligentsia union, to bring about any significant structural socio-economic changes in society meant that the social structure remained virtually intact, subject only to the objective mechanisms of change that operate as prolonged processes. However, whether they were acting by design or not the traditionalist parties did have a vested interest in maintaining the status quo which provided them with the undisputed loyalty of most of the population. Consequently, in view of their above-mentioned pragmatism, when these parties finally opted for Islam as their ideology, they did so in the most equivocal terms and perhaps with a single motive, namely to ban their radical opponents.

Consequently, one is led to believe that the leaders of the Traditionalist parties who opted for Islam on the basis of the latter's profound strength at the social level, had invoked the name of the Lord more for their own interests than out of a genuine desire to articulate a social demand.

The continued social strength of Islam and the ability of Traditionalist and Islamist parties to utilise this force ideologically had a very deep impact on radicalism. As we know, the radicals had virtually assumed the leadership of the intelligentsia and other modern forces following the demise of liberalism. Yet the vehement campaign against the Communists on charges of atheism had made the radicals extremely cautious and apologetic as far as Islam was concerned. The fact that they did not represent a major force *vis-à-vis* the population had made their task even more difficult. Furthermore, even among the small modern sector population, the Communists in particular did not command outright *ideological* influence, but rather a trade unionist, and at best a political one.[7] Consequently, radical secularism had not succeeded in becoming a sizeable alternative to either liberal secularism or Islamic conservatism. A testimony to this state of affairs is the conformist position of the CPS with regard to religion, as reflected by the party documents at the time:

> Imperialism and its local allies, the capitalists and feudal elements, try to falsify the Islamic religion by presenting it as a creed that agrees with class differentiation and opposes socialism . . . The CPS supports the forces of the revolution in their struggle against these colonialist and reactionary attempts; and works vehemently and patiently to free religion from this image and to set it on its natural course as a religion that fights against class discrimination and despotis.[8]

In view of the strength of the spiritual command of Islam over the majority of the populace, the CPS found it essential not only to pay due respect to it but even to attempt a reinterpretation of Islam in terms of equity and social justice.

With these considerations in mind we now turn to investigate the question of the 'Islamic constitution' that dominated the political scene in the second half of the 1960s.

II. THE CONTROVERSIAL CONSTITUTION

As in the 1950s, a National Committee for the Constitution composed of 44 members was elected by the Constituent Assembly during the government of al-Sadiq al-Mahdi (who had come to office in June, 1966).[9] The Constitution Committee which was headed by the Speaker of the Assembly, Mubarak Shadad, held its inaugural meeting on 12 February 1967. Another Associate Technical Committee of Constitutional Studies was formed with Muhammad Ibrahim Khalil as its chairman, and Hasan al-Turabi as secretary. This Technical Committee conducted its first meeting on 22 February 1967.

After a series of studies and discussions the Technical Committee proposed three options for a possible constitution:

1 A full Islamic Constitution, totally committed to the *shari'a* and its various obligations,
2 A constitution with an Islamic orientation, that is, one in which there is a general tendency towards Islam but which is not strictly constructed on the tenets of Islamic *shari'a* and jurisprudence.
3 A non-religious or secular constitution, that is, one in which the state would neither have an official religion nor would it meddle in the religious affairs of its citizens.[10]

The first option was proposed by the ICF, the second by the NUP and the third by the Southern representatives.

The National Committee endorsed the second option (of the NUP) and ruled that the 'Sudanese Constitution should be derived from the principles and spirit of Islam'.[11]

Accordingly, the National Committee drafted a proposal for the Permanent Constitution and submitted it to the Constituent Assembly on 15 January 1968 after a year of deliberations.[12]

Surprisingly, with all the propaganda about Islam and the expressed determination of the Umma, NUP and ICF (who dominated both the National Committee and the Assembly) to work out an Islamic Constitution the draft that was finally presented to the Assembly was not particularly Islamic in tone. In the whole text of the draft constitution there were merely the following clauses:

Draft Constitution – *Chapter One*,
(1) The Constitution of the Sudan shall be derived from the *principles and spirit of Islam*;
(2) The Sudan is a Democratic Socialist Republic that shall *be guided by Islam*, and comprises all citizens who live within its geographical boundaries;
(3) *Islam is the official* religion of the state, and Arabic its official language;
and, in *Chapter Four*,
(113) The Islamic *Shari'a* shall be the primary source of legislation:
(114) Every legislation passed after the adoption of this constitution in contravention with the provisions of *kitab* and *sunnah* (i.e. *Qur'an* and Prophet Muhammad authentic Tradition), shall be void, provided that such contravention did not in essence previously exist;
(115) All laws which contravene the provisions of the *kitab* and *sunnah* shall be repealed or amended to the extent necessary to remove the contravention and all unapplied provisions of the *shari'a* shall be enforced, provided that such repeal, amendment or

enforcement shall be gradual according to necessity and subject to the decision of the legislative;

(140) The state shall endeavour to spread religious (i.e. Islamic) consciousness among citizens and strive to purge society from atheism and all forms of moral corruption and lack of ethics.

Apart from these clauses the Draft Constitution categorically stipulated a ban on Communism; as is clear in *Chapter Three*, article No. 33 which reads: "All citizens are granted freedom of expression, publication and the press in conformity with the law. No one citizen is, however, either permitted to advocate communism or atheism or to act or advocate a change of the ruling regime either by force, terrorism or any other illegal means"; and article No. 34 which reads, 'Citizens have the right to form political parties, trade unions and associations according to the limitations of the law. No organization whose aims contradict the condition mentioned in the first article of this section (i.e. No. 33 above) is permissable'.[13]

Such were the Islamic elements of a vigorously publicised 'Islamic' Constitution. Reviewing it carefully, one quickly reaches the obvious conclusion that, apart from the stipulation of *shari'a* as the primary source of legislation, all references to Islam were rather symbolic and fall short of what could be expected from a constitution based on 'the spirit and guidance of Islam'. As for the categorical ban on communism and, for that matter atheism, there was nothing particularly 'Islamic' about it. The Communist Party was illegal during the 'non-Islamic' colonial state and continued to be so after independence under the 'secular' Transitional Constitution. As we know, it was only legalised after the October Uprising, since there was at least one recognised Communist minister in the Caretaker government.

Otherwise the main body of the draft constitution remained as secular as any other constitution based on secular principles. Indeed, both the memoranda of the Technical Committee as well as the deliberations of the members of the National Committee were noticeably influenced by the experiences of Western countries (such as Britain, France and the USA) which all constitute the birthplace of modern secularism.

Conspicuous by their absence were significant references to Islamic traditions, whether theoretical or practical, as far as the questions of power and politics were concerned. Thus when discussing, for example, the chapters related to the judiciary or the legislative authority, most of the committee members laboured with comparative studies of modern (mostly European) systems, as well as references to past experiences in the Sudan but not in Islam.

The significance of this attitude becomes clear if we recall that the draft constitution in question prescribed the Islamic *shari'a* as the basic source of legislation, a matter that would definitely have implications for the work of the judicial system and might entail its structural reorganisation. The Sudanese judicial system that developed under the colonial rule had a dual structure with the civil courts on the one hand, and the *shari'a* courts on the other, each with its separate hierarchical structures up to the level of the Court of Appeal.[14] The system had rested on two distinct sources of legislation, namely the Islamic *shari'a* for the *shari'a* courts and the secular (Indian and European) codes for the civil courts. Accordingly, one could imagine the impact of a constitution that stipulated the *shari'a* as the basic source of legislation. However, the committee's attention had rather focused on the question of the judiciary's independence and how best to guarantee it. Likewise, its deliberations on the legislative authority focused on issues such as whether to have one or two chambers in the legislative body, what would be the implications of an Executive President on the legislative authority and whether the system should be modelled on the American or French presidential patterns. None of the committee members including the representatives of the ICF, tried to present a formula based on the spirit of Islamic *shura* (consultancy), as practised during the early days of Islam, as an alternative to the European 'alien' models.[15]

The desire of some of the National Committee members was perhaps to draft a constitution based on the 'spirit and guidance' of Islam. Ironically, however, the spirit of their discussions remained secular and indeed guided by the well-known modern European traditions of liberal democracy, such as distribution of powers, human rights, universal suffrage, etc.[16] The issue here is not just a question of the knowledge and competence of the committee members, the majority of whom had, admittedly received a secular education, because there were equally influential members who were competent enough in Islamic jurisprudence (such as the former Grand *qadi* (chief *shari'a* judge) Hasan Muddathir, and the leader of the ICF Hasan al-Turabi). The issue is rather rooted in the ideological credentials of the champions of the Islamic Constitution themselves.

The most ideologically outspoken among these, the ICF, spearheaded the campaign for an Islamic constitution at all levels. Al-Turabi, who was also the secretary of the Technical Committee, distributed a memorandum wherein he listed the advantages of adopting an Islamic constitution:

1 The constitution should represent the will of the people and since the majority are Muslims their will should prevail.
2 Unlike other religions, Islam is a *religion and state* and it instructs (the believers) to govern in accordance with Allah's Revelation.
3 The adoption of non-Islamic political systems in the Sudan had not been in response to a popular demand, but rather a work of despotic rulers with Western culture and orientation.
4 The ostensibly Islamic states that ruled Muslims were bad models whose knowledge of Islam was very poor.
5 An Islamic constitution would be a rule of sacred *law* and not a rule of *men* because in Islam there is no place for *theocracy* or 'clergy men'.
6 Islam opposes dictatorship.
7 Islam protects private freedoms and guarantees freedom of opinion and participation in public affairs.
8 Islam encourages *'ijtihad*, because the final opinion is the public's and every individual, group of individuals or political party had the right to advocate their views and to work for the assumption of power through *shura*.
9 Islam recognised freedom of religion before Europe had ever thought about it and calls for the protection of citizens with other religious beliefs.
10 Islam calls for equality before the law and in public rights.[17]

Ahmad Safy al-Din 'Awad, who had contributed to the campaign for an Islamic constitution in the 1950s took up the same issue again. His endeavour was a continuation of his discourse in the 1950s with particular emphasis on controversial themes such as the position of women and religious minorities under the rule of Islam, the role of political parties and questions of democracy and human rights.[18]

'Awad goes some way to avoid the traditional conservative Islamic view on the positions of non-Muslims, and with it the usage of the term *dhemiyy,n* (i.e. non–Muslims under the protection and rule of Muslims). Yet when he touches on the issue of political parties the writer seems to have completely ignored non-Muslims' right to political activity 'An Islamic constitution would be the dividing line between the parties that call for Islam and who would enjoy the *right for political* activity, and those that do not call for Islam who would then be *banned*.'[19]

Once again we are faced with the obvious contradictory attitude of emphasising freedom of religion and equality of all citizens before the law on one hand, and restricting political activity to Muslims only on the other. It is not enough to state that Islam had recognised human rights, or that it had emphasised values of justice, equality and democracy several centuries before Europe, because the challenge still remains. How could the noble values of Islam be translated in practical terms and result not only in a democratic system like the European one but, essentially, a better one?

Yet far from working out a comprehensive blueprint or discourse the ICF seemed to have contented itself with the role of a pressure group that reminded influential politicians of the need to return to Islam as the root of 'our' identity. In this context the option of an Islamic constitution was viewed as the start of a process of progressive Islamicisation and accordingly details could be worked out in the course of time.

Furthermore, the ICF had remained predominantly a captive of sloganism: anti-communism, anti-secularism, anti-liberalism and anti-nationalism; pro-Islam, pro-*shura* and pro-social justice. Accordingly, it could not put forward any sound intellectual contribution to substantiate its relentless call for the adoption of an Islamic constitution.

If this was the position of the Islamic Charter Front, then what can we expect from the other parties such as the NUP and Umma which were less outspoken in their Islamist tendencies? As we know the former had been playing with the idea of an 'Islamic constitution' since the late 1950s and had deployed it mostly for reasons of political expediency. The same position continued in the 1960s, albeit with new variables, such as the search for a divergent position from that of the ICF, the 'patron' of the Islamic constitution.[20] Thus, as we have seen, the NUP had called for a constitution 'based on the spirit and guidance of Islam'. This formula, which was finally adopted by the National Committee, was convenient for NUP, as well as the other Traditionalist parties, as it gave the constitution a symbolic Islamic character, and banned communism.

For the Umma Party, the story was slightly different. By this time the UP was being effectively split into two factions one led by al-Sadiq al-Mahdi – the young ambitious leader of party, and the other by the latter's uncle and Imam of *Ansar*, al-Hadi al-Mahdi. Consequently, every faction was relying on Islamic ideology to make itself more credible in the eyes of the predominantly religio-political *Ansar* sect. Naturally, each faction called for its own version of Islamic constitution. Al-Sadiq al-Mahdi wanted to balance his call for modernism with strong Islamic overtones (sometimes vague, sometimes apologetic), while for his uncle al-Hadi al-Mahdi it was sufficient to present himself as the Imam of the *Ansar*, the custodian of the Mahdist tradition and essentially a formidable champion of Islamic values in society (indeed one of only two in the whole country).

All the same, no matter how divergent their motives, the right-wing parties were able to agree on a draft 'Islamic' Constitution and to defend it as such in the Constituent Assembly.

On the other hand, opposition to an Islamic Constitution *per se* came from a broad spectrum of secular parties and groups that included the Southern parties, the Communist Party and other leftist groups, regional groupings, the Republican Party, independent figures, especially in the press, as well as substantial forces within the civil service, and the army.

The immediate impression one gets from such a composition is that it was more ideologically diverse than the opposing camp of Islamicists. For both the civil service and the army, it was a question of adherence to long and well-established secular traditions, the alternative to which was at best unclear. However, these two forces could only make their views known discreetly or through gestures since they were constitutionally banned from direct political activity. The regional groupings (from Darfur, the Nuba Mountains and Beja) saw in the Islamic constitution an open attempt to consolidate the hegemony of North Central Sudan under the umbrella of Arabic-Islamic culture which would lead more than ever to their marginalisation. Interestingly, one force, the Republican Party, opposed the constitution from an Islamist platform on the grounds that there was nothing genuinely Islamic in the proposed constitution, rather it was a 'falsification' of Islam because the religion of Islam is 'not only the *shari'a*'.[21] As for the Southern and leftist parties, they viewed the issue as essentially a battle for survival and so campaigned against it fiercely.

A Southern representative, Natali Alwak, in the Technical Committee of the Constitution presented a memorandum on a par with al-Turabi's one, that favoured a non-religious or secular constitution. He argued as follows:

1 To establish a system of government and law on the basis of a certain religious ideology (even if it is the religion of the majority) would jeopardise the principle of equality of all citizens before the law and hamper the political and legal rights of citizens of religious minorities;

2 There cannot be real religious freedom unless the state either adopts a neutral position as far as religion is concerned or treats all religions on an equal footing;

3 A constitution based on Islam raises a number of important questions such as whether it would guarantee national unity, freedom and democracy; or whether it would be turned into a theocracy;

4 Judging by the objective political reality of the Sudan (which is characterised by the dominance of sectarian parties), an Islamic constitution would only consolidate the position of these Islamic sects – a matter which would not only widen the gap between Muslims and non-Muslims, but would also be detrimental to relations between Muslims themselves;

5 The Abolishment of interest (*ribba'*) would negatively affect the commercial and economic development of the country;

6 The possibilities of a negative international response.[22]

The leaders of the 'banned' Communist Party put forward the following views against the idea of an Islamic Constitution:

1 Political systems in Islam are very controversial and subject to various interpretations, yet those who advocate an Islamic constitution do not clarify how are they going to apply Islamic *shari'a*;

2 In Islam there are many values of co-operation and respect of humanity, but the rightists in their concentration on power have ignored those values;

3 This scheme of an Islamic constitution was nothing more than an abuse of Islam as a tool to defeat and abolish the revolutionary forces;

4 Under this banner of an Islamic constitution are concealed the 'rotten' capitalist values of corruption and exploitation which not only threatens the future development of Sudanese society but which even contradict the good faith of the Islamic tradition;

5 The multi-religious, multi-cultural composition of the Sudanese society and the rights of minorities.[23]

Although both the Southern and Communist parties were united in their rejection of an Islamic Constitution, their motives and arguments naturally differed. For the Southerners, the question was rather simple: an Islamic constitution questions the very political rights of non-Muslims and amounts to an enforcement and imposition of another religion. For the Communist Party, the issue was rather complicated, particularly with reference to the political circumstances of the time in which the CPS was dissolved on charges of atheism. For the CPS to oppose the idea of an 'Islamic' constitution would naturally be portrayed by its adversaries as a rejection of Islam as such. Therefore, the campaign of the CPS against the draft constitution was extremely cautious and rather apologetic. As can be seen, the essence of the above-mentioned reasoning is that Islam is good, but those who are raising its banner are not honest, they are using, or rather abusing the sacred name of Islam in pursuit of worldly matters. In other words, the polemics of the CPS *vis-à-vis* the idea of an Islamic constitution were political more than ideological.

This position, although obviously dictated by necessity, must have been convenient and perhaps sufficient for the communists. Convenient because it enabled the CPS to form a broader coalition of secular forces whose ideological grounds and motivation were otherwise divergent (intellectual, liberal, religious, regional and radical); and sufficient because the supporters of the 'Islamic' constitution, as we have seen earlier, were far from advancing a fundamentalist programme of progressive Islamicisation.

To sum up, one can say that rather than becoming a contest between divergent blueprints of 'Islam' and 'secularism', the draft permanent constitution was turned into another political controversy between influential forces who wanted to contain their opponents, and the latter's attempt to fight back.

Yet, the complexities of the socio-political reality were bound to affect the situation both in terms of the heterogeneous alliances that were forged in pros and cons as well as the divergent views held by the advocators of an Islamic constitution. Nevertheless, the latter, with all their political and social influence, failed to pass the draft of the 'Islamic' constitution, not because they could not agree on the document, because they did, but rather because of their squabbles and in-fights that induced the coalition in power to dissolve the Assembly before it was able to endorse the constitution.

The dissolution of the Assembly took place when it became apparent that the opposition led by al-Sadiq al-Mahdi was going to propose a vote of no confidence in the government. Consequently, both the Umma (Imam's faction) MPs, as well as a substantial number of the NUP MPs, tabled their resignations one day before the intended motion so as to give the government a pretext on which to dissolve the Assembly.[24]

III. THE BOURBON DYNASTY

The era of the 'second Republic', 1965–69, was characterised by the usual political manoeuvring and intrigues that had also characterised the first parliamentary period (1956–58). The party leaders, 'like the Bourbons, had learnt nothing and forgotten nothing'.[25] Evidence of this useless wrangling is the excessive number of changes of government for no other reason but personal disagreements and partisan intrigues. Thus in a period of two and a half years, three successive governments were installed. We need not here give the details of this governmental crisis, but one of its causal factors must be emphasised and briefly investigated, namely the above-mentioned split inside the Umma Party.

Prior mention has been made of the attempts of the Umma Party to modernise itself after the October Uprising, a process that was initiated by the new young leader of the party al-Sadiq al-Mahdi. Al-Sadiq al-Mahdi could not see through his programme of 'modernisation' without himself presiding over the government. Accordingly, as soon as he reached the age of thirty required by the law governing parliamentary membership al-Sadiq al-Mahdi joined the Assembly in an apparent bid for power.[26] This move, however, received neither the consent of al-Sadiq's uncle, al-Hadi al-Mahdi, (the Imam of the *Ansar* and patron of the Umma Party) nor that of the Prime Minister from the Umma Party, M. A. Mahjub.[27] Nevertheless al-Sadiq al-Mahdi insisted and became Prime Minister (June 1966) at the expense of a split inside his own party. Although the majority of the Umma MPs sided with al-Sadiq against Mahjub and *'Imam* al-Hadi, the split weakened the bargaining position of the Umma Party *vis-à-vis* the NUP (the latter had continued in a coalition with al-Sadiq's faction of the Umma Party).

Ostensibly al-Sadiq al-Mahdi had moved against the hegemony of the sectarian leadership over the Umma Party and had emphasised the necessity of separating the religious leadership of the *Ansar*, the *'Imam*, from the political leadership of the party. Presiding over the party he sought to address a wider spectrum of the population, especially the enlightened ones as a political force and not a religious sect.

110

Yet, to assess al-Sadiq's coalition with the NUP as an alliance between two forces of secularism to break the yoke of sectarianism would be a gross mistake. With all his talk about modernism, al-Sadiq knew only too well that whatever influence he enjoyed was drawn from the same constituency as that of his uncle's, that is, the strongholds of the Mahdist family. It was out of those considerations, as we know, that al-Sadiq al-Mahdi had opted for an Islamic constitution. As for the NUP, al-Sadiq's partner in government, the issue was nothing more than yet another intrigue. At first they formed a coalition with al-Sadiq's faction in order to deepen the crisis inside the Umma Party and to discredit its ambitious young leader. With these aims achieved they turned round and made a partnership with the Umma–'*Imam* faction (April 1967). As the split inside the Umma Party became unbridgeable the NUP joined ranks with the PDP and amalgamated with them to form the Democratic Unionist Party (DUP).

The revitalised DUP won a large number of seats – 101 out of a total of 218 in the elections which were called following the dissolution of the Assembly in February 1968. In contrast, the divided Umma suffered a damaging defeat as both factions won a total of 72 seats (38 '*Imam* faction, 34 by al-Sadiq's faction). Consequently, a new coalition was formed between the DUP and the '*Imam s* faction of the Umma. Al-Sadiq's faction led the opposition together with some regional groupings and the ICF (al-Sadiq al-Mahdi himself lost his seat in those elections, as did the Secretary General of the ICF, Hasan al-Turabi).[28]

This coalition suffered more disagreements than any previous one. There were differences inside the DUP contingency (between the former NUP and former PDP elements), differences between the DUP as a whole and their partner in the coalition the Imam faction of the Umma, differences between the two main coalition parties and the representatives of the Southern parties in the government, and, naturally, differences between the government and the opposition.[29] Meanwhile, the basic issues that had surfaced during the October Uprising such as economic development, the South, the constitution, and so on, remained unresolved. The continuous wrangling of the politicians as in the pre-November 1958 period, had diverted their attention from national issues, the only difference being that after October 1964 political disagreements were over the 'lesser and not the most important issues',[30] at a time when the above-mentioned problems (especially the Southern question) had reached unprecedented complexities. In so doing the politicians not only discredited themselves but even discredited the parliamentary system itself:

111

On 11 April 1969, the Umma split was finally healed and the factions merged, leading quickly to the deposition of the Mahjub government . . . The revitalised Umma and the DUP entered into negotiations over the nature of a new constitution, and announced agreement in early May. This was by now irrelevant, however, for the discredited politicians had, as in 1958, allowed for too long the subversion of the parliamentary system to personal advantage. When the army returned to power at the end of May 1969 the second parliamentary regime was to have as few defenders as the first.[31]

Chapter 5

From a Populist Leader to an *'Imam*

Thus the fate of the second parliamentary period in the Sudan was, like that of the first, an unceremonial end through a military intervention. For, on 25 May 1969 a group of junior army officers led by Col. Ja'far Muhammad Nimeiri (promoted to a Major-General after the coup) managed to assume power in a successful bloodless *coup d'etat*. Unlike the first military regime of Lt General Ibrahim 'Abbud which lasted for six years, this second military takeover established a regime that lasted for sixteen years, thus lasting longer than the combined periods of all the regimes that preceded it.

This chapter, however, is not going to account for the history of Nimeiri's or 'May' (reference to the month of the *coup*) regime.[1] Rather, the main preoccupation will be to focus on the experience of the enforcement of the so-called Islamic *shari'a* laws that were declared by Nimeiri in 1983 and which continued in force until 1991. The question that poses itself in this regard is how did the regime, which started as a victory of the forces of radical secularism, end up as the staunchest advocator of Islamic fanaticism? In an attempt to answer this question, this chapter looks into two areas: the internal political and ideological development of Nimeiri's regime; and secondly, the activities and rising ideological influence of the Islamist movements in the Sudan. At an impressionistic level it seems that the two processes have at certain point combined to produce the unique Islamicisation experiment of the early 1980s.

I. THE FORMATIVE YEARS

Prior to May, 1969, the political forces in the Sudan had virtually reached another state of polarisation as in the period that had immediately followed October 1964. To the left was the coalition of the 'Socialist Forces' (including the CPS and its tributaries in the mass organisations, the Arab Nationalists and Arab Socialists, and some leftist personalities),[2] to the right were the 'Islamic-oriented' forces (the DUP, Umma and ICF) who, as we have seen, had fortified themselves behind the project and motto of an 'Islamic Constitution'.

Judging by its first policy declarations the May *coup d'etat* appears to have taken power from the latter camp in the interest of the former. The new military regime had proclaimed itself as a successor not to the previous military regime of Lt General Ibrahim 'Abbud, but rather to the popular Uprising of October 1964, and duly included in its cabinet many of the personalities of the October Transitional Government.[3]

However, like other military regimes, the immediate problem that faced Nimeiri's was that of survival. In March 1970, the regime violently crushed a potential *Ansar* resurgence in Aba Island (the stronghold of the Mahdists). In July 1971 following an abortive *coup*, allegedly planned by the CPS, the regime once again ruthlessly suppressed the latter, executed its leaders, jailed the bulk of its cadres and banned its tributary organisations.

Following those events, Nimeiri hastened to give himself legitimacy through a referendum in September 1971, and was duly sworn in as the first president of the 'Democratic Republic of the Sudan'. (The officially declared result was 98.6 per cent for Nimeiri.) In January 1972, a 'Sudanese Socialist Union' (SSU) was launched as the sole political organisation in the country, i.e. the ruling party. Furthermore, an agreement was concluded between the government and the rebels in Southern Sudan in what came to be known as the Addis Ababa Accord, 3 March 1972.

One of the first declarations of the regime was the one known as the June Declaration (made on 9 June 1969), which provided a new reading of the Southern issue, recognising that there existed historical and cultural differences between the North and the South and that the Southern people were entitled to a kind of regional autonomy. To that effect a Minister of Southern Affairs was appointed by the regime (the first was Joseph Garang – a leading communist who was executed during the events of July, 1971). However, throughout the first two years, the goodwill and efforts of the said minister notwithstanding, no regional autonomy solution was worked out. The circumstances which followed the 1971 coup attempt (such as the regime's swing towards the West and the latter's relationships with the rebel movement, the appointment of a 'moderate' Southern politician [Abel Alier], and the regime's strive for political backing) appeared –

conducive to a settlement of the Southern question. Meanwhile, on their part, the rebels managed to reach a unified leadership, both military and political, under Major Joseph Lagu. He reorganised the Anya Nya movement under the name 'Southern Sudan Liberation Movement' (SSLM), a factor which facilitated north–south negotiations. Accordingly, a conference was conducted in Addis Ababa on 27 February 1972, after which the Addis Ababa Accord was reached on 2 March 1972; and, on 3 March 1972, the Addis Ababa Accord became the 'Regional Self-government Act for the Southern Provinces'. Among other things, the Addis Ababa Accord called for the grouping of the three Southern provinces into a self-governing Southern region with a Peoples' Regional Assembly and High Executive Council or cabinet.[4]

The significance of the Addis Ababa Agreement, apart from the termination of the civil war, is that for the first time in the history of independent Sudan the Southerners were fully integrated in the body politic of the country, both as a region as well as political forces. True, all along there were some Southern politicians in the Parliament or cabinet. Yet, far from being genuine representatives of the South in national politics, these Southern politicians were, in reality, little more than Southern 'faces' in the politics of the 'North'. Moreover, the conclusion of the agreement paved the way for a period of relative stability, and, for the first time since independence, a permanent constitution was promulgated in May 1973.[5]

The 1973 constitution established a presidential system and proclaimed the SSU as the sole political organisation in the Sudan. More substantially, however, the constitution tackled the two thorny issues that had frustrated previous constitutional efforts in the past: the status of the South, and the question of religion and politics. In the case of the South, the 1972 Addis Ababa Accord was enshrined in the constitution (Article 8) stipulating regional autonomy for the South within a unitary Sudan.[6] The question of religion and politics, and how best to reflect it in the constitution was more complicated, due to strong pressure from a group of Islamists inside the Assembly who wanted a constitution 'that enshrined Sudan's Islamic identity'.[7] Yet, after lengthy debates a formula was adopted and reflected in Article (16) of the constitution which reads:

a) In the Democratic Republic of the Sudan, Islam is the religion and society shall be guided by Islam, being the religion of the majority of its people, and the State shall endeavour to express its values;

115

b) Christianity is the religion in the Democratic Republic of the Sudan which is professed by a large number of its citizens who are guided by Christianity, and the State shall endeavour to express its values;

c) Heavenly religions and the noble aspects of spiritual beliefs shall not be abused, or held in contempt;

d) The State shall treat followers of religions and noble spiritual beliefs without discrimination as to the rights and freedoms guaranteed to them as citizens by this Constitution. The State shall not impose any restrictions on citizens or communities on the grounds of religious faith;

e) The abuse of religious and noble spiritual beliefs for political exploitation is forbidden. Any act which is intended or is likely to promote hatred, enmity or discord among religious communities shall be contrary to this constitution and punishable by law.

Article (9) also says: 'Islamic law and custom shall be the main sources of legislation. Personal matters of non-Muslims shall be governed by their personal laws.'[8]

Meanwhile opposition to the regime continued unabated. In August 1973, a state of unrest and a series of student demonstrations were staged primarily by the National Front (the opposition alliance of right-wing parties that included the Umma Party, the DUP and the ICF) which led to the closure of the universities and mass arrests. In 1975 the regime foiled another *coup* attempt led by Lt Col. Hasan Hussayn who advocated a programme along the same lines of the pronounced positions of the National Front opposition. Furthermore, the regime survived yet another, and major challenge in the form of an invasion from abroad by the militia of the National Front who were trained and armed abroad. They stormed the army headquarters in Eastern Khartoum and various divisions, and managed to capture some strategic bases of the regime. This attempt, although initially successful, was eventually foiled after about 72 hours of bitter fighting and great loss of life.[9]

In 1977, Nimeiri pledged a 'national reconciliation with the opposition, particularly the National Front. The offer was accepted by both Sadiq al-Mahdi, leader of the Umma party, and Hasan al-Turabi, of the Muslim Brothers. They both accordingly returned with their aides from exile, or were released from prison, and received appointments in the politburo of the SSU. Other quarters of the opposition like al-Sharif al-Hindi, leader of the DUP, and the CPS declined the offer of reconciliation. The former remained in exile, while the latter continued its underground activities.[10]

Although the national reconciliation process had helped to neutralise and deter the danger of an armed opposition (most probably from abroad), other forms of opposition to Nimeiri's regime continued. From 1978 onwards strikes, marches and similar protests became constant phenomena that occurred almost annually, especially among professionals, white-collar workers and students. Reasons for these outbursts are to be sought not only in political discontent but also in the increasingly ailing economic situation and in the general failure of the regime (that became more clear in the second half of the 1970s) to deliver the promised progress and prosperity to the country and its people. Ultimately, it was the accumulation of these types of civic protests that toppled Nimeiri's regime in April 1985.

On another level, the 'national reconciliation' may be regarded as a watershed in the process of the political and ideological discourses of the regime as we shall see below.

II. POWER AND IDEOLOGY

The 'cult' of development

As we know, the regime came to power in 1969 riding on a leftist wave and so had overtones of socialism, development and social progress. Following the predominant trend in the Middle East at the time, the May regime was then classified as yet another populist military regime in the region. Within the particularity of Sudanese politics it was a victory for the forces of radical secularism.

However, the leftist coalition in power was a rainbow coalition dominated by three main currents: the Communists, the Arab Nationalists and the left of centre Social Democrats; others, including Nimeiri himself, were apolitical or a 'nationalist of a sort'.[11] In such a coalition differences and ideological disagreements naturally appear. Yet in the Sudanese context the issue was even more complex because of the weakness of the ideological credentials of the leftist forces. As put by one critic, the leftist forces in the Sudan suffered a 'multiple ambiguity' in that they failed either to identify with the Sudanese reality, with due appreciation of its particularities and complexities, or to adhere completely to the tenets of their particular ideology.[12] This assessment may be true in a sense. As pointed out earlier, the CPS had succeeded politically, especially during the 1960s, in becoming a force in national politics and particularly in the hard-core of the left, basically by appealing to the general discontent of the public electorate. On the other hand, both the Arab Nationalists and Social Democrats were intrinsically ideologically weak and politically insignificant.

Such a situation had indeed hampered the ideological clarity of the regime's initial period. Progressive? Yes. Socialist? Certainly. But what kind of socialism and which means were to be used to achieve it? What sort and form of popular participation was there to be?

These, and similar crucial questions had no clear answers. Yet in the absence of clear blueprints the supposedly ideological dispute appeared, more often than not, as personal conflict. Meanwhile, the regime was giving people only slogans. Indeed, the situation was not helped by the violent collision with and suppression of the CPS.

What followed after 1971, as mentioned earlier, was a gradual but clear swing to the right in terms of the regime's practical policies, especially as far as foreign and economic policies were concerned. Nevertheless, commitment to socialism and populism was still expressed in the highest circles of the regime, as manifested in the establishment of the Sudanese 'Socialist' Union (SSU) the ruling political organisation. The SSU was modelled on the Egyptian Arab Socialist Union (ESU) with an ostensible Marxist imprint in both its structure and programme, 'The Charter of National Action'. The permanent constitution stipulated that the Sudan would be a 'Democratic Socialist Republic' (article 1). Furthermore, although the five-year plan, which was initially elaborated by communist members in the Cabinet in 1970, was amended in 1972, it still bore some references to socialism as the ultimate target.

In reality, however, there were no sufficient grounds for socialism. Collision with the mainstream CPS, the disillusionment of the faction that chose to co-operate with the regime, the demise of Nasserism in Egypt, the severing of relations with the Soviet Union and other countries of the 'socialist bloc' of the time, had all left virtually no room for the development of a serious socialist experiment. Nevertheless, if the idea was to work out a socialist experience of a particular 'Sudanese' brand, it was neither elaborated theoretically nor pursued pragmatically. The regime continued its adherence to socialism as an ideological appeal, as something reminiscent of its initial populist phase which even became enshrined in the constitution and the basic statutes of the ruling party. The latter, with no clarity about the practical value of the formula of 'the Alliance of the working forces', became the umbrella under which anybody who cared to associate with the regime could find a place. Thus the organization became full of opportunists, 'sycophants and cheerleaders". In the course of time the services of the latter were perhaps more needed than those of the ideologues because the SSU role had increasingly become not one of 'guidance, education and mobilisation', but rather one of being a bulwark to give the regime an air of popularity during particular occasions, such as anniversary parades.[13]

The substance of the policies pursued after 1971 and the presence of a number of able technocrats in the state machinery indicate a high degree of pragmatism as far as the regime's practical policies were concerned. Yet socialism continued to be the order of the day until well after the mid-1970s. It was useful for the regime to present itself as socialist in the face of the right-wing National Front opposition and it was also a useful tool to 'whip into line' any official who dared to disagree with the powerful president.[14]

Apart from the general slogan of 'socialism' the regime employed other slogans based on certain achievements such as 'national unity' (on the basis of the settlement of the Southern question) and 'economic development' (on the basis of developmental plans already implemented or under implementation). In retrospect it may be argued that the concepts of both socialism and national unity helped to legitimise and perpetuate a totalitarian regime in its worst manifestations. In the name of socialism and national unity a one-party system and a presidential republic were established.

The slogan of 'development', on the other hand, was advanced as a promise, a living hope to the poverty-stricken Sudanese people 'in whose interest the May Revolution broke out'. Moreover, the thesis of development even trapped many of the pragmatic technocrats who hoped that their association with the May regime would still serve a national purpose, that is, development. 'Development' had become the 'cult' of the regime.

On another level, the regime retained a secular character which, unlike that of the Traditionalist parties in the 1950s, appeared as secularism by design. The secular constitution, the populist/secular basis of the SSU, the integration of the South into national politics, and the legacy of radical secularism all helped to maintain and perpetuate the secular nature of the regime. In essence this resulted from the character of the forces that the regime associated with during its formative years such as the various leftist forces, the South, the technocrats and naturally the army itself. Yet, as we shall see below,

119

this picture was to change radically. The overtones of socialism and the overwhelmingly secular politics gradually gave way to a more powerful and emotive ideology – Islam.

Pan Islamism

In spite of the zealous socialistic phase in the early 1970s, Nimeiri did not pose as an ideologue then. On the contrary, he affirmed that:

> I do not belong to any school of thought. This revolution was a war on ready-made moulds and preconceived solutions; a war on things copied or arrived at by speculation. Sudan is free to go along any path and embark upon any experiment; there are no obligations save the preservation of independence, self-esteem and values.[15]

This approach may be called pragmatism, but it enabled Nimeiri to be socialist or otherwise as he deemed necessary. In fact, during the same period he started a cautious adherence to Islam – as demonstrated by his publicised attendance at Friday Sermons, the appointment of some Islamic-oriented figures in his cabinet, and the encouragement of some small *sufi* orders as well a the Republican Brothers.

Furthermore, in 1975 Nimeiri sent a circular around the Ministries entitled *Guided Leadership*, in which he asked Ministers and senior officials to refrain from drinking alcohol and to observe good conduct in general.[16] In his 1977 programme for a second term of office he voiced a vehement, though vague, attachment to Islam. It was on the basis of this that he contracted the 'national reconciliation' agreement with the opposition leaders. From 1977, onwards Nimeiri's ideological adherence to Islam became more pronounced. In 1977 he established a committee to revise the laws in accordance with the Islamic *shari'a*.[17]

Yet no significant practical steps were taken in the direction of the Islamicisation of politics and legislation except for the presentation of a bill of 9 revised laws (in conformity with the *shari'a*) to the People's Assembly (which never discussed it).[18]

Moreover, an experiment in Islamic banking began in 1978 in the private sector but with the provision of facilities and encouragement by the state.[19] In 1980, Nimeiri published a book called *al-nahjj al-islami limatha*? 'Why the Islamic Method'. The book emphasised the role of Islam in the life of the individual and society and called for the necessity of reconstructing Sudanese society on Islamic grounds through the gradual application of Islamic principles.[20] In 1983, Nimeiri stood for a third term of office offering a 'comprehensive political programme' based on the 'Islamic method'. Finally, in September 1983, in a sudden and dramatic step Nimeiri declared the immediate enforcement of Islamic *shari'a* laws. This was not, however, necessarily a culmination of the president's renowned Islamism. As we shall see later, it was primarily dictated by the particular circumstances of the time.

Apart from the strong roots of Islam in Sudanese society, the recourse of Nimeiri to Islamic ideology may be viewed within both the context of domestic politics as well as the wider context of Middle Eastern politics. In the latter, although a number of radical secularist regimes had come to power in several countries during the late 1960s, Nasser's defeat in the 1967 war with Israel and then his death in 1970 were heavy blows to the whole of radical Arab politics. Nasser's successor Sadat left no stone unturned in his efforts to destroy Nasser's legacy. Sadat's signing of the peace treaty with Israel was a step that led to the loss of Egypt's leadership of the Arab world and to its isolation.

Owing to the increased economic power of the oil-rich Arab countries resulting from the oil boom of the 1970s, the leading role in the region passed not to the radical Arab states of the time such as Syria, Libya or Iraq but to the moderate Saudi Arabia. The radical Arab regimes (associated mostly with Arab Nationalism and Socialism) were discredited by their failure to deliver domestic progress, Arab Unity and the liberation of Palestine.

In the Sudanese context, socialism without any kind of socialist experiment or blueprint had eventually become irrelevant at a time when the regime was effectively liberalising the economy. Regardless of the declared intentions of the regime to adhere to some form of socialist ideals, its head lacked the solid commitment to propagate them effectively. Nimeiri's eclecticism (if one wants to be lenient), but more probably his lack of commitment to any political principle, meant a constant search for one policy after another. This also meant a constant making and breaking of various political associations, alliances and allies. As a result of this opportunism nothing better than Islam, the religion of the majority and the ideology of the opposition, could serve the purpose of Nimeiri. Hence, the pragmatist/opportunist president lost no time in adhering to the latter sacrificing in the process the populist character of his regime and its institutions.

II. DOVES AND HAWKS

Whatever the general or particular considerations of the regime might have been, its gradual drive towards Islamicisation created an atmosphere in which Islamic-oriented groups emerged in various degrees and at various periods advocating their own versions and interpretations of Islam. This phenomenon can be divided into two phases: 1972–77, when the regime clearly swung to the right, though its institutions remained secular with 'socialistic' overtones and 1977–83, when the regime became reconciled with the Islamic-oriented opposition groups (namely the Umma party and the Muslim Brothers) amid expressed gestures of gradual Islamicisation of the system's politics and legislation.

During the first phase, owing to the continued enmity between the regime and the Islamic-oriented opposition parties, the arena was clear for two forces to flourish: some minor *sufi* orders and the Republican Brothers. Both are treated here as the 'doves'of Islamism as they did not attempt to inflict change on the existing politico-ideological framework of the regime. In contrast, the second phase witnessed the increased activity of the veteran Islamic-oriented forces, such as the Umma and *Ikhwan*, whose well-known views on the role of Islam in politics and society may safely place them as the 'hawks' of Islamism.

The Doves

Nimeiri's personal Islamicisation after 1971 was like that of a layman, the more so as it was closely associated with *sufism* in its most superstitious form rather than its scholarly one. It was like the adherence of somebody seeking salvation and protection (mainly for his survival as a ruler).[21] This *sufist* 'penetration' of the regime as symbolised by the attitude of its president did not have a clear impact on the ideological discourse of the regime. Yet as we shall see later, it greatly influenced Nimeiri's brand of Islam that manifested itself more vigorously after 1983 when he declared himself the *'Imam* of the entire Sudan.

Equally mystical but more sober were the Republican Brothers, formerly the Republican Party, the Neo-Islamist group led by Mahmud Muhammad Taha. In the 1970s, the Republican Brothers advocated the same ideas that Taha had put forward since the early 1950s, albeit in a more elaborate and revised form. The fact that the

May regime had at least ostensibly eradicated sectarianism provided the Republican Brothers with sufficient grounds to pledge their support, overlooking as they did many of its arbitrary policies. In return the regime not only tolerated their curious version of Islam, which was viewed by many other Islamist group as *heresy*, but even allowed its free propagation. Consequently, Taha's ideas became more publicised and increasingly influenced some quarters of the intelligentsia and the urban community and the ranks of the Republican Brothers expanded remarkably.

Taha's 'neo-Islamist' ideas were a mixture of theology and mysticism. They offered a new theological interpretation of the Quranic texts (divided between Meccan and Medinan texts), and, at the same time, provided a mystical conception of the relationship between man and God. Furthermore, Taha offered a formulation of a socio-political blueprint for a neo-Islamist alternative based on his interpretation of Islam as consisting of two kinds of messages: a universal message which is embodied in the Meccan Quranic texts, and a limited message for the circumstances of 7th century.[22] Questions of theology aside, Taha's progressive views on matters of human rights, law, socialism and women's rights seem to have been among the most attractive of his ideas.

At first sight there appeared to be a contradiction between Nimeiri's 'clumsy' *sufism* and the more scholastic neo-Islamist views of the Republican Brothers. Yet, on close examination this apparent contradiction vanishes. Nimeiri, as we know, was not an ideologue, so he did not care much about the ideological credentials of his allies as long as such an alliance served his purpose. In this context the significance of Taha's ideas apart from their political passivism was that they appeared to have the potential for growth at the expense of both the Communists and *Ikhwan* (hitherto the dominant forces among the intelligentsia). As for the Republican Brothers, their tolerance of Nimeiri's brand of Islamism is to be regarded as part of their overall tolerance of his entire regime regardless of its policies and practices. Crucial for the Republican Brothers was the unprecedented possibility to advocate their ideas freely.

The Hawks

As pointed out above, the doves did not attempt to influence the body politique of the May Regime or its ideology, and the president did not translate his Islamist orientation into practical policies during the first phase of the regime (1972–77). Meanwhile, the Islamist parties continued their opposition to Nimeiri's regime in spite of the latter's apparent swing to the right. Their opposition continued to be underscored with Islamic pronouncements. For them Nimeiri's regime had started initially as atheist/communist and after the collision with the CPS had remained essentially secular. They were particularly critical of the regime's political organisation, the SSU, of the regime's socialist appearance, of its constitution, and so on. In reality, however, the fundamental cause of enmity between Nimeiri's regime and the National Front Opposition – the initial leftist orientation of the former – had been removed as a result of the events of July 1971. It was no great surprise therefore that after three successive attempts to overthrow the May regime (1973, 1975, 1976), the National Front Opposition accepted Nimeiri's offer of 'national reconciliation' in 1977.

With the reconciliation the political arena was virtually free from both radical secularism, which was suppressed, and liberal secularism, which had long lost its zeal and had effectively disappeared by 1969. As for the secularist forces of the May regime itself, whether in the SSU or in the government, they were basically preoccupied by defence of their positions in power *vis-à-vis* the newcomers. Hence they effectively defended the authoritarian structure of the SSU and the political system as a whole; an exercise that only helped to discredit their 'cause'. In contrast, by posing as champions of democracy and calling for the reform of the system the various Islamist groups were in a better position to put forward their views on Islamicisation. This was not their only advantage.

Reconciliation with its pronounced Islamic connotations triggered increased activity and the flourishing of various Islamist groups, particularly the hawks of Islamism. Moreover, the Iranian Revolution of February 1979, with its zealous Islamist character and leadership, had made a profound impact on the entire Muslim world. The Sudan was no exception. 'The Islamic revolution in Iran', according to al-Sadiq al-Mahdi, 'confirmed the contemporary revolutionary role of Islam.'[23] Furthermore, it was during this period that Nimeiri issued his above-mentioned book *al-nahjj al-islami limatha?* (*Why the Islamic Method?*). The book, with its equivocal and generalised formulations, was intended to placate the various Islamist groups regardless of their divergent positions and viewpoints. Yet, at the same time its emphasis on the gradual application of Islamic teaching and on piety and education was meant to caution the hawks who were calling for the acceleration of Islamicisation.[24] Nevertheless, Nimeiri's book was praised by almost all the Islamist groups, including the Republican Brothers.

Thus conditions conducive to increased activity by the Islamist groups, particularly the hawks, were created after 1977. These activities took three principal forms: individual preaching (e.g. in the mosque, marketplaces, educational institutions and the like) which dealt mostly with theological questions and controversies; conferences and-seminars (sponsored by both the government and non-governmental organisations) that addressed wider questions pertaining to the role of Islam in society and other politico-ideological connotations, writings which naturally dealt both with spheres of theology as well as with politico-ideological questions.[25]

Here we are not concerned much with purely theological matters, but rather with politico-ideological implications. We will examine the contributions of two prominent veteran Islamists, namely, al-Sadiq al-Mahdi the leader of the Umma Party, and Hasan al-Turabi, the leader of the *Ikhwan*. Both are treated here as the hawks of Islamism in the post-reconciliation era.

Al-Mahdi, and al-Turabi adopted the same view as far as the history and 'Islamic potential' in the Sudan and its future prospects. They shared a rejection of 'traditionalism' and emphasised the necessity of original *'ijtihad* within the context of present-day circumstances. Moreover, the two more or less shared a common analysis of the history of the 'Islamic' movement in the Sudan and they both accorded a particular place to Mahdism as the most vigorous attempt to link Islam with politics in the history of the Sudan. Yet, while al-Sadiq al-Mahdi attributed to the Sudanese Mahdist tradition the potential of contributing to the unity, revival and radicalism of the contemporary 'Islamic resurgence', al-Turabi emphasised only the Mahdist political activism as an *asset* to the modern Islamic movement in the Sudan (by which he essentially meant his party, the *Ikhwan*).

On a practical level, in spite of the fact that both leaders had agreed to the national reconciliation and had accepted the SSU as the only political organisation in the country, we have seen that al-Sadiq al-Mahdi later resigned from the SSU politburo and henceforth kept himself and his followers outside the boundaries of the regime's political activity. Al-Turabi, however, continued to work inside the SSU as a member of its politburo, and was even appointed to the ministerial post of Attorney General together with a number of his fellow *Ikhwan* leaders who assumed other occupations. The strategies of the former allies diverged and so did their discourses, as we shall see presently.

AL-MAHDI'S PAN ISLAMISM

Al-Sadiq al-Mahdi, though in reality a sectarian leader, emerged in the 1970s with peculiar formulations. He pledged to foster a pioneering and inspirational role for Islam which would deliver both spiritual salvation and material prosperity to Muslims in the modern world. This important role and Islam's great potential was something that could be achieved through political activism because 'it is impossible to depoliticize Islam without emptying it . . . Islam does not recognise a distinction between secular and sacred matters; its two cardinal principles are belief in unity of God and the institution of justice'.[26]

With regard to the type of 'Islamic' political system, al-Mahdi argued that 'Islam does not oblige us with a specific model of the state at all times and in every place.' There are certain principles which Islam presents to us in the world of politics:

a) General principles; *shura* (counsel), *'adl* (justice), *al-wafa' bi'l-'ahd* (fulfilment of promises) *'ada' al-"amanah* (honesty), *ri'asat al-jamma'a* (community leadership);
b) specific legislation, including *hudud*.

He went on to say that 'observation of these principles is all that is requested from us by Islam in the sphere of politics. Otherwise . . . we are completely free to form whatever we like of political systems, institutions and means of participation.'[27] Furthermore, he maintained 'Islam provides for peace among people with different creeds and ideologies [and] it accepts pluralism, but limits it to the basis of the teachings of Islam on human rights and minority rights'.[28]

With reference to the particular Sudanese situation, al-Sadiq al-Mahdi emphasised the great potential of Islam in the Sudan and predicted for Islam a bright future. He argued that the fact that Islam had taken root in Sudanese society without significant assistance from the state had made it both popularly based and characterised by a high degree of tolerance, whether between Muslims and non-Muslims or between the various Islamic factions. Yet he conceded that the great potential of Islam in the Sudan and its bright future were faced by a number of challenges and obstacles. These obstacles were: (a) divisions (e.g. Sufism, Mahdism, the *salafiyya* movement, the Muslim Brothers);

(b) traditionalism (lack of *'ijtihad* and rethinking); (c) the secular system, (d) over-enthusiasm; and (e) foreign intervention. Likewise the movement faced a number of challenges such as modernisation, development, liberty, peace, neo-Islamism (the Republican Brothers) and the status of the Southern Sudan.

However, al-Mahdi asserted that the Islamic movement in the Sudan, with its established traditions of tolerance and activism, was capable of overcoming all the obstacles and of meeting the challenges. It would rebuild Sudanese society on the foundations of a newly conceived Islamic thought, one which incorporates the positive achievements of modern Western civilisation but avoids its negative aspects.[29]

Al-Sadiq al-Mahdi moreover believed that the Islamic movement in the Sudan in reality had something to contribute to the Islamic movement throughout the world on the basis of the Mahdist tradition in the Sudan: 'Firstly through the principle of transcending sects and schools of law and drawing legislation from original sources, on the understanding that "there are different ways for different circumstances and different leaders for different occasions". Secondly, by serving as a bridge between Shi'ism and Sunnism, based upon the Sunni concept of theology and the Shi'ite concept of leadership. Furthermore, the Mahdist tradition initiated Sudan into *its leading role* in the rebirth of Islam and forged a permanent link between it and Sudanese patriotism . . ."[30]

AL-TURABI'S REALISM

Al-Turabi sought to develop a new approach towards the religious faith *al-'Iman* by emphasising its relevance and positive implications not only in the after-life but in this world as well. Belief in God and in the Hereafter, argued al-Turabi, is underlined by our expectation of the eternal rewards and fear of punishments. It is this reward-punishment mechanism which acts as a motivational force for Muslims, inciting them to worship and making them endure hardships and sacrifices. Accordingly, believers will have more incentive for hard work even in pursuit of their worldly affairs as they have submitted their lives to the command of *Allah*. If they prosper then this is an 'advance' reward to them in this life, for which they should express gratitude. If a crisis beset them then they should exercise patience and restraint and ask for forgiveness. Whatever happens a true believer should not worry because his/her reward is certain in paradise.[31]

An essential theme in al-Turabi's treatment of the question of faith is his concept of *tawhid* (monotheism or unification). Primarily, *tawhid* means belief in one God, but al-Turabi employed the concept in a more comprehensive way to denote unity of the natural and supernatural, reason and revelation the worldly and the other-worldly, the material and the spiritual. As the Muslim submits him/herself to *Allah* they at the same time liberate themselves from nature and its obstacles or temptations. This concept of *tawhid* is manifested in, and complemented by al-Turabi's concept of worship. It is through worship that the Muslims could aspire to achieve the unity between the material and the spiritual. As this world is only a transition to the hereafter, then all actions of Muslims, including their worldly engagements may be utilised as objects of worship. Within such a wider concept of worship every material activity is capable of becoming a spiritual medium if the intention is there.[32]

Al-Turabi's unique concepts of *tawhid* and worship were substantiated by his emphasis on *tajdid* (renewal) of Islamic thought and jurisprudence. In al-Turabi's scheme, *tajdid* is necessitated first by the lengthy stagnation of the Islamic thought which became notoriously preoccupied with details so that it has become almost incapable of advancing a comprehensive vision or holistic view on anything. On another account, al-Turabi is convinced that renewal is a pressing matter in view of the dominance of the Western civilisation and the challenges it poses to Muslims' lives and societies today.[33]

To achieve the required *tajdid*, al-Turabi argued that there is a dire necessity not only to consider new answers to new problems but also to reconsider how to revitalise the methodology (*'usul*) of Islamic jurisprudence (*fiqh*). Because the foundations on which traditional *fiqh* was established were the work of the first generations of ulama who were guided by the sciences and methodology of their time, *fiqh* has in the course of time stagnated. It is no longer capable of providing answers to current problems. In particular traditional Islamic *fiqh* was deficient in its treatment of public affairs such as politics, administration, and the economy. The reason for this deficiency, in the eyes of al-Turabi, is that throughout most of their history Muslims had not ruled their societies in accordance with the spirit and principles of Islam and therefore the *fiqh* was not inspired to develop in these fields and concentrated instead on issues related to personal and individual matters.[34]

Al-Turabi emphasised the point that Islam is essentially a progressive religion that welcomes any change (e.g. material progress), the facilities of which Muslims can utilise *for the worship* of God. Yet for Muslims to be able to do so it is important to swing the door of *'ijtihad* wide open for all Muslims who are willing and competent, and then to rationalise and co-ordinate their findings through regular consultations under the auspices and guidance of Islamicised authorities that could then enforce the *consensus* of the *'ulama.*[35]

What should be underlined in this regard is that al-Turabi emphasised the necessity and perhaps primacy of an Islamic (political) revolution which would then pave the way for the required revolution in jurisprudence. For such an Islamic revolution to take place a method of Islamic propagation (*da'wa*) was needed that would start with the individual and move up through society until it was adopted by the state. Because the state is part of society and the character of any society is derived from the souls of the individuals that compose it (i.e. individual Muslims).[36]

The way to change individual Muslims was through peaceful propagation (*da'wa*) (a pious Muslim would lead to a pious society, which in its turn would produce a pious state).[37]

Al-Turabi suggested that whenever a number of Muslims become inspired enough by the Islamic *da'wa* they form a group or party which endeavours to become a microcosm of a possible pious and righteous Muslim society. Yet, for such a pioneer group to become successful it must observe certain conditions. Of paramount importance among these are: an established system of leadership and consultation and a strong popular base. As a matter of approach members of the vanguard group should receive an intensive 'Islamic' education, whereas the larger popular base of the movement may be mobilised on the basis of generally formulated discourses, such as the call for the application of Islamic *shari'a*, the observation of Islamic code of ethics, the denouncement of non-Islamic approaches from the state or adversary parties. Furthermore, Al-Turabi underlined the necessity of the establishment of social and economic institutions, 'to serve as examples and models of an Islamic-oriented social change'.[38]

As for the method of change (i.e. the Islamicisation process) to be carried by the above-mentioned Islamic movements it involves peaceful propagation, education revolutionary means (by which is meant the use of force). In this process, 'if the Islamic movement attains power whether peacefully or by force then it adds the force of the state to its means of changing reality'. And, 'whenever in power, an Islamic movement can either adopt a gradual or radical approach to society's Islamicization . . . *both are legitimate methods*'. Yet al-Turabi argues that 'a complete Islamic system involves both specific legislation (such as the sanctioned laws of penalties and other *shari'a* laws); and general principles (pertaining to *shura*, and the selection of the ruler, as well as other principles such as social justice, etc.)'. The first aspect that deals with particular legislation is more tangible and easily applicable whereas the second entails more rethinking and naturally requires a longer time span. In view of this 'it might be more appropriate to start with the particular legislature and to move towards realisation of the general principles'.[39]

Al-Turabi sees no contradiction between his initial emphasis on the salvation of the individual as a foundation for the establishment of a pious society that would automatically produce a 'pious state', and his latter approach which, considers the state itself as a tool of change of society in the Islamicisation process. That is because he was essentially a politician with a considerable degree of pragmatism. As the emphasis shifted from the individual as a tool of change to the state, whatever means that are used to attain power and/or influence it become virtually legitimate.

As pointed out above, the Muslim Brotherhood organisation, led by Hasan al-Turabi, had agreed to work within the institutions of the May regime after the national reconciliation, a decision that was achieved at the expense of a split inside their movement. A small faction of hardliners led by Sadiq 'Abdalla 'Abd al-Majid (a founding member of the *Ikhwan* and editor of *al-ikhwan al-muslimun*, the official publication) broke away on the grounds that preaching and the education of society came before political strategies. Nevertheless, the mainstream *Ikhwan* movement sided with al-Turabi.[40]

Al-Turabi's aim from the reconciliation was basically a search for legitimate activity and power that would facilitate the political action of his organisation.[41] Therefore, unlike al-Sadiq al-Mahdi he did not demand the reform of the regime's institutions as a condition for participation but rather joined in it. He publicly declared the dissolution of the *Ikhwan* who would thenceforth work within the one-party system together with other forces for a common purpose, namely the Islamicisation of Sudanese political, legal and economic structures.[42] In the process al-Turabi and his followers tended to pose as *Islamists* in the broadest possible sense of the word:

The modern Islamic movement (in the Sudan) has never existed on a sectarian basis, but has always tried to function through popular participation. Islamic development is ideally designed to follow a peaceful and gradual course. The majority of the Sudanese are Muslims, and if some elements have the facility to lead Islamic awareness and thought then their activities will gain legality through being supported by Islamic society. There is fortunately no conflict between the modern Islamic movement and the traditionally-based ideologies of the *sufis* or Mahdists. Hence these will form a base, a form of Islamization [sic] which combine the modern and the traditional. We even want our Islamic movement to interact with the Christian. Our programme is religiously comprehensive, excluding only non-religious ideologies such as Marxist and secularist creeds and those opinionated movements which claim to hold direct mandates from God [by which he means the Republican Brothers].[43]

Here once again we encounter al-Turabi the politician who tries to forge a broadly based *religious* alliance which includes not only the various Islamist groups and movements but even Christians versus the secularists and atheists (Marxists). In this respect al-Turabi's movement no longer posed as a puritanical, 'fundamentalist' movement but rather as a broad *Islamic* (sometimes religious) platform.

To separate reality from fiction, the above-quoted statement should be treated as propaganda meant to placate and/or pacify. Al-Turabi's real motive was to create the necessary pressure, through such a broad Islamist platform, for accelerated Islamicisation. As a matter of fact the *Ikhwan* continued to exist as an organisation despite the publicly pronounced self-dissolution. They kept their organisation within the student movement, the trade unions, and so on, publicly intact and continued to operate within the SSU and the People's Assembly as a distinct group. They sought to overcome what they regarded as fatal mistakes in the experience of their adversaries – the CPS' – alliance with Nimeiri's regime during its initial period. Thus, rather than posing as an independent identity with a vigorous ideological stand on each and every policy of the regime, they opted to utilise the latter's renowned Islamism and their positions in power to rebuild and expand their movement and in the process to press for further Islamicisation. Their strategy included, among other things, the intensification of their grip on the student movement, the infiltration of the army, trade unions and the judiciary, and significantly, the establishment and control of 'Islamic' financial and economic institutions.[44]

To sum up, the fact that al-Sadiq al-Mahdi had accepted reconciliation and then declined participation has greatly informed his posture of a 'think-tank' of pan Islamism. Although his reformist views on the role of Islam in modern society converge with al-Turabi's on many issues they did not share the latter's pragmatism which was greatly informed by his active participation in the Establishment. It was at this point that the courses of the two diverged widely to the extent of assuming opposite positions towards Nimeiri's 'enforcement' of the *shari'a* laws as we shall see presently.

III. SEPTEMBER 1983

In May 1969, Ja'far M. Nimeiri, as the leader of the military *coup* declared that one of the primary objectives of the 'May Revolution' was to tear off the 'yellow paper'. This was a clear reference to the project of the Islamic constitution (1968, noted earlier) Yet, in June 1984 the same Nimeiri presented a bill of 'constitutional amendments' to the People's Assembly that amounted to a redraft of the (1973) constitution on 'Islamic grounds'. Therefore, what started as a victory of radical secularism appeared to have ended up as victory of conservative Islamism. The course of events that produced such a roundabout result has been referred to earlier in this chapter, hence what will be emphasised here is the particular experience of the enforcement of new laws based on the Islamic *shari'a* that later necessitated the above-mentioned project of constitutional amendments.

In a sudden and dramatic move, Nimeiri announced to the nation on 8 September 1983, a decree stipulating the establishment of a new penal code for the country that include the five canonical Islamic penalties or *hadd* sanctions.[45] The new law which was to replace the penal code of 1974, was accompanied and/or followed by new laws of criminal and civil procedures and a law of the Sources of Judicial verdicts. Furthermore, a number of laws designed to reorganise the legal systems such as the Judiciary Act, the Attorney General's Act, and the Bar Act were all passed in 1983.[46]

The laws that dealt with the legal system involved a substantial reorganisation of the courts and procedural considerations, as well as the personnel of the judiciary, the Attorney General's Chamber and the Bar. The expressed reason for these laws was to reorganise the legal system so that it could deliver 'instantaneous justice'.[47]

As for the substantive laws such as the penal code, the most significant changes were first the introduction of the controversial *hudud* sanctions, and secondly, the incorporation of the arbitrary state security Act 1973. As for the *hudud* sanctions, they provided for punishment of the crimes of theft, adultery, the drinking of alcohol, murder and false accusation.[48] According to the new penal code, the *hadd* sanction for theft prescribes the amputation of a hand while for armed robbery or repeated theft the penalty is the amputation of a foot as well as a hand. In both cases what is stolen must be valued at Ls 100 or more in order for the *hadd* sanctions to apply. Public lashings have been stipulated for both alcohol drinking and adultery, 40 lashes for the former and 80 lashes for the latter where the adulterer is not married. Should the adulterer be married then the sentence is one of execution. In all cases of adultery, however, the *hadd* regulation requires the testimony of four respectable and reliable eye witnesses in order to secure a conviction. Finally, murder was made punishable by execution, but with the alternative of *diyya* (a compensatory fine) should the family of the victim agree.[49]

Besides the '*shari'a*' basis of the new laws as its major credit and a value in itself, it was also argued that the new laws 'in fact diminish suffering . . . because unlike in the traditional system, the penalties [of lashes or amputation] are borne by the criminal alone without affecting his family (as in the case of imprisonment), while there is also room now for the restitution of the victim of that which was taken (i.e. in case of theft)'.[50]

No sooner had the new laws been issued than a heated debate arose. The controversy involved the media, politicians, jurists and other interested circles both inside and outside the country. Issues pertaining to the possible motives behind the new laws, their relationship to *shari'a* and secular laws and questions of practical application have figured high in the debate. The remainder of this chapter will confine itself to a condensed treatment of the politico-ideological connotations of these laws; many other learned contributions exist which deal with its legal and religo-political aspects.[51i]

One issue that loomed large in the controversy over these laws was a strike by the judiciary that continued for about three months before the enforcement of the laws and in relation to which much of the 'reorganisation' of the legal system was devised. Yet on its own the judiciary crisis did not cause the enforcement of the *shari'a* laws, though it may have prompted its timing.

While much of the initial criticism was directed towards the abrupt nature of the laws' declaration, the regime's officials and media channels wanted to make-believe that the September laws 'have been neither hasty nor abrupt'. Elaborating on this point the Chief Justice at the time Daff 'allah al-Hajj Yusuf said: 'The truth is that from the first days of the May Revolution there was an Islamic orientation, but this orientation adopted a gradual approach. At first, laws were issued prohibiting alcohol drinking during *Ramadan*, then local orders were issued for the closure of brothels. Subsequently, the president issued a directive for enlightened [i.e. guided] leadership as well as a ban on gambling. This was followed by the President's book. "The Islamic Method – Why", and, finally, came the comprehensive political programme for the third presidential term'.[52]

Superficially it appears so; yet the reality is rather different. As we have seen above, the gradual Islamicisation of Nimeiri should not be regarded as a reason for the implementation of these laws. A testimony to this was the bill of Revised Laws (to conform with *shari'a*) which was presented to the People's Assembly at least two years before the dramatic laws of September, but were neither discussed by the Assembly, nor decreed by the president as he used to do more often than not. Moreover, when the September laws appeared they had nothing to do with the 'Revised Laws' save one.[53] In terms of ideological pronouncements it is true that enough Islamic overtones were expressed by Nimeiri, as we have seen above, yet the reasons behind such a dramatic and daring step as the *shari'a* application should be sought not in these ideological overtones but rather in the political circumstances – that from Nimeiri's viewpoint – necessitated such a choice.

As far as Nimeiri's motives are concerned, it has been argued that Nimeiri took such a step for the following reasons:

- To take the wind out of the sails of the Sudanese Islamic movements (the Muslim Brothers, the *Ansar*, and the *Khatmiyya*);
- To avoid dealing with chronic internal problems and to turn people's attention from government mismanagement, reflected in the total collapse of services, unemployment, [and] soaring inflation;
- To divert attention from government corruption to the corruption of individuals (e.g. alcoholism, adultery, theft).[54]

With varying emphasis it may be commonly agreed that Nimeiri had political motives for the *shari'a* declaration. The roots of these political motives are to be sought in the political and economic situation of his regime during the early 1980s. As mentioned above, the regime had intensively played on its achievements in the field of national unity (the settlement of the Southern question) and in the field of economic development. However, by the early 1980s, there were hardly any objective grounds for such self-congratulation. No matter how great the achievement of the Addis Ababa Accord, it soon fell victim to the political needs of both Nimeiri and the Southern leaders, and had fallen apart by 1983.

The magnitude of the tragic situation in the South was best demonstrated by the reappearance of armed resistance to the regime, first in the form of a separatist group calling itself *Anya Nya II*, which was soon overshadowed by the more powerful Sudanese People's Liberation Army (SPLA) led by Col. John Garang.[55]

In the field of development, it is true that the regime had launched a large number of huge and smaller projects (mostly agricultural) comparable only to those of the 'Abbud regime. Yet 'inattention to existing works, poor maintenance, shortages and other problems led to a decline in agricultural production, even as the area under cultivation was expanded by four million acres.'[56]

The huge development projects had either fallen victims to the renewed civil war in the South (such as Jonglei Canal and the oil exploration projects) or implemented at a very high cost and low productivity such as the Kenana and Rahad schemes. This was worsened by corruption, which 'becoming rampant, has deleterious effects on the economy'. By the early 1980s, the government, unable or unwilling to undertake efficient recovery measures, had lost control of the economy. By the mid-1980s, the Sudan, rather than being the breadbasket of the Middle East, as was thought possible in the mid-1970s, was suffering from famine, and its economic problems of an enormous foreign debt, inflation, shortages, devaluation's and ever-declining production had become virtually insoluble.[57]

The regime clearly could not continue to play the tune of national unity and development at a time when there was civil unrest in the North because of the mounting economic hardships and armed resistance in the South. Accordingly, the declaration and application of *shari'a* law in this context served to divert the attention of the populace from the regime's failures and to tighten the regimes' grip on the opposition. This was basically done through the ideological challenge that opposition to a renowned Islamic *'Imam*, who has the credit of re-establishing the sacred *shari'a* law is something very close to heresy. Thirdly, the declaration of *shari'a* law, served as a new window display in place of the defunct ideology of 'socialism'.

Indeed, when the laws were enforced the regime utilised them in just this way. A man by the name Salah al Din al-Misbah was arrested at the mosque and sentenced to five years imprisonment because he wanted to perform his classical Islamic right of *shura* (Counsel) to the *'Imam*, Nimeiri, after a Friday sermon.[58] Moreover, four members of the Ba'ath Socialist Party – Country of Sudan, were also tried on charges of 'secularism' and anti-Islamic convictions, the initial charge being that of preparing and distributing a 'subversive' document. Thirdly, the late Mahmud. M. Taha was tried and executed in January 1985, on charges of apostasy, though the initial charge also was that of preparing and distributing a 'subversive' document. The execution of the 76 year-old Islamic reformist deeply shook the nation and in a way triggered the civil unrest which eventually resulted in the popular *Intifada* of march-April 1985. Thus, after the 'Islamic' laws were invoked the usual political opposition to the regime was increasingly described by the latter in religious terms and tried accordingly.[59]

Thinking that he had finally subdued his enemies and won the hearts of the majority of Sudanese Muslims, Nimeiri proclaimed himself *'Imam* of the whole of the Sudan (non-Muslim citizens included). Accordingly, he received oaths of allegiance (*bay'a*) wherever he went and would lead public prayers in mosques, especially during Friday sermons. Nimeiri, the soldier by profession, suddenly became a doctor of Islamic jurisprudence and philosophy.[60]

After being proclaimed the *'Imam* of the Sudanese people, Nimeiri sought to constitutionalise his neo-theocratic rule and to reorganise the political system accordingly. Thus in June 1984 he proposed a number of constitutional amendments that amounted to a repeal of the Constitution as they involved 123 articles out of a total of 225. Significant among the new amendments were the ones that dropped article (8) that incorporated the Southern Provinces Regional Self Government Act 1972, and consequently the reference to its inviolability, amended article (16) by dropping references to Christianity and noble aspects of spiritual beliefs and replaced it by an equivocal reference to 'religious freedoms', and made Islamic *shari'a* as the only source of legislation. In short, the draft amendments seemed to undo the very articles that made the 1973 Constitution an acceptable document to non-Muslims. On another level the scheme of amendments affected the articles dealing with the role, powers and duties of the powerful president (who became an *'Imam*). According to the scheme of amendments the president was to become 'the leader of the faithful *qa'id al-Mu'minin,* and the shepherd of the Sudanese nation' as well as the head of state. The president was to be invested according to an oath of allegiance *bay'a* as president for life. Furthermore, on assuming office the president would swear an oath of loyalty to God.

Finally, the president was to have assistants, instead of deputies, who would swear an oath of obedience to him. Moreover, the amendments substituted the People's Assembly with a *majlis al-shura* (council for consultation) which was to be composed of the President of the Republic (as its president), the First Secretary of the central leadership of the SSU (as deputy) and as members: the members of the Executive Bureau of the Central Leadership of the SSU, speakers and members of the People's Assemblies (national and regional) and members of the President's Council (government). Members of this *majlis,* furthermore, would have to swear an oath of obedience to the president.

Unsurprisingly, the proposed amendments met with fierce opposition from the Southerners and some remnants of the SSU 'old guard'. Both of the prominent Southern figures, Abel Alier and Joseph Lagu, addressed a memorandum to the President which expressed their relentless opposition to any amendment that touched on who should be the president of the country, how he would be elected and who would elect him, the character of the state, the status of the South and the situation of religions as laid down in the 1973 Constitution. In other words, they were opposed to any amendment that affected articles No. 8, 9, 16 and 80–110.[61]

Faced with such strong opposition, Nimeiri withdrew his scheme of amendments for further study, and then brought it back to the Assembly with some changes such as the reinstatement of the Southern Provinces Self Regional Act, the role of the SSU and the deletion of the provision of life presidency and the right of the incumbent to appoint his successor. Nevertheless, the 'amendments to the amendments' also met with opposition, and after a lengthy discussion 97 MPs (including all the Southern MPs) tabled a petition to the president requesting that the issue be referred for further discussion. Nimeiri's response to this 'mutiny' was to dissolve the Assembly altogether and shelve the constitutional job indefinitely, indeed until he was toppled in April 1985.[62]

The announcement of Islamic laws, regardless of Nimeiri's motives was bound to produce an emotional response from the various Islamist groups. Unsurprisingly, Mahmud M. Taha and his followers the Republican Brothers rejected the laws – a position that was based on their neo-Islamist view regarding the question of the traditional *shari'a* and in line with their previous opposition to the projects of an 'Islamic constitution' as we have seen earlier. Moreover, several months before the September declaration the Republican Brothers had fallen out of the regime's favour and some of their leaders were jailed, including Mahmud Muhammad Taha himself. They were released shortly before September 1983, only to be re-arrested when they pronounced their opposition to the new laws.

The notorious trial of Mahmud Muhammad Taha and his execution was meant by the regime to be a warning to its opponents such as the Communists, the Ba'athists and al-Sadiq al-Mahdi. The latter, in spite of his known stand with regard to Islamicisation, also opposed Nimeiri's laws on the grounds that:

– the laws, in spite of their importance, were issued by a presidential decree without ample study and discussion by the legislative chamber;
– the Islamic canonical penalties were issued as part of a penal code that did not respect the basic freedoms of citizens while Islamic *shari'a* gives due respect to these rights;
– that these Islamic penalties should be applied only 'within an Islamic social order which fights crime by spiritual, moral, social and economic means', and the institution of justice in general.[63]

Furthermore, al-Mahdi maintained that Nimeiri's political exploitation of the *shari'a* was only paying lip-service to the cause of Islam. He expressed these views from the pulpit of his grandfather's mosque at Umdurman, from where he was arrested and jailed for several months.

On the other hand, al-Turabi and his party were the staunchest of Nimeiri's supporters in his new adventure, leading the campaign of explaining and defending the laws, acting as judges in the emergency or 'speedy justice' courts, mobilising demonstrations of support for the *shari'a*, and so on. Al-Turabi in 1980 said that:

"The application of the *shari'a* is the application of a comprehensive legal and moral system. This is why we said that councils and institutions should be established to assist in the application of these laws, by launching campaigns among the public, especially as regards drinking and *zakat*. We must use guidance in addition to the law . . . Existing laws – even where they do not conform to the *shari'a* – *serve a certain interest.* [Therefore] If the People's Assembly approves, *we guarantee that shari'a law will be introduced gradually*'.[64]

The same Al-Turabi, however, argued in 1983 that 'the new laws [of September 1983] appear sudden only to those who for whatever reason do not really support them'.[65] He went on to denounce any other non-Islamic law and particularly European secular laws, as *worthless.*

Such a position has been dictated by al-Turabi's pragmatist strategy which sought to utilise the feverish wave of Islamism in order to ascend to high positions in the regime and to empower his organisation. Consequently, the *Ikhwan* were considering whether to inherit the earth after Nimeiri's death or, at a ripe moment, to stage a palace coup against him and rule the country thereafter. Nimeiri who was well aware of their designs, struck first. All of a sudden, all the prominent leaders of the *Ikhwan* found themselves behind bars, denounced publicly and dismissed from their high positions.[66] As the *Ikhwan* were then the only political force behind the regime, their removal from power only helped to accelerate the collapse of the regime which had been in a slow decline since the beginning of the 1980s.

If any proof is needed for the failure of Nimeiri's calculations with regard to the political utility of the enforcement of the *shari'a* laws, it was the collapse of his regime in less than two years after that dramatic declaration. Nevertheless, the collapse of Nimeiri's power notwithstanding, the experience itself has left a tremendous impact on Sudanese society and politics.

At the social level the laws affected a number of social and individual habits (e.g. alcohol drinking, relations between the two sexes). Furthermore, they also affected the lives of several unfortunate individuals who unjustly lost their limbs, property or lives, or were subjected to public humiliation under the notorious emergency courts. Nevertheless, in spite of the intensive campaign that clouded the declaration of these laws, the actual experience had neither brought a significant decrease in crime nor improved ethical standards. On the contrary, due to the rampant economic and social hardships and the release of seasoned criminals (Nimeiri had declared a general amnesty for all inmates upon the declaration of *shari'a* laws), armed robbery became more widespread than ever before.

With regards to the economy the experience had added new problems and controversies connected basically with the issues of introducing the Islamic principles of *zakat* and prohibition of *ribba'* (usury or interest). On both issues the regime's policies fluctuated between a projected Islamicisation of the taxation and banking systems (by introducing *zakat* to replace the taxation system and the abolition of the interest rate from the banking system) on the one hand, and the practical requirements of the economic system that rendered these measures unrealistic. A testimony to this is that no sooner had these measures been introduced than they were repealed.[67] Such confusion added new scars to the ever ailing economic situation of the Sudan. However, the experience seemed to have enhanced the position of the 'Islamic banks' that had been operating since the late 1970s under the tutelage of the *Ikhwan*.

In political terms, the experience undoubtedly brought Islam to the centre of Sudanese politics more than ever before. However, on closer examination the 'September laws' seem to have raised new questions rather than provided answers to the thorny issue of the Islamicisation of politics in the Sudan. In the first place, the laws have aggravated the second civil war in the South to unprecedented levels as the latent religious factor in the conflict became an expressed one. Furthermore, judging by the complex legal, social and economic consequences of the experience, the question of Islamicisation has become more controversial than ever, as demonstrated by the course of events in the post-Nimeiri era.

Chapter 6

The Post-Nimeiri Sudan

AN INTRODUCTORY NOTE

The politics of the post-Nimeiri Sudan (1985–89) bear curious resemblance to those of the 1960s, particularly the era of 1964–69 that preceded the *coup d'état* of May 1969. The trend of events is almost identical: civil unrest, similar to the events of October 1964 which brought down general 'Abbud's junta (this sparked the downfall of Nimeiri's regime); a transitional government and constitution; a partial 'general' election; a Constituent Assembly; a series of coalition governments punctuated by partisan squabbles; a civil war; and finally, a *coup d'état* (30 June 1989) imposing yet another military dictatorship.

Yet, despite this ostensible replay of the politics of the 1960s, the underlying issues and problems were radically different. The Sudan of 1985, even if judged by the natural passage of time, was hardly the Sudan of 1964–69. Surprisingly, however, one is left with the impression that the major players in the politics of the period in question acted as if nothing had changed, despite the lengthy intervention of a notorious regime with a heavy-handed approach to the entire matters of state and society.

If this assumption explains the above-noted superficial similarities between the politics of the 1960s and 1980s, a key to an understanding of the divergent problems that underlay the politics of the 1980s (the post-Nimeiri period) resides in the adequate appreciation of Nimeiri's legacy.

Without doing any injustice, it can be safely stated that Nimeiri's legacy was one of a political confusion, economic ruin, and social disorder. At the political level, the state apparatus suffered from the deleterious impact of a one-party system, which was further drastically transformed into a highly personified 'one man rule'.

The civil war which erupted for the second time in 1983 both resulted from and added to the political confusion – the product of a decade and half of an erratic regime. The imposition of the September (*shari'a*) laws of 1983, was perhaps one of the most conspicuous manifestations of political confusion and controversy in a multi-religious, multi-cultural country which spent most of its independent history searching for a suitable political system.

As for the economic situation, it is perhaps too obvious to be emphasised. By 1985 there was a famine and a huge foreign debt, with significant arrears to the IMF and other creditors.[1] Production was at its lowest levels (some sectors collapsed completely), industry in tatters, and the whole economy was suffering from the impact of the state's immense fiscal problems: a cash-strapped treasury, a devalued currency, a persistent deficit in balance of payments and trade balance, and a rocketing rate of inflation.

To these may be added the impact of Nimeiri's disastrous Islamic experiment on taxation and banking systems; and the impact of a civil war, the first casualties of which was the halt of the oil exploration and drilling schemes as well as the Jonglei canal project.

What should be emphasised here is that the crisis did not stem just from the failure of the May regime to implement its projected development programmes to achieve the promised economic and social transformation. Emphasis on agricultural development ensured the country's continued dependency on an unpredictable and often disadvantageous world market, as well as its continued reliance on the ever-expensive imports. This was compounded further by the failure of the regime's plans to achieve self-sufficiency in essential consumer commodities (such as sugar and grain), despite huge and costly ventures in that regard.

Furthermore, emphasis on expansion of road transport at the expense and negligence of rail transport, had resulted, among other things, in the dramatic rise of the oil imports bill, which added new burdens to the ever-complicated fiscal situation that failed to improve despite continuous intervention by the IMF since 1978.[2] Additionally, some of the development strategies generated their own related economic and social problems. A case in point is mechanised farming, which was pursued feverishly during the 1970s and 1980s, with disastrous impact on environment (deforestation, land exhaustion and pressure), and extreme pressure on the communities of traditional farmers and herdsmen.[3]

Away from the state and macroeconomics, the crisis manifested itself to the population in the continuous and unprecedented rise of the cost of living, persistent shortages in basic necessities and related hardships. The response of the population to these problems varied with different sectors. Few sectors of organised labour and professions took to militant forms of civil protest. The commonest forms of response, however, were rural-urban migration and out-migration to the oil rich Arab countries. Fairly widespread but undocumented was the corruption of state officials and par-state corporations. Other responses were smuggling and inter-tribal clashes and raids (primarily connected with economic deprivations and the irrational expansion of mechanised farming).

The situation in its totality – rural-urban exodus, brain-drain, collapse of local security – created a state of social disorder resulting in a merciless and abrupt destruction of subsistence economies and traditional systems of social control in the countryside, and a horrific disfigurement of the urban socio-economic structures. In their turn, these effects generated further mechanisms of economic deterioration and social disorder. On the eve of Nimeiri's departure the country had become literally ungovernable.

Despite the euphoric atmosphere that accompanied Nimeiri's departure, no sensible person would have thought that the horrendous problems generated by the flawed economic planning and policies of the May regime would evaporate following the collapse of that regime. In fact the challenge for Nimeiri's successors was so great that only a government guided by resilience, decisiveness and prudence, and blessed with domestic and outside co-operation, could have positioned the country once again on the track of recovery.

Yet, despite so great a challenge Nimeiri's successors did not pay the expected attention to these problems. Other questions of more 'pressing' political and legal nature seemed to call for immediate attention. Of this class are Nimeiri's notorious September (*shari'a*) laws, and the second, but far more devastating, civil war in the South.

However, because of the politicians inattention, the above problems and complexities of economy and society were allowed to escalate and produce new hazards in an already desperate situation. Hence an important source of discontent was allowed to degenerate resulting in a dismal erosion of whatever popularity the democratic regime, that succeeded Nimeiri, had enjoyed in the beginning. Worse still, Nimeiri's successors failed even to address seriously enough the questions identified by them as the first priorities; namely, the civil war and *shari'a* laws that dominated the political scene of the third republic. Reasons behind this curious state of affairs are twofold. On

143

the one hand, it has to do with the composition of the power structures and arrangements that succeeded Nimeiri which dictated its own logic of priorities and attitude to the country's main problems. On the other, it is related to the internal dynamics and politics of the civil war and *shari'a* laws.

I. NIMEIRI'S SUCCESSORS

The Transitional Period

In April 1985 Nimeiri's regime was overthrown by a combination of a popular *Intifada* and a military *coup* led by the General Command Army and headed by its chief of Staff and Defence Minister Lt General 'Abd al-Rahman M. Hasan Suwar al-Dhahab. After assuming power and deposing Nimeiri the army's General Command formed a Transitional Military Council (TMC) composed of fifteen senior army officers. The *Intifada*, on the other hand, was sparked by the government's announcement of a new package of austerity measures that involved price increases of essentials. Student demonstrations that took to the streets during the last week of March 1985 soon became nation-wide protests. On 3 April, an amalgamation of Trade Unions and Professional Organisations declared a general strike. On the early hours of the 6 April, the senior Trade Unions and political parties combined to from the National Alliance for National Salvation (NANS) and agreed on an *Intifada* Charter as a working programme for the next period. A few hours later the army announced its *coup*. The two parties, TMC and NANS entered into a process of prolonged and complicated negotiations that ultimately resulted in the formation of a civilian Cabinet on 25 April. The cabinet was composed largely of trade Unionists (or people nominated by Trade Unions), with the exception of the ministries of defence and interior which were given to the army and police respectively.[4]

Despite the fact that the TMC's intervention was triggered by the *Intifada* it insisted on acquiring, and assumed, effective control of the state's power by retaining both the functions of a head of state and legislative authority. Accordingly, the civilian Cabinet became, by and large, a mere executive body with very little say on major policy designs.

Retrospective assessment of the trend these events have taken might come up with different answers to this question: why did the TMC prevailed despite the 'fact' that the *Intifada* leaders were the champions of people's power and will? Yet it may be argued that this arrangement, regardless of what exactly had led to it, reflected the effective balance of power at the time.

The post *Intifada* political scene was dominated by three active forces: the army, represented by the TMC; the trades unions which were represented, chiefly but not exclusively, by the Trades Union Alliance (TUA); and the political parties.

The army's command which took power and formed the TMC was spurred into action by pressure form middle and junior rank officers who saw no reason of continuing to pledge support for a regime that had long lost the confidence of the Sudanese people and lost its ability to govern the country. The declaration of the army command that it reflected and responded to the will of the people, the representative composition of the TMC (from all Divisions), the seniority of the officers in charge, all ensured the unity of the army's rank and file around the TMC throughout the transitional period.

The same cannot be said about the other two centres of political activity: the trades unions and political parties. Most of the latter were allied to the TUA within the National Salvation Alliance (NANS). Yet for reasons that have to do with the differing nature of the two forces – their belated alliance and agreement over the *Intifada* charter – concerted action was not smooth, and each force was acting almost single-handedly. Hence the weaknesses of each were there to proliferate.

The TUA suffered initial injuries when the leaderships of two heavy-weight unions, the workers and farmers refused to join the protest actions of the *Intifada* and continued to support Nimeiri's regime until the last moment. Hence, and in the absence of an alternative leadership the said unions were excluded from the TUA. In retaliation, the leaderships of the former attempted to form another centre of trade union movement. Although the move did not hold any ground, it somehow weakened the bargaining power of the TUA. Moreover, the TUA suffered from a disunited action with regard to the decision on lifting the general strike declared on 3 April. Some trades union leaders were of the opinion that the strike should continue 'until total victory' despite the intervention of the army's command on the side of the *Intifada*. In the end, however, the majority of the Unions' leaderships had to give in to the overwhelming rejoicing mood in the streets following the announcement of Nimeiri's overthrow. Accordingly the strike was finally lifted, with some confusion, and the TUA leaders sat with the TMC and political parties to work out a formula for the next era.

Here a number of miscalculations were committed by the TUA leaders. First, it appeared as if the latter were concerned more about outmanoeuvring the political parties than facing the new challenge posed by the TMC. By insisting on an apolitical Cabinet, the TUA leaders thought that they will have a monopoly over the government, not realising perhaps that power had already been monopolised by the TMC. Furthermore, by allowing the latter to vet the candidates for the ministerial posts, the majority of the personalities chosen in the end were in no way measuring up to the designs of the TMC.

In the political parties front things were rather different. By their very competitive nature, unity between political parties could only be conditional and string attached to a particular programme or action. Theoretically, such a programme was provided by the *Intifada* charter to which three of the main Northern parties (Umma, DUP and CPS) were signatories. The fourth, the Muslim Brotherhood, which re-emerged under a new name the National Islamic Front (NIF), had neither signed the charter, nor was it invited to do so.[5]

For the *Intifada* parties there was the common problem of the lengthy Nimeiri years which had its varied impact on their strength, influence, and organisational structures. Furthermore, the fact that these parties signed the charter only on 6 April due to their failure to establish a common opposition front earlier was bound to leave a weakening impact both on their effective commitment to the document and their interworking relations. The problem was compounded further by the latent or professed rivalries, and hostilities, such as the historical rivalry that exists between the DUP and Umma parties, as well as the ideological dichotomy that exists between these two and the Communist party.

Consequently, the *Intifada* parties were not able to move as one front or even to articulate their positions and vision, *vis-à-vis* the TMC on the basis of the *intifada* charter as the guidelines for the post-Nimeiri era. Yet, the above-mentioned notwithstanding, there is a point of caution here. Why would the Umma and DUP work to outdo the TMC in favour of a charter signed with radically-minded trade unions in exceptional circumstances of civil unrest and quasi power vacuum? The question appears cynical but is not irrelevant. If the DUP and Umma regarded themselves as the natural successors to Nimeiri, and they did, then their potential adversaries were the trades unions rather than the army. In any event its safe to suggest that the Umma and DUP were ambivalent both in their commitment to the charter and their attitude towards the TMC.

As for the NIF, the only political party that continued in alliance with Nimeiri until the eve of his departure, it had, unsurprisingly, emerged in an extremely hostile atmosphere. However, rather than adopting an apologetic or low profile posture, the NIF leadership, shrewdly enough, placed all its bets on the TMC. The latter was more than willing to strike an undeclared alliance with the NIF. As one (NIF) writer has put it the two needed each other desperately. The TMC needed the NIF's support to deflect the pressures cast on it from the *Intifada* forces to adopt their policy designs and vision. As for the NIF the TMC provided an invaluable shield of protection in an extremely hostile atmosphere.[6]

As always, the South occupied a very marginal position in the minds of the major players and, consequently, in the power arrangements that took place during the transitional period. The usual number of three insignificant ministries were assigned to 'represent' the south. Accordingly, any potential or actual influence on the national politics of the era has to come almost exclusively from the rebel SPLA/M, which by then had been engaged in active fighting against the government since the end of 1983.

In view of all this, the balance of power was undoubtedly on the side of the TMC. Thus, when the dust of the momentous days of the *Intifada* cleared, the TMC was indeed in effective control of the transitional government.

The TMC's declared agenda was to hand over power to the people after a 'specific transitional period'. This was later translated into holding power for one year and then handing it to an elected government. Accordingly, the TMC saw its primary task during the transitional period as that general elections were to be held at the end of that period. The rest was routine.

As for the civilian cabinet its terms of reference were theoretically the *Intifada's* charter which calls for more than holding parliamentary elections. Conspicuously it calls for eradication of the vestiges of the 'May regime', rehabilitation of the economic situation, abrogation of September laws, and solution of the Southern problem.[7] In reality, however, the charter has become nothing more than a 'declaration of principles' without any *de jure* obligation to the government. This happened because the prolonged civilian-military negotiations that dominated the post-*Intifada* political scene had focused more on people who would compose the cabinet than the legalisation of its guiding principles.

Hence, in the absence of a *constitutionalised Intifada* charter, the

TMC decrees became the only terms of reference for the government; whereas its vision of leaving everything 'untouched' for the consideration of the elected government, became the undeclared programme of the transitional cabinet.

The second factor that contributed to the prevalence of this state of affairs was the very composition of the transitional government itself. As pointed out earlier, the majority of individuals who formed the cabinet were by and large people with no experience of politics or statesmanship. Worse, some of them were in effect partisan to the designs of the only party that did not sign the *Intifada* charter, the NIF.[8]

Thus the TMC's vision prevailed and elections became the sole and only achievement of the transitional government. This time there was no controversy as to when elections were to be held. Almost all the political forces (except perhaps the SPLM) were agreed on the date. However, there were two problems regarding how these elections could take place: the first was the request of the TUA of securing representation of the 'modern forces' in the elected assembly; the second was the civil war in the South that continued despite Nimeiri's downfall.

As for the question of modern forces representation the case was lost by the TUA and those political forces who supported the idea. A joint session of the two transitional councils voted by a majority to retain the old formula of the 1950s and 1960s of geographical constituencies on the basis of one man one vote, but with particular constituencies devoted to the graduates (this time graduates of university and higher institutes only). Once again the balance of power proved not in favour of the forces who 'triggered' the *Intifada*.

The civil war, on the other hand, threatened elections in two respects: first, the question of necessary security conditions, particularly in the South; secondly, the negative political impact of holding parliamentary elections under the shadow of a civil war. Hence it was widely believed that a peaceful settlement should precede the general elections. Despite the undeniable prudence of such a line of thought, nothing of the sort was done. The only agreement which was achieved between the SPLA/M and a majority of the political parties, represented by the NANS (but boycotted by the DUP and NIF) on the eve of the elections was ignored by the TMC, its cabinet and even one of the major parties that signed it (the Umma party), and elections went ahead. However, they were postponed in a majority of constituencies in the South (37 out of 71 constituencies) because of the non-conducive security situation.

The elections resulted in a good performance of the Umma party (101 seats), followed by the DUP (63 seats), the NIF (51 seats), the regional parties from the south and Nuba mountains (33 seats); and the CPS (3 seats).[9]

Of significance was the growth of the NIF from a minority party competing with communists in student politics and some urban areas, into the third parliamentary party that challenged the 'historical' influence of the mainstream or Traditionalist parties.

As a result of the outcome of the elections, which did not accord the Umma party with sufficient majority to form a government alone, the president of the latter, Sayyid al-Sadiq al-Mahdi decided to put together a coalition government with his traditional rival and partner Sayyid Muhammad 'Uthman al-Mirghani, the head of the DUP.

As a result of the transitional government's ineptness, manipulation and stalling tactics, the complex problems of the country were handed over to the elected government. Some of these problems, such as the civil war, had alarmingly escalated after Nimeiri's departure and widened in scope. Therefore, the challenge facing the elected government was unreservedly immense. Yet, the genesis of failure resided less in the magnitude and complexity of the problems than in the approach of the power holders, the new old guard of Sudanese partisan politics. Either because of a lack of vision, indecisiveness or sheer indifference, it appears as if the eyes of the latter were cast somewhere else, away from the country's immediate or long-term problems. As we shall see below the record of the 'third Republic' was one of continuous making and unmaking of coalitions with no clear sense of purpose. This is why the term *episode* seems most appropriate.

The Third Democratic Episode

Between the elections of April 1986 and the *coup d'état* of June 1989, five coalition governments were formed under the premiership of Sayyid al-Sadiq al-Mahdi, the Umma party leader. The making and remaking of five governments in three years is in itself sufficient indication of the political instability and pointless squabbles that have generally characterised the Sudanese parliamentary politics. This time, however, the situation was more complex. An overview of the events might shed some light on the forces in question and the politics of the 'third Republic'.

The first two governments, which lasted for about two years (from the general elections till May 1988), had basically rested on a coalition between the Umma and DUP with participation from the Southern parties' bloc. The coalition broke twice as a result of disagreements between the two main partners: Umma and DUP. For a given period (August 1987–April 1988) the country was technically without a government for lack of an agreement between the two coalition partners.

In any event, throughout those two years relations between Umma and DUP were tense and full of intrigues and differing views as if nothing was common between them except the power they shared.

Another problem that devastated the coalition governments was their gross failure to tackle any of the country's immense problems; such as the ever-deteriorating economic situation, the escalating civil war, and the rapidly collapsing public services and infrastructures. The conspicuous failure of the coalition governments even to address any of these problems after two years of Nimeiri's downfall was perhaps best described by a leading journal which stated that the country 'was drifting aimlessly'.[10]

The government position was not at all helped by the attitude of the chief opposition party – the NIF, which not only waged a fierce and merciless campaign against the government and its failures both through Parliament and its huge press network, but also resorted to occasional flexing of its economic and 'popular' muscles in the face of the paralysed government.

When the Umma–DUP coalition was finally undone in April/May 1988, the subsequent (third) government included the NIF in addition to the traditional coalition partners. Some 'Southern' faces were also retained. However, the bulk of the Southern bloc (22 out of 33 MPs), took to the opposition under the name of the Union of Sudanese African Parties (USAP).

Inclusion of the NIF in the government has been justified, by the Prime Minister, as an attempt to broaden the governmental base in order to boost its abilities in tackling the immense and multi-faceted problems facing the country at the time. Yet, Premier al-Sadiq himself had once dismissed the idea of NIF's inclusion when he was about to form his first government after the general elections as something that 'would weaken the government's ability to address non-Muslims concerns, decrease the chances of inter-action with modern forces, and hamper our co-operation with the outside world'.[11]

Hence, the decision to include the NIF in al-Sadiq al-Mahdi's government came as a surprise, not just because of the above-mentioned statement, but also given the overt tension that characterised the Umma-NIF relations since the *Intifada*. However, one has to recall that both parties strategically share common ideological grounds, particularly in their designs for a future Sudanese state based on Islam, varying emphasis and interpretations notwithstanding. Such a strategic harmony may be contrasted by the restless relationship which existed during the Umma–DUP partnership.

On the other hand, with the next elections drawing nearer the Prime Minister saw the opposition seats which the NIF occupied as too comfortable. To include them would mean sharing responsibility and blame. Hence, by including the NIF al-Mahdi wanted both to eliminate its potential opposition, as well as to find a way out from an uncomfortable coalition with the DUP.

The DUP, however, viewed the situation differently. The NIF which has grown at the expense of DUP's influence (most of the NIF's 28 geographical constituencies were gained in the DUP traditional sphere), threatens the latter's share in power. The DUP file felt that they were pushed aside by the NIF's presence, which appeared in more harmony with Umma leadership. Nevertheless, the DUP reluctantly joined the government as a peripheral partner. Indeed, its conduct throughout the seven months it spent in the *wifaq* (concord) government was that of half opposition, half government.

Consequently, despite of its strong political and parliamentary support (the three parties between them commanded the support of 215 MPs out of a total of 262), the 'concord' government suffered from persistent disagreements and disputes; primarily between the Umma/NIF on the one hand, and the DUP on the other. This was both a result and a reflection of the DUP's marginal position in the government.

Furthermore, that government found itself in a rather embarrassing situation as a result of USAP's opposition. With the pronounced Islamic overtones of the three northern parties that composed the government, the situation bore the potential of religious, racial, ideological and regional polarisation.

These were by no means the only problems. Inclusion of the NIF meant a redefinition of the government's priorities. Policy number one became the enactment of alternative *shari'a* laws to replace Nimeiri's 1983 *shari'a* laws within a two-month deadline. That was the NIF condition for participation to which the other parties succumbed. Consequently, the question of peace retreated, the civil war escalated, and the economic crisis deepened.

It was during that period that industrial actions were extensively used by the trades unions in the face of the worsening economic situation. At the same time, the issue of peace came to assume additional importance because of the continuous deterioration of the economic situation which was further worsened by the expanding military budget, and the other impacts of war such as the disruption of production, and the additional burden of displaced population. Gradually, peace became a popular demand.

It was at this juncture that the DUP succeeded in signing a joint agreement with the SPLA/M called the 'Sudanese Peace Initiative', on 16 November 1988.[12] The agreement received overwhelming enthusiasm and support from most political forces in the country except the NIF which declared that the agreement was a 'surrender to the rebels'.

Yet when the issue was tabled before the Constituent Assembly it was not considered as a basis for a comprehensive peace process. On the contrary, the Prime Minister requested the Assembly to mandate him 'to undertake all the necessary measures for the holding of the constitutional conference by the 31 December 1988. With the support of the NIF this motion was carried, much to the dismay of the DUP leaders and MPs. Furthermore, since the vote took place at the end of the third week of December, it was not at all clear how the Prime Minister could convene a *constitutional conference* on the future political system of the Sudan in a single week.

In protest against this dubious attitude of the Prime Minister and his reluctance to endorse the 'Sudanese peace initiative', the DUP withdrew form the government on 28 December 1988. The DUP's quitting coincided with popular unrest caused by the government sudden decision to increase the prices of some essential commodities such as sugar by 500%. The move alarmed the entire trade union movement which declared an open strike until the government withdrew the increases. Demonstrations broke out in Khartoum and other major cities around the country for three successive days. On 29 December the third consecutive day, the strike paralysed the national capital.[13]

The government had no other option but to back down and revoke the increases. However, the other questions raised by the DUP upon its walkout were not addressed. The DUP move was regarded by Sayyid al-Sadiq and his new allies, the NIF, as simply an attempt by the DUP leadership to 'fish in troubled waters'. Thus to outmanoeuvre the latter, the cabinet was reshuffled on 1 February 1989, and recomposed from the Umma and NIF to make up for the DUP withdrawal.

If the new partners thought that they had won the day they were mistaken. The next shot came from none other than the army itself. For, on 20 February the General Command of the Armed Forces submitted a memorandum to the Chairman of the State Council in his capacity as the Supreme Commander of the Armed Forces. The memorandum pointed to a number of concerns, some of which were of a technical character such as the poor shape of the army's equipment, training, logistics, and so forth; others, however, were of clear political nature like the questions of national unity, security, and the country's economic situation. The memorandum concluded by calling for the *enlargement of the government's base* within the framework of democracy, unity, and national sovereignty.[14]

The armed forces memorandum had eventually invoked the collapse of the Umma–NIF short-lived coalition. After a lengthy and prolonged process, the fifth government was formed under the title of the 'United National Front'. As its name suggests, the UNF government was indeed abroad-based grouping of all the influential political forces, except the NIF, which declined to participate on grounds that the 'NIF will not participate in a government that does not commit itself to the *shari'a* or include trade unionist who does not have a political mandate'.[15] Noteworthy is that for the first time in Sudanese parliamentary history the cabinet included representatives of trades unions, and the Communist Party of Sudan (CPS).

The 'provisional programme' that provided the guidelines of the UNF government called for: adherence to the constitution, democratic rule and multi-party system, independence of the judiciary, and preservation of the basic rights and freedoms; adequate support for the Armed Forces, and the dismantling of all kinds of militia forces; consolidation of internal unity; improvement of living conditions, and due consideration for a solution to the economic crisis; and, significantly, *convening of the national constitutional conference* in the nearest possible future within the framework of the *official acceptance of the Sudanese peace initiative of 16 November 1988.*[16]

It appeared as if at last things had started to move in the right direction after a waste of four precious years since the collapse of Nimeiri's regime. The question that poses itself in this regard is why did the very forces that finally agreed on the March programme of the UNF government – the army, trade unions, and political parties (with the exception of the NIF which had its own agenda) – fail to take such step in the immediate post *Intifada* period.

In view of the transitional government's composition and its strategy of handing over power to the elected regime as the one and only priority, the question becomes rather irrelevant. As for the 'democratically elected government', it had problems of another character. First among these were the pointless or rather suicidal squabbles as conspicuously manifested in the continuous breaking up of coalitions over minor differences. It is with regard to this particular feature that Sudanese affairs at the time looked very much like a repeat of the politics of the 1960s. For the third time the people realised that the Sudanese 'Bourbons' had failed to learn the lesson. Yet the problem was not solely the making of the Traditionalist parties that dominated the parliamentary politics after the 1986 elections. In the absence of a restructuring of the political system, and a clear-cut redefinition of priorities by a consensus of major forces nationwide, a return of the old politics was unavoidable. A partial election under the shadow of a persistent civil war should have served as an unmistakable indication of what was to come. Once in power, the Traditionalist parties, unsurprisingly, became concerned more with office rewards, especially after a decade and half in the cold, than the heavy responsibilities of managing a country ruined by war, economic collapse and social disorder.

Related to this is the failure of the 'other' forces that proposed a different strategy – the left, the 'modern forces' of the South and other 'marginalised' regional forces – to impose their agenda on the power holders. The Sudanese left which has been historically dominated by the Communist party, was marginally represented in Parliament. Furthermore, the CPS, whether for political calculations or structural wekness or both, has maintained a very low profile throughout the third democratic episode.

As for the celebrated 'modern forces', that played a 'vanguard' role in the *Intifada*, they suffered from intrinsic and extrinsic problems. Though the main force was a sectoral one, i.e. the trades unions, it was largely dominated, especially in its professional sections, by liberal and leftist ideologies. In itself this factor ensured the suspicion of the Traditionalist parties and open hostility (in the case of NIF). However, despite common ideological orientation, the leaders of the professional organisation, did not share, politically and organisationally a united front, apart from the loose forums of the Trades Union and National Alliances. On the other hand, the leaderships of the all-important trades unions of workers and farmers, who were composed basically of elements of SSU (Nimeiri's single party), decided to affiliate to the DUP. Thus, lacking an intrinsic unity of purpose and action, the 'modern forces' were outmanoeuvred twice: first effectively marginalised in the post-*Intifada*; and then prevented from sectoral representation in the Parliament. Consequently, after elections they were reduced to a little more than what the other politicians wanted them to be: interest groups pursuing the economic concerns of their ranks.

The failure of the regional forces, other than the south, to maintain the 'Rural Forces Solidarity Movement' and substantiate it with electoral gains, has meant that the demands of the backward areas (such as Darfur, Nuba mountains and Eastern region) remained virtually inarticulate, or at best dependent on the pressure groups inside the 'mainstream parties'.[17]

As for the Southern bloc, inside Parliament its position was more precarious. In the first place its legitimacy and representative weight were in question due to the postponement of election in 37 constituencies (out of 71 in the whole region). Even in those constituencies in which elections did take place registration and voting were very low. To this is added the impact of a continued civil war in the region. Continuity of the war in the south had a counterproductive effect on the strength of the southern MPs on at least two accounts. First, the continuous and massive displacement of people from their constituencies to the capital and other major towns in the north created additional burden on the Southern MPs and made them more vulnerable to pressures from their northern counterparts. Secondly, the negative response the continuation of the war had created among the Northern public opinion, especially after the widening of the war zone to parts of the north.

Continuation of the war led to the hardening of positions on both sides of the conflict and by 1988 the situation had reached a point of almost complete political and military intransigence between the government and SPLA/M. Such a situation had imposed on the Southern bloc in the assembly and government to choose between either siding with the 'Northern Establishment' or the SPLA/M. In the absence of a convincing share of power both in Khartoum and the Southern region the majority of the southern parties, the USAP group, chose the latter. Once in opposition, following the formation of the Concord government, the USAP group assumed positions and stances that looked extremely similar, if not identical, to that of the SPLA/M's discourse.[18] On the other hand, a minority group of the Southern bloc decided to side with the government largely due to inter-southern differences or personal ambitions.

Thus, the 'Southern politics' closely mirrored the military situation in the field whereby the main contenders were the SPLA and government's with 'friendly forces' on both sides. However, with the majority of Southern forces siding with SPLA/M and rallying around its programme, the 'Southern' view on national politics has virtually become that of the SPLA/M.

To sum up, each of the forces that proposed change had a limitation of a sort that impeded its ability to heed its programme, or effectively mobilise the public around it. Consequently, the Traditionalist parties were left to concern themselves primarily with making and breaking of coalition governments and to squabble over petty matters. Their main worry was the increasing challenge that the NIF succeeded in imposing on their socio-political constituencies by its strenuous calls for the application of *shari'a*. Accordingly, it was the NIF – in opposition throughout the first two years of the coalition governments – which was setting the agenda for the government.

Hence, the formation of the *wifaq* government, with its above-noted programme, represented a gallant victory for the NIF and its agenda. Ironically, significant as it was, that victory proved to be the most that the NIF achieved during the parliamentary period. From then onwards its fortunes started to decline.

Once in power, the NIF lost the privileges of an active opposition party versus a paralysed government. It soon became clear that the inclusion of the NIF in the government had by no means improved the performance of the latter or increased its ability to tackle major or even routine problems. The only 'achievement' of the NIF in government was the draft 'criminal bill, 1988' which postulated even harsher application of *shari'a* codes.

The Concord government then suffered a blow 'from within', when the DUP broke ranks with its partners in power and signed the Sudanese peace initiative of 16 November 1988 with the rebels. The reluctance of the Umma and NIF to endorse that agreement set the scene for popular discontent, which was soon translated into active opposition when the government recklessly chose that very moment to introduce its highly unpopular price increases. The slogans of the December massive demonstrations called for the government to quit.

The main force behind the December 'uprising' were, as always, the trades unions. By 1988 the trades unions movement had accomplished the formation of its elected structures at all levels and even formed a joint supreme council for consultation and co-ordination. Furthermore, several unions had individually or jointly tested their industrial muscles more than once over disputes with the government. Hence, the trades unions leaderships enjoyed undisputed legitimacy and were therefore equipped with the potential of exerting more influence on national politics.

One impact of the December events has been the DUP's pulling out from the shaky tripartite alliance that formed the basis of the Concord government. However, both Umma and NIF chose to stay in office despite the unmistakable popular rejection. The last straw came with the army's memorandum which spelled out the collapse of the NIF–Umma government.

The armed forces memorandum was indeed unusual in every respect, especially in a democracy wherein the army either abided by the legal authority or staged a *coup d'état*. The Sudanese situation, however, was by no means a normal one by any standard. A democracy that operated under the shadow of a civil war and within a continuous state of emergency is a rather dubious one. When it come to armies in politics, the Sudanese army had been barely three years ago, the ultimate sovereign of the country and its legislature. Before that it had ruled the country twice for a combined period of twemty-two years.

Yet, the most obvious factor behind the army's action was the civil war, the burden of which was naturally shouldered by the armed forces. Continued intransigence meant that the army was dragged in an increasingly escalating and devastating war. Worse still, it soon became clear that the army was fighting an unwinnable and rather humiliating battle, as was demonstrated by its repeated losses of one garrison after another to a largely non-professional rebel army.

Consequently, the armed forces became convinced that the government of the day had to make a clear and unequivocal choice: either to work for a lasting settlement and therefore save the army the burden of fighting an unwinnable war and the country the consequences of this, or else, create the necessary conditions for its army to prevail. That was the substance of the armed forces memorandum in a nutshell.

Clearly, the Umma–NIF government was not able to shrug off the army's protest as it did with the massive popular discontent, and pretend that it was still in effective control. It had to acquiesce.

The collapse of the Umma–NIF coalition signalled a new process wherein peace was regarded as the first priority if the country's major problems were to be addressed seriously. Yet, failure to reach peace from the outset in the post-Nimeiri Sudan was not just the making of imprudent politicking. It had a lot to do with the dynamics of the dichotomous processes of war and peace, to which we now turn.

II. WAR AND PEACE

The start of the second civil war in the Sudan is commonly set as May 1983, when the garrisons of Battalion 105, stationed at Bor, Pibor and Fashalla, refused orders to be transferred to the North and fled to Ethiopia with their arms, after being attacked by the government's army on 16 May 1983. Yet the mutiny of Battalion 105 was the climax of a lengthy process of discontent, and tensions that had been brewing for years in the Southern region despite the Addis Ababa Agreement of 1972 which accorded regional autonomy to the South. For the genesis of these tensions and discontent we have to look into two areas: the traditional North–South dichotomy and how it was transformed/ handled in the post Addis Ababa arrangement; and the politics of the Southern region, 1972–83.

Some of the problems and tensions of the latter sprang out of the discontent of certain 'absorbed' Anya Nya(I) elements with, and after, the Addis Ababa Agreement. This included the infighting and divisions of the Southern politicians, the generational differences between the senior ex-Anya Nya politicians, who monopolised the regional government and the younger and more educated Southern politicians, who were denied access to power, and the financial constraints of the regional government that intensified its internal power struggle and made it more vulnerable to intervention and manipulation by the central government and its autocratic president, Ja'far Nimeiri.

On the other hand, the central government's inattention to economic development in the South, its mishandling of the question of the discovery of oil in the South, and its attempt to redraw the 'borders' of the Southern region in a flagrant contravention to the Addis Ababa Agreement, had all cultivated deep apprehension and dismay among the Southerners.[19]

All these tensions, problems and discontents that were accumulating exploded on a wider scale when the central government imprudently decided to crush the Bor mutiny.

Furthermore, Nimeiri's high-handed approach, which culminated in his complete abrogation of Addis Ababa agreement, and his later decree of imposition of *shari'a* laws throughout the country (September 1983), ensured the quick transformation of the Bor mutiny into a full-scale rebellion. Thus, before the end of 1983 the South was, once again, in a state of a civil war, just as it was when Nimeiri took power in 1969.

Yet, the second civil war was different from the first one in at least two respects: first, the wider scale of the conflict and its rapid proliferation and escalation; and secondly, the nature, composition, and programme of the Sudan People's Liberation Army (SPLA), and its political wing, the Sudan People's Liberation Movement (SPLM).

The SPLA/M, which was founded in July 1983, appeared – unlike Anya Nya I – better armed, well organised, and with a great deal of political and ideological sophistication. Furthermore, unlike its predecessor, it has rapidly consolidated its hold and grown into prominence and strength. By 1988/89, just five years after its inception, the SPLA/M was in effective control of about 75% of the Southern region. Politically, the movement had become not only the major force in the south, but also one of the chief players in national politics. Yet, of greater significance, perhaps, was its declared objectives and programme.[20]

In its founding manifesto, the SPLA/M emphatically proclaimed that far from being a secessionist movement, it was indeed fighting for the liberation of the whole Sudan; and that its ultimate aim was the creation of a *new Sudan*.[21]

This SPLA/M call for unity or 'liberation' of the whole Sudan was viewed by the majority of Northern Sudanese with a good deal of curiosity and even cynicism, because it was a breakaway from the usual norm of Sudanese politics wherein Southerners were singularly concerned with the Southern region's problems. Nevertheless there are a number of considerations that might explain SPLA's position.

In the first place there was the experience of Addis Ababa agreement as a result of which Southerners became more integrated in national politics besides their control of the regional government. Furthermore, the decade of peace created conducive conditions for more education to Southerners and training of administrative and professional cadres, as well as better contact with the North and interaction with national problems. Accordingly, more Southerners, particularly the younger and more educated generation, came to regard themselves more in terms of their belonging to a wider dominion of the Sudan rather than the *Southern* Sudan. So when this younger generation of Southerners became dissatisfied both with the attitude of central government towards the South, as well as with the squabbles of the senior Southern politicians who monopolised the regional government, they decided to bid for their share of power in Khartoum itself. Hence, together with army deserters they formed the SPLA/M with its agenda of liberating the *whole* of the *Sudan*.[22]

Other considerations may be associated with the SPLA/M's 'socialistic' ideology, which was conspicuous throughout the first three years of the movement's existence. The 'socialistic ideal' generally emphasises liberation of the 'oppressed masses' rather than the secession of particular ethnic or cultural groups. The SPLA/M's socialist discourse may also be viewed as a product of the Ethiopian influence at the time. For its part, Ethipia would likely emphasise unity of Sudan for reasons connected with Ethiopa's own problems with cessionist movements.

Moreover, it may be argued that the Nilotic tribes – particularly the *Dinka*, who formed the hard-core of the SPLA and its main recruiting ground – because of their proximity to, and historical links with the North, were more inclined to remain within a united Sudan rather than to opt for secession.

In any event, the SPLA/M produced a new phenomena of a Southern-based *national* party that aspires to a fundamental *restructuring* of the Sudanese socio-political order on a new basis. The movement remained loyal to this thesis despite the collapse of Nimeiri rule in April 1985, and throughout the transitional and parliamentary periods.

In the opinion of the SPLA/M leadership, the failure of a majority of political forces in the North, particularly those who succeeded Nimeiri in power, to understand or accommodate this new vision of the SPLA/M, had led to their inability to pursue any successful dialogue with the movement and ultimately their failure to achieve a political settlement to the conflict.

That seems true enough, for despite the SPLA/M's founding manifesto and subsequent statements, prior to and after Nimeiri's downfall, the transitional government had nothing to offer apart from the re-invocation of the Addis Ababa agreement. To the SPLA/M that was equivalent to nothing since the movement regards its cause as far more than just the agreement in question, or the 'Southern problem' for that matter. Furthermore, the movement had from the outset refused to recognise the TMC as the legitimate authority in the country, and accordingly declined any proposals to talk with the Generals. Hence, the question of peace, just like everything else then, had to wait for the elected government. Alas, the latter proved as ill equipped in dealing with the question as its predecessor, and hostilities were bound to continue. Yet, it may be argued that the vital and most ripe moment for a just settlement was the 'historic' moment of the *Intifada* and its immediate aftermath. To some, that moment was wasted by the SPLA's 'intransigence'. Even those sympathetic to the SPLA/M and its programme thought that had the movement come after the *Intifada* it would have affected the balance of power and consequently the transitional arrangements.

Whether, the SPLA/M was right in its outright rejection of the transitional power arrangements remains a controversial theme in contemporary Sudanese affairs. What should be stressed here is the failure of the forces that led the *Intifada* to build a wider coalition capable of accommodating the SPLA/M as an integral and national (versus regional) component, and the latter's inability to reach the *Intifada* forces in the North in a manner that would make its vision and programme more comprehensible and appreciated.

Failure to achieve this concerted action between the forces that might potentially share similar objectives, meant that the question of peace became hostage to the half-hearted designs of the TMC Generals, and, subsequently, the Traditionalist politicians. Thus, the war continued and even escalated beyond any foreseeable dimensions. Continuity of the war, and its escalation added new complexities to the situation and generated new mechanisms that in its turn influenced the political scene as a whole.

THE IMPACT OF WAR

The most immediate impact of the war was the increasing suffering of the civilians whose death toll dramatically exceeds that of soldiers on both sides. With the continued prosecution of war, civilians were increasingly drawn into its yoke and suffered from its related disasters such as related famine, which became the most conspicuous element in the conflict. In its turn, civilian suffering had become a focus of both domestic and international humanitarian concern – a matter that increased pressure for a peaceful settlement.

War disasters, on the other hand, had caused mass displacement of hundreds of thousands of Southerners, the majority of whom moved to the North, particularly the capital Khartoum, to the extent that by the late 1980s the south was suffering from 'a haemorrhage of people'. Such a situation caused serious disruption to the demographic and socio-economic structures of the South, and created serious pressures in the North by imposing new constraints on an already catastrophic economic situation.[23]

Yet, the war by itself generated its own econometrics. By the late 1980s the war was costing the government an average of US$1 million per day on military expenditure. Such a situation left the government unable either to reform its budget by cutting expenditure (as the IMF was insisting), or to meet the demands of the salaried strata and workers who were experiencing rapid deterioration of their purchasing power as a result of the 'war economy'. This is why the workers had increasingly resorted to press the government, through their unions, to move in the direction of a peaceful settlement.

By contrast, there was another group that appeared to have a vested interest in the continuation of war. This was the 'military-commercial complex' that appeared during Nimeiri's period in the form of the 'military economic corporation' and continued, unofficially, after Nimeiri was overthrown. This group greatly benefited from the disruption of regular transport with the South on the account of war, and were able to extract huge profits in trading with the beleaguered region.[24]

At the military level, the period in question witnessed growing advantage of the SPLA over the government's army. The Sudanese army was drastically under-equipped and incapable of pursuing a protracted war. Accordingly, by 1989 the rebel army was in effective control of most of the South, while the regular army became confined to a few garrisons in the provincial capitals. As stated earlier it was this humiliating situation that led to the senior army officers pressing for peace.

Furthermore, the government's economic problems and the poor condition of its army had led to its pursuance of a disastrous policy of arming militias or 'friendly' forces to fight the SPLA on its behalf. Most conspicuous in the government 'friendly forces' was the Anya Nya II that continued to fight the SPLA on the side of the government until early 1988, when a majority of its forces changed sides and joined the SPLA. For its part, the latter also had its own friendly forces. Being undisciplined, unreliable and difficult to control the militia war had the most devastating effect on villages and disrupted all traces of normal life in the region. Furthermore, the ruthless pursuit by the government of its militia policy had deepened the dismay among the army officers and men and fuelled their discontent.[25]

All in all, the continuity of war tended to deepen the enmity between the two main sides of the conflict – the government and SPLA – and to harden their respective positions on the prerequisites and substance of negotiations. For a government that was rapidly losing grounds to the 'rebels', the primacy of a military advantage or negotiation from a position of *strength*, was an obvious, though thinly disguised, policy. As for the SPLA it was more inclined to continue a war in which it was increasingly having the upper hand. Therefore, the two sides appear to have found it easier to make war than peace.

Notwithstanding this deadlock between the two main warring parties, one has to take into consideration the conflicting pressures, particularly on the government, for peace or war. As pointed out above, there appeared certain groups with vested interests in the continuation of the war, such as the 'commercial military' complex. Other forces were also interested in the continuation of war because of their belief that a military victory should precede negotiations in order to dictate the terms of the settlement. These forces were represented mainly by the NIF and a faction in the Umma party (that included the Prime Minister), and a faction in the DUP. As for the 'peace party', it included, in addition to some factions in Umma and the DUP all the liberal and leftist forces, whether organised in political parties, associations, trade unions, and certain personalities, as well as the Southern bloc on whose land the war was (and still is) being waged.[26]

Furthermore, the continuous military intransigence has had its input in shaping and reshaping public opinion at large. Therefore, when the general expectations of reaching a political settlement with the SPLA after the *Intifada* were not realised, a climate of growing disappointment with, and even hostility to, the movement developed gradually. The NIF was quick to utilise such a mood to the maximum to breed its militarist strategy, as demonstrated by its organisation of the 'security of Sudan (*'aman al-Sudan*) march' as early as September 1985 when the great expectations generated by the *Intifada* were still alive.[27] From then onwards, the anti-SPLA feeling was rising in the North until it reached its highest levels with the former's occupation of Kurmuk and Gaysan in the Southern Blue Nile in December 1987, thus bringing the reality of the war to the North.

The hysterical response, both by the government and the public, to the occupation of Kurmuk and Gaysan, exposed the latent racialist factor in the conflict, and demonstrated beyond any doubt that the civil war had hitherto been treated as a *Southern* war. Nevertheless, it also signalled a countdown to a change in the mood of public opinion in the

163

North in favour of peace. The demonstrated possibility that the war could easily spill over into the North had led the majority to start thinking about the merits of a definite political settlement over a doubtful military victory. This factor was further compounded by the growing economic impact of the war, alluded to earlier, on the urban middle and lower classes. By 1988, the overall public opinion in the North had witnessed an almost complete transformation in favour of peace, despite the fact that the government of the day (the *wifaq* government) was the least prepared to pursue a policy of peace, as demonstrated by its reluctance to endorse the DUP-SPLA/M peace initiative.

If the dynamics of war had left a strong impact on the political situation, including the generation of an antithetical process of peace, the latter, like war, had its own dynamics, internal politics and significance.

BEHIND THE PEACE PROCESS

Between 1985 and 1989 there were several peace initiatives, contacts, mediations (both domestic and external), as well as a sizeable number of agreements, declarations and position statements. The length of the list in itself indicates that there was a real concern about the conflict, and an expressed (if not always genuine) desire for its political settlement from several quarters, including the two main warring parties – the government and SPLA/M.

Yet, despite this 'feverish' drive towards peace, the gloomy reality remains that no peace process was effectively unleashed, as demonstrated by the absence of a solid agreement between the government and SPLA/M. Nevertheless as far as this study is concerned, the literature associated with the quest for peace is quite useful, indicative and revealing.

The constant factor in all the agreements, declarations, and so on is the SPLA/M. That is to say, the agreements were always ones between the SPLA/M and one or a number of political forces in the country (both North and South). Furthermore, with one exception, the SPLA/ M signed agreements with practically all the political parties and associations in the country. This situation has been cited by the SPLA/ M and its sympathisers as an indication of the movement's seriousness and its genuine interest in peace. On the other hand, from the viewpoint of the SPLA/M's opponents, failure to reach a settlement was attributable to the movement's intransigence. Realistically, however, the whole process points to the difficulty and complexity of the problem which takes more than declarations of good intentions to be solved. Rather than listing here all the agreements and the like, it will serve the purpose to cite representative examples.

There were two main categories of agreements signed between the SPLA/M and other forces in the country: a) agreements signed between the movement and one or more major players in the stage, such as the Koka Dam Declaration, 24 March 1986 (signed between SPLA/M and NANS) and the Sudanese Peace Initiative, 16 November, 1988 (SPLA/M-DUP); and b) agreements or joint actions carried between the SPLA/M and a particular group or groups with which the movement shared common ideological or regional grounds such as the communiqué of the Addis Ababa Peace Forum, 5–7 July 1988 (SPLA/M-USAP) and the final statement of the Ambo Workshop 4–7 February 1989 (organised by the SPLA/M and attended by a number of academics, trades unionists and certain regional groups). Whereas, the first category bears direct implication on the national situation including the possibility and/or the eventuality of a settlement, the second represents a co-ordination of strategies between groups which share similar views or grievances.[28] The focus of this study obliges us to examine only the first category represented by the Koka Dam Declaration, and the Sudanese Peace Initiative.

The Koka Dam Declaration was signed between the SPLA/M and the National Alliance for National Salvation (NANS), which was then grouping most of the political parties (except the DUP and NIF) and trade Unions and associations. The Declaration main points are as follows:

In the preamble, the signatories express their commitment to the creation of a *new Sudan* and state that the formation of a new Sudan should begin by convening a *National Constitutional Conference*. The two sides then agree that 'essential prerequisites which would foster an atmosphere conducive to the holding of the proposed national constitutional Conference are:

a) A declaration by all political forces and the government of the day to discuss the *Basic Problems of Sudan* and not the so-called problem of Southern Sudan and that shall be in accordance with the agenda agreed upon in this "declaration".
b) The lifting of the state of Emergency.
c) Repeal of the "September 1983 Laws" and all other laws that are restrictive to freedoms.

d) Adoption of the 1956 Constitution as amended in 1964 with the incorporation of "Regional Government".
e) The abrogation of the military pacts concluded between Sudan and other countries and which impinge on Sudan's National Sovereignty.
f) A continuous endeavour by the two sides to take the necessary steps and measures to effect a ceasefire.'

Furthermore, the two sides agreed that the agenda for the Constitutional Conference should comprise the following:

'(i) a) The Nationalities Question.
   b) The Religious Question.
   c) Basic Human Rights.
   d) The System of Rule.
   e) Development and Uneven development.
   f) Natural Resources.
   g) The Regular Forces and Security Arrangements.
   h) The Cultural Question, Education and the Mass Media.
   i) Foreign Policy.
(ii) The Two sides have agreed that the above agenda are not exhaustive.'[29]

The Koka Dam Declaration is often regarded as a watershed in the conception of the conflict and the possible outlets for its resolution because of its recognition and commitment to discuss the 'Basic Problems of the Sudan'. It was also significant because the 'party' which concluded the ageement with the SPLA/M was led by the then highly respectable and representative NANS.

However, important as it was, the Koka Dam Declaration was immediately devastated by two factors: DUP-NIF opposition; and the holding of the general elections (April 1986). The DUP-NIF then had a lot in common. Both were outside NANS (DUP resigned in November 1985), both were opposed to the repeal of September (*shari'a*) laws, and both were co-ordinating stances against the Umma Party which was then apparently enjoying a surge of popularity. The opposition of these two 'senior' parties of the North somehow watered down the significance of the Declaration, and, crucially enough, encouraged the TMC and transitional Cabinet to go on with elections despite the Declaration.

Yet, the responsibility of holding a partial elections under the shadow of a civil war does not rest only with the TMC *et al.* Some of those forces that signed Koka Dam have their share as well, either because they did not campaign seriously for its postponement in order to attend first to the conflict, or because of their *active* campaigning for elections that 'will put everybody in his rightful place' (believed to be the opinion of the Umma party). Having said that, it is equally correct to state that a lot of forces, including those who regard the civil war as a priority, wanted elections to rid them off the many uncertainties of the transitional period.

The holding of elections and their results brought about new balance of power and, consequently, a re-alignment of forces. One of the elections' results was that NANS was 'voted' out of the scene, and the left, the most active in campaigning for peace was reduced to a negligible minority in Parliament. Significantly, elections' results accorded three of the 'major' northern parties – Umma, DUP, and NIF – with about 72% of the Assembly seats. Among these three it was only the Umma party which was a signatory to Koka Dam. Nevertheless, as the party that headed the elected government, the Umma was expected to initiate a move that would put the peace process, within the framework of Koka Dam, on track.

Yet, it soon became clear that Sayyid al-Sadiq al-Mahdi, the chairman of the Umma party and Prime Minister, was having second thoughts about Koka Dam. In the light of the elections' results, the immediate concern of the Prime Minister was cast on the potential threat that both his partner, the DUP and opponent, the NIF, posed to his power. He therefore started to talk increasingly about the necessity to accommodate 'those who rejected Koka Dam', that is, DUP and NIF. The position of the Prime Minister could not have been more controversial. He was either attempting the impossible by becoming all things to all people; or, worse, trying to outdo his conservative rivals in their militarist overtones and Islamist sloganism.

In any event, if al-Mahdi's government was looking for a pretext to stall the peace process and eventually retreat from Koka Dam, the SPLA gave it one by shooting down a civilian plane over Malakal (capital of Upper Nile province) on 16 August 1986. Thenceforth, negotiations were shelved indefinitely amidst heated accusations of 'treason' to everyone who attempts to talk with the 'rebels'.

What followed was a period of overwhelming militarisation on both sides punctuated only by some efforts from third parties (domestic and foreign) to broker a political settlement. The two main parties, however, remained entrenched into a quasi 'zero-sum' options.

One of the multi-dimensional impacts of escalation of the war, alluded to earlier, was the radical shift of Northern Sudanese opinion in favour of peace. This mood was clearly apparent in the last quarter of 1988 when the DUP made its peace agreement with the SPLA/M – the Sudanese Peace Initiative (SPI).

The SPI reiterated the commitment of the two parties to the holding of the National Constitutional Conference, 'as a matter of national necessity and urgency', with the following pre-requisites:

1 'Although the firm stand of the SPLA/M remains the repeal of the September 1983 Laws and to be replaced by the 1974 Laws, it nevertheless, and because of its keenness on the convening of the National Constitutional Conference', agreed that the '*Hudoud* [sic] and related articles be frozen and that there shall be no legislation on any laws that contain such articles', until a final agreement is reached on 'the alternative laws' in the Constitutional Conference.
2 The abrogation of the military pacts concluded between Sudan and other countries and which impinge on Sudan's national sovereignty.
3 The lifting of the state of emergency.
4 Ceasefire.

The two parties also agreed on 'the necessity of holding the National Constitutional Conference by 31st December 1988 provided that the prerequisites mentioned in this agreement would have been implemented to the satisfaction of the parties concerned'.[30]

The SPI was also a very significant development in the peace process, not just because it was worked out by the DUP – a new convert to peace – but also because it was having the potential of achieving a settlement (or at least the convening of the constitutional conference) on account of its terms and the apparent conducive climate that surrounded it.

The political situation in which the Sudanese Peace Initiative was concluded has been described earlier. Many observers believed that the motive behind the DUP's peace drive was its attempt to regain some of its lost ground and attract new partners in view of its marginalised position in the *wifaq* government. Prior reference has also been made to Umma and NIF opposition to the peace initiative. They were bent on preventing the DUP from getting away with all the applause. Furthermore, if the latter was likely to gain from the agreement the former would undoubtedly be the losers.

Again, the SPI, like Koka Dam before it suffered from the opposition of two 'senior' Northern parties. Yet, unlike Koka Dam, the NIF–Umma opposition to the peace initiative, although initially successful in blocking the process, ultimately eroded their own power as demonstrated by the collapse of the short-lived NIF–Umma coalition government. That is to say, while the political situation – the elections' results and politicking of the major players' was dictating the trend of the peace process in the aftermath of Koka Dam; with the SPI the reverse was true, it was primarily the peace agenda that set the political scene.

So much for the political circumstances and considerations with regard to the peace efforts. Of crucial importance are the issues involved. Here it is noteworthy to observe that the SPLA/M had managed to impose its vision on the framework and even agenda of dialogue on the respective political forces in the country. Despite the overt or covert hostility of the bulk of the latter, they all finally accepted the SPLA/M call for the holding of a constitutional conference to discuss the 'Basic Problems of the Sudan' rather than the 'Southern problem'. The agenda of that Conference were also virtually accepted by the respective forces. Indeed, in the course of time the Constitutional Conference became the panacea of Sudanese politics. Yet, as is clear from both Koka Dam and the SPI certain 'prerequisites' were to be met first by the government of the day before a constitutional conference could be held. These prerequisites proved to be the real bone of contention throughout most of the third democratic episode.

The said prerequisites involved matters of procedural nature such as a ceasefire and the lifting of the state of emergency. These – as conventional items in conflict resolutions – were dependent in their implementation on the political will of the two warring parties. Other points were of a more specific nature such as the SPLA/M demand of abrogation of the military pacts with other countries. Both the transitional and elected governments were reluctant to endorse this demand on conflicting grounds that varied between denial of the existence of such pacts or questioning the right of the 'rebel' movement to *dictate* the state's foreign policy conduct. Nevertheless that point was equally possible to implement if the political will was there, as was later demonstrated by the UNF government (formed in March 1989) which officially adopted the SPI (April 1989) and started to implement some of the prerequisites.

All in all the lengthy squabbles around the prerequisites reveal important undercurrents. The governments of the day (1985–89) regarded the SPLA/M prerequisite as an unacceptable condition that a government should give in to a rebel army. Negotiations, they maintained, should be conducted without preconditions, since *all matters* would be discussed in the Constitutional Conference.

As for the SPLA/M, its insistence on committing the main political forces in the north reflects a deep mistrust, not just of the power holders in Khartoum but perhaps of the North in general. Building on previous experiences the movement apparently did not want to be 'tricked into an agreement only to be dishonoured later'. Moreover, consistent with the SPLA/M's proclamations and objectives the said prerequisites were regarded by the movement as necessary for the existence of an atmosphere conducive to a 'dialogue between equals'.[31]

If such a gulf separated the respective concepts of the two main parties with regard to negotiations/dialogue, what about the substantive issues of the conflict? This is an area that involves two distinct but interrelated categories: a) the forces involved; and, b) their respective *visions* of the substance of the conflict.

Given the multiplicity of the political forces involved during the period in question, it might not be appropriate to speak of 'two sides', as is the case in the military field, or of two visions. Yet, with regard to the ideological polarisation that accompanied the conflict escalation, it is possible to identify two main conflicting visions each espoused by one of the forces involved. One of these is obviously the SPLA/M; the other being the NIF. The latter, though not having the upper hand in the government of the day, was conspicuous by its constant absence from, and fierce opposition to the countless agreements, declarations, and communiqués signed between the SPLA/M and the rest of the political forces in the country, whether bilateral or multilateral. Hence, an NIF that failed to meet the SPLA/M half way even in a 'declaration of principles', may be regarded as the opposite pole of the latter.

A key to the SPLA/M's vision for the overall problems of the Sudan is its concept of a 'new Sudan'. As for the NIF it elaborated its own version of a new Sudan in a document called the 'Sudan Charter', issued in January 1987.

The SPLA/M thesis for a new Sudan had been around practically since the inception of the movement. Initially, it was perhaps presented as an alternative to the limited and traditional 'Southern' objectives of secession and/or regional autonomy. Subsequently, the call continued to appear in the movements' position and policy statements with little elaboration beyond general principles. Eventually, however, the movement, through its department of information, presented an elaborate document explaining what it meant by its call for a new Sudan. A paper was presented to the Bergen Forum (23–24 February, 1989), under the title: 'On the New Sudan'.

The paper started by stating what the proponents of the 'New Sudan' do consider wrong with the present or *old* Sudan, such as:

- the 'cognital deformity' that afflicted the Sudan and 'has always threatened its viability as a single united country'.
- 'As a multi-national, multi-religious, multi-cultural and multi-lingual society, it continues to be at serious odds with its own realities.'
- 'The ruling class is drawn from one nationality, that is the Arabicised Sudanese who also profess Islam.'
- For the past three decades of its political hegemony, this ruling class has not only consolidated its rule, but has also pursued a policy that 'accentuates domestically and projects externally the image of an exclusively Arab and Islamic Sudan'.
- Accordingly, Sudan has come 'to be defined only in terms of the perceived identity and aspirations of the ruling clique'.

The paper then went on to state that the 'new Sudan' as a concept 'strives to establish a new cultural order in the country'. Furthermore, the establishment of this new order, 'demands of necessity a radical restructuring of state power to establish genuine democracy and to follow a path of development that will lead to far reaching changes'.

What follows is an elaboration of the projected 'Content of the New Sudan', which includes:

a) Resolution of the Nationality and religious questions within a secular democratic context. On the nationality question the paper proposed that, 'the diverse nationalities making up Sudan can and will have to coalesce into a Sudanese Nation (National Formation) with its own distinct formation . . .'. On the issue of religion, the paper stated that, 'nothing short of strict secularism will do in Sudan'.

b) Overhauling the power structure in a fashion that:
  i) Enables members of the different Sudanese Nationalities to enjoy opportunities of taking part in decision-making process in Khartoum at all levels; and,
  ii) ensures the devolution of authority on authentic autonomous regional governments, whatever form these governments assume.

Here the project does not exclude a federal option, but puts more emphasis on 'who should be charged with the responsibility of operating the Central government among whose key duties is the transfer of a measure of its authority to the regions'.

The paper then went on to reflect on areas such as the economy, the army and foreign policy (points c, d, and e respectively).

The rest of the paper, was devoted to the 'Mechanisms for the Formation of the New Sudan'. In this regard the measures to be adopted rested on a combination 'of a mass political action with the armed struggle' in 'a broad based National Democratic Alliance'.[32]

The NIF's Sudan Charter: National Unity and Diversity

The document is divided into four main parts:
The first: religious affiliations and the nation, states:

- The Sudanese are one nation united by common religious values, and by the bonds of co-existence, solidarity and patriotism, and;
- Diversified by the multiplicity of their religious and cultural affiliations.
- The Muslims are a majority in the Sudan, and 'they are Unitarian in their religious approach to life', and they 'do not espouse secularism or accept it politically'.
- The Muslims, therefore, 'have a *legitimate right* by virtue of their religious choice, of their democratic weight and of natural justice, to practice the values and rules of their religion to their full range – in personal, familial, social and *political* affairs'.
- Furthermore, in Sudan there is a large number of those who adhere to African religions, a substantial number of Christians and a few Jews.
- These 'Non-Muslims shall, be entitled freely to express the values of their religion to the full extent of their scope – in private, family or social matters'.
- The state is a common affair among all believers and citizens of the Sudan; and that: 'None shall be barred from public office only because of his adherence to any religious affiliation".

In the sphere of law, the state shall establish a legal system in full consideration of the will of the majority as well as the will of non-Muslims.

Thus:

'Islamic jurisprudence shall be the general source of law, [as] it is the expression of the will of the democratic majority'.

- Family law shall be personal.
- To the Muslims shall apply the *shari'a*.
- To scriptural religious denominations shall apply their respective church laws. To the followers of local cults shall apply their special customs. Any of these or others can of course choose to be governed by *shari'a*.

The Charter then projected that, 'the effectiveness of some laws shall be subject to territorial limitations considering the prevalence of certain religions or cultures in the area at variance with the dominant religion in the country at large, and regarding the matters where an exception can be made from the general operation of the legal system'.

With regard to power-sharing, the Charter projected that

- A federal system would transfer to the federated regions matters of an even wider scope, but more importantly attribute to regional measures immunity from interference by central authorities through participation or abrogation, except with regard to a matter specifically designated as concurrent.
- The Charter then went on to enumerate 'some of the major powers normally *reserved* to the centre', and some of the matters that are 'normally *assigned* to the regions'.

Furthermore, the Charter was careful to list a number of 'provisions' indispensable from, or complementary to the projected Federal structure such as how to make the system workable as well as ensuring a balance between the 'Centre' and the 'Region'. Two of these provisions are worth referring to here:

- Provision for 'a defined emergency regime that permits the national authorities to transgress the normal limits and equations, of power sharing to the extent of the necessity (wars, calamities, constitutional collapse . . . .'
- ' . . . the parliamentary system might be preferred, as it is based on collegiate executive power and allows for any political convention or usage governing regional representation or balance'.[33]

173

These extracts from 'On the New Sudan' and 'The Sudan Charter' shows that the two documents address similar issues and problems, such as the questions of Sudan's identity, diversity, religion, power sharing, and so forth. The approach and treatment are, however, radically different. While 'On the New Sudan' emphasises questions of *identity* and *nationality* as key concepts, the 'Sudan Charter' emphasises *religion*.

Thus, although both documents recognised diversity, they differed on what was meant by that. For 'On the New Sudan' the centre of gravity was the country's different nationalities, all of which should receive an equitable share of power and wealth. Whereas, for the 'Sudan Charter' there is a religious diversity in the Sudan, but with a 'Muslim majority' which must prevail with some concessions to other religious minorities.

Furthermore, the respective approaches of the proponents diverged sharply. While the SPLA/M espouses a fundamental restructuring of state and society in a manner that will redress the present status quo, which they regarded as prevailing 'at serious odds with its own realities', the NIF proposed a scheme of assigning *privileges* and *concessions* within the existing status quo.

Accordingly, for the NIF all matters are treated on the basis of majority and minority. Hence, the Muslims, because of their 'democratic majority' are entitled to define the country's political system, which has to be Islamic since Muslims 'do not espouse secularism'. By the same token 'Islamic jurisprudence shall be the general source of law'. Within this framework the rights assigned to non-Muslims are primarily their rights to be exempted from *shari'a* laws, and their right to follow their religious teachings and tradition in personal and family affairs.

To substantiate this rather delicate arrangement, the NIF proposed a Federal structure for the system of government in order to allow for diversity of legislation and law application. The detailed manner in which the federal scheme was reflected in the 'Sudan Charter' indicates that the proponents regarded it as a solution by itself to Sudan's problems of regional disparities and religious and cultural diversities.

The SPLA/M, on the other hand, proposed a system of government that ensures 'devolution of authority' to regional bodies, but went on to emphasise that 'what really matters is for all the Sudanese without distinction to be able to exercise the right of administering their country at both the regional and central government levels . . .'. The proponents of 'On the New Sudan', moreover, strongly deplore 'a situation where a particular nationality or ethnic group takes upon

174

itself to dispense rights to and determine the duties of the rest of the nationalities and thereby decide their destinies'.

For a SPLA/M that equates Islamism with the hegemony of the Arab 'Nationality' the 'Sudan Charter' is doing just that. The latter, however, attempted a half-hearted concession by stating that 'none shall be legally barred from any public office only because of his religious affiliation'.

If the 'Sudan Charter' was directed to the South and primarily to the SPLA/M, as one presumes, then the latter was not impressed. It has emphatically rejected any involvement of religion in politics by stating that 'nothing short of secularism will do in the Sudan'.

At this juncture the position of the two parties becomes diametrically irreconcilable. One calls for a 'strict' secularism as the only system that ensures indiscriminate participation of all citizens regardless of their religious affiliations, whereas the other champions an Islamist system with token concessions to non-Muslims on the justification that the Muslims are the majority in the country. This polarisation focuses attention on the thorny issue of the *shari'a* which proved to be the stumbling block in the peace process and one of the most important substantiative issues of the conflict.

III. THE POLITICS OF THE *SHARI'A*

Despite Nimeiri's overthrow, the *shari'a* laws imposed by him in September 1983 remained in the books. Indeed, *shari'a* is one of the most controversial issues in the post-*Intifada* Sudan. The matter would not have taken such a turn, had Nimeiri's successors taken the decisive, albeit difficult, step to abrogate the laws as the majority of forces were demanding. The demand of laws abrogation was based on the following reasoning:

- the laws were part and parcel of the legacy of May regime which must be liquidated in accordance with the *Intifada* charter;
- the laws were issued in the absence of legitimacy and in pursuance of narrow objectives of a dictator, and had nothing to do with Islam or the society's reform;
- the many legal problems associated with the laws and the draconian way in which they were applied;
- the obvious impact of the laws on the escalation of the civil war in the South;
- other views rejected the September laws on merits of law, religion, or ideology.

Thus it appeared that there was an overwhelming opinion (including those who adopted an Islamist position), that demanded the abrogation of the September laws. In fact no political force explicitly demanded the retaining of the controversial laws except the NIF, which raised the emotive slogan *la tabdil li shar'Allah* (no change to the *shari'a* of God). The NIF, however, moved gradually to adopt a position that called for the replacement of September laws with an *Islamic* alternative.

Yet, despite this broad consensus on the necessity to repeal the laws, successive transitional and elected governments were not able to do so. This failure is attributable to a complex of causal relationships and processes, that in their totality indicate the extent to which the question of religion has assumed central stage in Sudanese politics. Viewed closely, the controversy around the laws has a three-dimensional complex: legal, political and ideological.

On the purely legal sphere, problems of a practical nature appeared with regard to the continuity of the September laws after the *Intifada*. In general, the laws were at odds with a political system that adhered to the principles of liberal democracy, pluralism, and human rights. In particular it contravened the spirit of the Universal Declaration of Human Rights, to which Sudan is a signatory, and the letter of some of its articles (such as article No. 5). Likewise, the laws contravened articles 18 and 29 of the Sudan's Transitional Constitution, 1985.[34]

For these and other considerations of political sensitivity, the transitional and elected governments saw to it that, although the laws remained in the books and courts continued to pass sentences accordingly, execution of *hudud* penalties in particular was suspended. The same rationale, however, had not persuaded those in power to scrap the politically sensitive laws altogether. One problem was finding the suitable alternative.

Agreeing on a set of alternative laws proved far more difficult than agreeing on abrogation of September laws. In this connection two classes of opinions appeared. One (adopted by the Bar Association, the TUA, the CPS and other leftists, SPLA/M, and the Southern bloc) called for the replacement of September laws by 1974 laws, or any other laws of *secular* nature. The second (adopted by the NIF, DUP, and, Umma) demanded the enactment of an *Islamic* alternative to the September laws.

This polarisation was not formed immediately after the *Intifada* when the issue of the laws and their abrogation was raised for the first time. Then the atmosphere was rather different, and so was the alignment of forces.

On the morrow of the *Intifada* the political scene appeared with a good deal of polarisation between the forces that led, or joined in the *Intifada* (the *Intifada* forces); and the forces that continued to support Nimeiri's regime until the last moment. While most of the active forces were listed in the first category, the NIF and the leaders of the defunct SSU were listed in the second. In reality, however, there were no sufficient grounds for this polarisation to hold.

In the first place, there was the all-important weakness and disunity within the *Intifada* camp, alluded to earlier. Secondly, the situation was not helped by the weak allegiance of the *Intifada* forces to their own charter, the latter's lack of *de jure* powers, and the bizarre composition of the transitional government. Furthermore, some of those who had collaborated with the defunct May regime were quick to reappear among the *Intifada* forces with new labels.

All these factors have created a fertile ground for the NIF to engineer a redrawing of the political map on its own terms using the issue of *shari'a* laws as a tool. Advancing the question of the laws as its *raison d'être*, the NIF targeted the Traditionalist parties – the DUP and Umma. Conscious of the historical rivalry and sectarian constituencies of the latter, the NIF aimed either at outmanoeuvring them or winning them over to its line of thought. It was not long, however, before both parties were converted to the 'cause' of the *shari'a* as the most important task to be realised.

The first convert was the DUP which, as pointed out above, resigned from NANS in protest at 'the imposition of the opinion of leftist minorities with regard to the laws'.[35] Thenceforth, it drew closer to the NIF to the extent of forging a quasi-alliance with the latter. After the *Intifada* the DUP appeared in a poor shape pronged with factionalism and loss of direction. With the death of al-Sharif Hussayn al-Hindi and breakaway of most of its reputed leaders, the *Khatmiyya* leadership (al-Mirghani brothers) came to assume a direct role in the party's affairs. The latter, who adopted a passivist approach throughout the lengthy Nimeiri years and even participated in some of its political structures, were perhaps worried about the heated calls for the liquidation of the 'remnants of May'. Their greatest worry, however, was the rising popularity of the Umma party under the leadership of al-Sadiq al-Mahdi, and the latter's closeness to the radicals.

In any event the *shari'a* laws became a legitimising cover for the DUP–NIF alliance during the transitional period. As can be recalled, it was from such a platform that both parties had opposed the Koka Dam agreement of March 1986.

By contrast, the Umma party was a strong advocate for the abrogation of September laws throughout the transitional period. Its position on this matter may be regarded as an extension of its outright opposition to the September laws the moment they were issued in 1983. It may also be considered within the Umma strategy at the time of appearing as a champion of the *Intifada* objectives and slogans. The Umma's harmonious relations with the left may be seen within this framework. Furthermore, the calculation of the party's leadership is that an alliance with the left might bring it nearer to the radical-minded 'modern forces' and enhance the prospects of negotiations with the rebel SPLA/M.

Thus, the demand for abrogation of September laws provided a common platform for both Umma and the left in the same way as the opposition to the laws' abrogation constituted a common platform for DUP and NIF.

As noted earlier, the general elections brought significant changes in the balance of power. As the largest political party in the Parliament the Umma party was more inclined to distance itself from a substantially weakened left. As the head of the executive authority the Islamist al-Sadiq al-Mahdi would not wish his name to be associated with the *repellence* of the *shari'a*. Hence al-Mahdi was quick to cling to the thesis of preparing an Islamic alternative *first* before abrogating the September laws. Increasingly, his tone became one of drawing attention to the 'fact' that *shari'a* was the people's choice since the three parties that got a majority of votes – Umma, DUP, NIF – were all *Islamic-oriented* parties. Accordingly, it was the consensus of these 'major' parties that September laws could only be replaced by an *Islamic* alternative.

In reality, however, the matter was not as straightforward as it appeared. On the one hand, there were the pressing problems that confronted the government (e.g. war, economy, famine). On the other hand, the distribution of the 'Islamist parties' across the benches: two in government and one in the opposition deterred them from a concerted action. With regards to the magnitude of the national problems, particularly the war, the question of issuing yet another set of *Islamic* laws in place of the September ones was as problematic as retaining the latter. As for the interrelationships of the three 'senior' parties, the question of the *shari'a*, like that of peace, had become a pawn in their struggle for power. What mattered more was who would be rewarded or blamed for enacting or abrogating the laws.[36]

Taken together, these two factors might explain the failure of al-Mahdi's successive governments to produce an alternative to the September laws in whatever form. That is not because of a shortage of draft alternative laws. In fact several draft bills, fluctuating between secular and Islamist, were presented to or by the Attorney General's chamber representing different views of political forces, legal profession and so forth. Significant among these are two sets of draft laws; the first was presented by an *ad hoc* committee called the National Concord Committee, and the second by the NIF.

The Concord Committee was composed in October/November 1987 on the initiative of Khalid Farah, the editor of the Daily *al Siyassa* (who was apparently encouraged by the Prime Minister). The Committee included in its membership representatives of all political forces in the country together with prominent lawyers and other personalities form all walks of life (Muslims and non-Muslims). The Committee examined various drafts, looked into Sudan's previous laws (such as 1974, 1929, 1925); and the country's legal precedents. Finally, after about five months' work, the Concord Committee presented five draft bills (a penal code, criminal and civil procedures, evidence and traffic). The committee agreed also to refer the controversial question of the *hudud* to the projected constitutional conference.[37]

The significance of the Concord Committee is in its representateness and the serious manner in which it had conducted its business. Hence its draft bills represented a consensus both in legal as well as political terms. Accordingly, if such a consensus was possible in this area, then also was a political settlement to the conflict or at least an agreement that would pave the way to the holding of the much talked about constitutional conference. The politics of the period, or more precisely the main contenders for power, saw to it that such a possibility would never ever be translated into a reality.

For, shortly after the Concord Committee had accomplished its task, al-Mahdi's third or 'Concord' government (no relation to the Concord Committee) was formed in May 1988. Ironically, the 'Concord' government did not find the draft laws that were painstakingly elaborated by the 'Concord' Committee worth of consideration. Instead, it championed a draft bill that had been proposed by the NIF. As we know, the latter had joined the said government with a pledge of *applying* the *shari'a* in two months. Thus, the NIF leader, al-Turabi, who became the attorney General and Minister of Justice in the Concord government, converted his party's project into the government's Criminal Bill, 1988 (hereinafter CB) that was presented to, and discussed by the Constituent Assembly.

The CB provided for all the *hudud* offences and penalties, including that of *ridda* (apostasy), and the stoning of a married adulterer, besides *qasas* (retribution), and *diyya* (bload money). The CB, however, 'purported to exempt the Southern region from the application of *hudud* penalties, unless the accused specifically request their application on him'.[38]

The Criminal Bill generated fresh controversy and dispute. Apart from emphasising the points that had essentially sparked rejection of September laws, that is, their religious nature, the CB was even more orthodox in its *hudud* provisions and therefore harsher than the former. Several criticisms were directed, on legal as well as political merits, against its device of exempting the South from the *hudud* penalties.

What induces a government confronted with a devastating civil war waged partially because of conflicting views over the role of religion in politics to issue such a bill that was bound to generate more complications? The prime connection was obviously the NIF which had continuously waged a zealous campaign for the *shari'a* 'cause'. Despite its participation in all the deliberations of the 'Concord' Committee, once in power the NIF ignored the Committee's work and fell back on its own uncompromising project. Its rationale was, why bother with compromises if there was a chance of imposing 'our' version of a fully-fledged Islamist public law?

Yet, since the NIF was not the only, or even the major, party in the government it would be unfair to place responsibility on it alone. I would suggest that the Prime Minister al-Sadiq al-Mahdi actually bore most, if not the whole responsibility. Essentially, it was the Prime Minister who insisted on, and achieved the inclusion of the NIF in his third government on the latter's agenda which gave priority to the *shari'a*. Hence, the CB was a legitimate child of such an arrangement.

Yet, there is more to the Prime Minister's position than his politicking. As pointed out above, after assuming power, al-Mahdi came to subscribe more explicitly to the thesis of an 'Islamic alternative first'. His pledge was to work out a formula that would both 'realise the Muslims aspirations' (i.e. to be ruled in accordance to their divine revelation) and respect the rights of non-Muslims.

Despite its essential Islamist frame, the pledge was meant to be conciliatory. This is why al-Mahdi encouraged the formation of the Concord Committee to work out a compromise and followed closely its deliberations. When the latter concluded and filed its report the Prime Minister found its work praiseworthy and promised to take it from there.

Yet, it was the same Prime Minister who had effectively wasted the Committee's efforts by endorsing al-Turabi's CB 1988, and even defended it in the Constituent Assembly. One possible explanation is that by proposing the exemption of the South from the *shari'a* penalties the CB provided al-Mahdi with a 'short cut' for his unusual (and practically impossible) formula of emphasising the Islamic nature of law while appeasing the non-Muslims. In other words, *ideologically*, al-Sadiq al-Mahdi found himself more at home with the NIF project than with that of the Concord Committee. This brings us to the third dimension of the controversy around the laws, and that is its ideological realm.

As stated earlier the formation of the 'Concord' government indicated a new polarisation of forces along the broad lines of 'Islamic' or 'secular' orientations. With the presentation of the CB the latent ideological metaphor became an expressed one. Accordingly, the forces were distributed along clearly demarcated lines between proponents of an Islamist orientation, and opponents of that orientation who may be termed secularists. The Islamist group are of course represented by the Umma, DUP, and NIF; while the second include SPLA/M, CPS, trades unionists, other leftist groups, and some factions in DUP and Umma.

THE ISLAMISTS

All the parties in this camp raise the slogan 'Islam is the solution', yet they are neither clear nor united on what is meant by that. The most equivocal in this group is the DUP. As we know, the DUP's Islamism is historically ridden with political expediency. Moreover, there were historically various currents and factions in the DUP, some of which identify themselves with the liberal tradition of the Graduates' Congress, others closely associated with the party's strong base among the merchant class. It is, however, important to point out that the DUP of the post-Nimeiri era appeared more conservative in its outlook with strong overtones of Islamism. This is broadly attributable to the resignation of several of its liberal-minded cadres, who tried unsuccessfully to re-create a non-sectarian NUP; the death of the dynamic al-Sharif Husayn al-Hindi, and the direct assumption of the party leadership by the *Khatmiyya* patrons. The party leadership was also increasingly worried with regard to the strong rivalry posed by the NIF on its constituencies. Yet, the DUP leadership and its rank and file emphasised a centrist approach to the country's affairs. Accordingly, apart from slogans the party was not extending any ideological discourse, and its approach remained as pragmatic as ever, as demonstrated by its alliance with the NIF at one time and its conclusion of a peace agreement with the SPLA/M at another.

More ideological is perhaps the Umma party, the discourse of which is personified by that of its chairman al-Sadiq al-Mahdi. Al-Mahdi tried to present a vision called *nahj al-sahwa* (method of the [Islamic] awakening). It is based on presenting Islam as the best system within the available options: communism, which suppresses individual rights, and capitalism, which neglects social reform aspects. The argument claims that, by comparison, Islam combines the best values in both systems. Moreover, al-Mahdi also ascertains that Islam protects the rights of non-Muslims because of its inherent values of justice and respect of human dignity.

Sadly, despite all these lofty ideals, al-Sadiq's *ideological* pro-gramme appears as vague as the DUP's *pragmatic* discourse, and so does his practical model of an Islamic political system. Furthermore, al-Sadiq emphasised that his scheme is capable of engulfing the several 'bipolars' in the Sudanese society (such as Islam versus secularism; traditionalism versus modernity; and so forth) which is literally impossible. As for his pledge of a legal system that respects the non-Muslims rights it had failed the first test as we have seen above. Yet, to his credit perhaps al-Mahdi seemed to believe that the popular will – i.e. free elections – was the only way of realising his Islamist blueprint.[39]

Surprisingly, the NIF, which was the most outspoken in its call for Islamicisation was rather ambiguous in its projection of an Islamic blueprint. Its discourse fluctuated between apologist, as represented by its 'Sudan Charter' 1987 and orthodox, as in its emphatic call for the application of the *shari'a* laws. The 'Sudan Charter', as we have seen earlier, was meant to placate non-Muslims by extending to them a federal system of government and propounding to exempt them from the application of the *shari'a* laws. However, the same liberalism that induced the authors of the Sudan Charter to give concessions to non-Muslims did not prevent them from suggesting the most orthodox interpretation of the *shari'a* as in the case of the CB 1988.

Having said that, one observes a degree of inconsistency in the call for the enforcement of *shari'a* itself as formulated in the emotive slogan '*la-tabdil li shar' Allah*'. This 'infallible' *shar' Allah* was sometimes presented in its Nimeiri version of September 1983, or al-Turabi's version of September 1988. Likewise the NIF was not explicit either in its project of an 'Islamic order '*al-nizam al-islami*, or in the most suitable way of achieving it. It was suggested that 'al-Turabi believes that no option should remain closed in the fight to establish an Islamic order'.[40]

In view of the above it is fair to argue that al-Turabi's, and for that matter the NIF's, ambiguity was deliberate and dictated by pragmatism. Being cynical about parliamentary democracy, the NIF leader viewed the Sudan's democratic episode as a chance of maximising his party's gains and improving its chances of attaining power by whatever means available. Thus, rather than formulating a clearly defined strategy (in terms of an Islamic order, state, or blueprint), the NIF resorted to pressure tactics in the question of the *shari'a*, primarily to embarrass its Traditionalist rivals (Umma, and DUP), while simultaneously making overtures to win over non-Muslims.

Thus, the Islamist company were either ambivalent in their call for Islamicisation of the state and society, as in the case of Umma and DUP, or deliberately ambiguous as with the NIF. However, both Traditionalist parties appeared more pronounced in their calls for Islamicisation than it was the case hitherto. This is perhaps attributable both to the strength of Islamist drive in the Middle East and North Africa at the regional level, and the potential threat of the NIF to their constituencies locally. In any event, the three parties seemed to have agreed upon the application of the *hudud*, but they also differed in their approaches to that particular matter. Furthermore, while the DUP discourse is characterised by dominance of sloganism and absence of specific ideological, or even policy statements (typical of *Khatmiyya*), that of both Umma and NIF were personified by their leaders, al-Mahdi and al-Turabi respectively.

Prior analysis was given to the views of both al-Mahdi and al-Turabi to the question of Islam and politics during the 1970s, and early 1980s. Both seemed to have tried to adjust their discourse to the pluralistic atmosphere generated by the *Intifada* and its subsequent political system. Yet, while al-Mahd believed that he is capable of creating a platform that would accommodate each and everyone, al-Turabi's main concern was how to outmanoeuvre the rest in his race for power.

THE SECULARISTS

The secularists, on the other hand, contested the view of Islamicisation of state and public law projected by their adversaries the Islamists. They call for separation, or 'differentiation' between state and religion and rejected the concept of a 'religious state'. Most of the components of the camp are agreed, with various degrees of emphasis, on the alternative of a 'civil democratic state' based on the recognition of Sudan's political, religious and cultural pluralism. Ideological visions and discourses among this group are best represented by the CPS and SPLA/M.

The CPS did not call explicitly for secularism, the establishment of a secular state, or even for separation between religion and state. It was the CPS that emphasised the thesis of a 'civil democratic state', and concentrated its discourse on the rejection of religious state and laws of a religious nature. The communists' reasoning rested on the premise that because of Sudan's multi-cultural and multi-religious nature, blueprints of a religious stigma are divisive and disastrous.[41]

It is true that the CPS has always been very cautious with regard to its stand on religion for fear of alienating its predominantly Muslim constituency in the North. However, in the 1980s the CPS appeared even more apologetic than it was during the 1960s. Then at least it was calling for socialism, new democracy, and significantly separation between religion and politics. There are three possible explanations for this apologetic position of the CPS during the period in question.

First, the bitter experience of the CPS dissolution (1965) under the pretext of atheism, had bestowed the party's leadership with extreme caution, lest the act be repeated.

Second was the strong wave of Islamism in the Middle East and North African region and its noticeable impact on the Sudanese scene. This was compounded by the dismal retreat of socialist slogans due to the stagnation (and ultimately disintegration) of the Eastern Bloc, and the failure of the populist regimes in the region which were operating under the banners of socialism and secularism.

Third was the CPS insistence on maintaining the broad based *Intifada* alliance and its adamant rejection of establishing or joining in a 'left' or progressive front. This stand, coupled with the party's avowed commitment to parliamentary democracy, has undoubtedly induced its leadership to become more cautious and apologetic with regard to the question of religion, lest it alienates the increasingly 'conservatised' Northern public opinion.

184

At impressionistic level it appeared as if the SPLA/M had stepped into the shoes of the CPS, since it was explicitly calling for secularism and socialism. Yet, as was discussed earlier, the SPLA/M key concept was 'nationality' not 'class', with emphasis on the necessity of reconstructing the Sudan's political system and the establishment of a new Sudan.

As pointed out earlier, the SPLA/M was very explicit and assertive in its call for a secular system of government. The SPLA/M being an armed rebel movement with its main constituency in the South (non-Muslims), did not feel an obligation of making concessions of any sort. This is why the movement has become a source of attraction for some radical-minded groups and individuals in the North, who viewed the CPS cautious line and its readiness to enter into alliances with 'sectarianism' with great distaste.

Ironically, the two factors that enabled the SPLA/M to present a more assertive view on secularism; namely, its non-Muslim constituency and armed 'struggle', were also its weakest spots. Hence the movement's main constituency remained in the South, while its continuation of violence in a *parliamentary system* could easily became a liability. In any event, the SPLA/M view on democracy, particularly parliamentary democracy, was not clear at all during the period in question.[42] However, in view of the SPLA/M's call for a united Sudan, its demand for a secular system carried more weight, and was having potential implications if a constitutional conference was ever held.

Thus, as in the 1960s the Sudanese political scene was polarised on the question of Islam. This time, however, both the main contenders involved as well as the substance of the question, were different. The main ideological contenders were not, as in the 1960s, the Muslim Brothers and Communists, but the former (who constituted the hard-core of the NIF) and the SPLA/M. Furthermore, the contention was not one between Islamism and socialism but between *Islamism* and *secularism*.

In addition, within the Islamist camp the call this time was not for an Islamic constitution, as in the 1960s, but for the application of the *shari'a* laws. The primacy of the laws came about because of Nimeiri's enforcement of them in 1983 and the demand advanced by the *Intifada* for their abrogation. As we have seen above, such a situation put the Traditionalist parties in a very critical situation because of their reluctance to abrogate laws that claim a relation to Islam, and particularly in view of the NIF relentless campaign for retention of these very laws.

Yet, emphasis on the laws has generated a mechanism that proved somehow different from the controversy surrouding the constitution (Islamic or secular). In the first place the laws, because of their practical implications, would entail pressing actions and responses. Secondly, the laws' controversy, unlike that of constitution does not *automatically* and explicitly vote out certain forces (such as secularists and non-Muslims), though the implication is there. Because of its legal and practical nature the dispute around the laws finally centred around the question of the *hudud*, which arguably covers a very limited area of criminal law. Such a situation created some room for compromise, as in the case of the prudent approach of the Concord Committee which, by referring the question of the *hudud* to the Constitutional Conference, paved the way for a consensus on the alternative laws. Another attempt at compromise may be seen in the NIF's device to exempt the South from the *hudud*. Such a 'concession' was at best extremely difficult under an 'Islamic' constitutional project. As had been evident in the controversy around the constitution in the 1960, by its very categorisation and 'Islamic' constitution questions the very principle of equality of rights between Muslims and non-Muslims.

These variations notwithstanding, a common factor between the controversies surrounding the laws and constitution was the similarity of the forces which espoused both projects, and their dominant Islamist orientation. Therefore, as in the case of the draft Islamic constitution in 1968, the Criminal Bill 1988 was voted to the second reading in the Constituent Assembly due to the parliamentary majority of the three Islamist parties.

In the end it was the contradiction between the avowed ideological discourses of the Islamist company and the political realities of the country that broke the *impasse* of the *shari'a*. Thus when the situation became virtually intractable following the formation of the Concord government and the introduction of the CB, it was the 'centrist' DUP that, by its own calculations, broke rank with its Islamist partners and contracted a deal with the SPLA/M.

The re-introduction of peace as a priority had spelled out a re-alignment of forces and generated a new political process that culminated in the composition of the UNF government. Accordingly, the political manifestation of the Islamist–secularist polarisation receded, giving way to a new polarisation along the lines of 'peace' and 'militarism'.

If the long awaited Constitutional Conference was ever held as scheduled on 18 September 1989, the discussion as to whether Sudan should be ruled by a secular or Islamic constitution would have definitely surfaced. A deadlock would have been possible, but a compromise, inherent in the peace process itself and such positive experiences like that of the Concord Committee, would not have been ruled out. The atmosphere of parliamentary democracy and pluralism might have proved conducive for such a compromise.

Sadly, this possibility was rendered purely speculative by the fact that the UNF government did not live to see the light of day of 18 September 1989. Once again, a group of hitherto unknown army officers seized power in a *coup d'état* on 30 June 1989.

Chapter 7

Pax Islamica

The *coup d'etat* of 30 June 1989 was led by Brig. 'Umar Hasan Ahmad al-Bashir, who formed a Revolutionary Command Council (RCC) from fifteen middle to lower ranking officers. Al-Bashir immediately promoted himself into a Lt General and became the Commander in Chief of the armed forces, and the RCC chairman. The RCC appointed a civilian cabinet and issued three 'Constitutional Decrees'. The first suspended the transitional constitution of 1985, dissolved the Constituent Assembly, the State Council, and the council of ministers and vested both executive and legislative authorities in the Revolutionary Command Council (RCC), the head of which acts as a head of the state, prime minister and minister of defence. The second decree banned all political parties, trades unions, and the non-governmental press and information institutions. It also declared a state of emergency under which the new power-holders enjoyed unlimited authority, ranging from arrests, detention, dismissal of public servants, restriction of peoples movements, to market regulation and the confiscation of property. Furthermore, under the state of emergency, opposition to the new regime, strikes, and political gatherings were considered criminal offences punishable by law. The new leadership referred to their power take-over as the 'Revolution of National Salvation'.[1]

In 1992, the RCC appointed a Transitional National Assembly to act as a legislative authority until the election of a legislative chamber. In 1993, the RCC dissolved itself and appointed Umar al-Bashir as president of the Republic. A state-organised Conference on National Dialogue held in 1989 opted for a federal administrative structure, which was subsequently decreed by president al-Bashir and the country was divided to about twenty-six states. Another Conference on 'National Comprehensive Strategy', which was held in 1991, resolved to establish a political structure called the 'Congresses System' to act as the governing political organisation of the country. The Congresses System closely resembles the ruling parties of totalitarian system with its structure constituted from the base to local and national levels. The constituent process of the Congresses System started in 1992 and was accomplished in 1995 with the election of the National Congress from both geographical and sectorial (that is, representing mass, professional, cultural, and other social organisations). An NIF member, Ghazi Salah al-Din al-'Atabani, became the General Secretary of the National Congress. In December 1995, the president approved constitutional Decree No. 13 which provided for the election of a National (Federal) Assembly and President of the Republic.[2] These elections were held in March 1996 and as was expected Umar al-Bashir was 'confirmed' as the elected president of the Republic. Elections for the National assembly returned a House dominated by the leaders and cadres of the National Islamic Front. Other forces had unsurprisingly refused to be associated with a political process that was regarded by them from the start as both illegitimate and unacceptable. The NIF leader Hasan al-Turabi became the Speaker of the new 'elected' Assembly.

Given the *modus operandi* of partisan politics, and the multi-dimensional crisis of the state and society in the post-Nimeiri Sudan; the demise of the 'third Republic' was hardly surprising. Neither, of course, was the military intervention itself, which was fairly expected by the beginning of 1989. Rather the question was, whose *coup* was it?

That the *coup* was not led by the top brass of the army had from the very beginning ruled out the emergence of a military regime which virtually enjoys the support of the whole army along the lines of the military interventions of 1958 and 1985 (led by Generals 'Abbud and Suwar al-Dahab respectively). A *coup* led by a group of lower and middle ranking officers immediately shifts the attention from the army as a whole to a faction inside it and the likelihood of a political force backing such a faction.

After some initial speculation, the Sudanese public gradually came to the conclusion that the National Islamic Front (NIF) was somehow connected with the new regime. In the course of time what was speculative became a reality, with the NIF emerging as the dominant force in al-Bashir's regime. Hasan al-Turabi, though without an official post until his election to the National Council in March 1996, had been widely regarded as the real power behind the throne; while most of the key ministerial and departmental posts were occupied by the NIF cadres and leaders including the organisation's deputy secretary-general 'Ali 'Uthman Muhammad Taha. Has the NIF planned the seizure of power through a military *coup d'etat*; or has it simply recognised and supported a de facto situation created by an independently planned and executed military takeover?

So far the NIF leaders have persistently held to the claim that their organisation has nothing to do with planning and implementation of the *coup*, and that it has only pledged its support to the new regime on the basis of a shared 'Islamic orientation'.[3] However, the thesis that the NIF pledged its support to an essentially non-partisan regime does not seem to hold any reasonable ground. The first striking fact is that the NIF in effect had never publicly issued a declaration explicitly pledging its support to the new regime; neither in the first period never ever afterwards. Secondly, if the ground of the NIF's support to the new regime is the 'Islamic' agenda of the latter, this was not manifest in the first policy statements of the RCC leadership:

> the revolution of national salvation is a genuine revolution; it has a Sudanese goal. It is a revolution of the people who suffered scorn and degradation and where passionate, despite their wounds for years . . . It is a revolution with a pan-Arabist orientation. Not to the left nor to the right; non-partisan, and non-factionalist, non-May, non-tribalist and non-racial.[4]

Thus, the new regime may be eloquently populist and even pan-Arabist but not Islamist. When the new leaders provided their first policy statement two days after the *coup* it emphasised issues such as strengthening the armed forces, peace economic crisis, and improving Sudan's foreign relations. For the second time in a major policy document the new regime failed to refer to Islam in whatever form.

As we recall the NIF had declined participation in the last parliamentary government, the UNF government, on the grounds that the latter had backed down on the question of the *shari'a*. Why should it then support an alternative regime that does not promise an imminent application of the *shari'a*? In fact, the new *coup* leader, 'Umar al-Bashir, actually promised a *referendum* on the question of the *shari'a*. Had this been proposed by any force independent from, or opposed to the NIF, the latter would have charged it with blasphemy, for how could one put the divine *shari'a* to human vote! The referendum suggestion turned out to be a smoke screen. In retrospect, the whole painstaking exercise of ascertaining the non-partisan character of the new regime was a calculated step to disguise its real character as a regime installed by the National Islamic Front.

Therefore, contrary to the thesis that the NIF has only pledged its support to the al-Bashir regime after the takeover, the present writer suggests that the NIF had actually planned and oversaw the takeover. As such the main power base of the new regime is the NIF constituency rather than the army. The latter was merely used as a tool to effect the necessary ascent to power. The rise of the Islamists to power was by no means an overnight development; neither had it started with the recruitment of the officers who instigated the *coup*.

I. GENESIS OF THE NIF ASCENT

The ascent of the Islamists may be put in perspective through a quick review of the movement's history and development. As noted earlier the Muslim Brotherhood organisation (*Ikhwan*), the offshoot of the NIF, was officially founded in 1954. Throughout the 1950s, the *Ikhwan* remained ineffectual and divided regarding their identity and political strategy. They succeeded during the immediate post-independence era (1956/58) in forging a temporary Islamist coalition pressing for the enforcement of an 'Islamic' constitution. However, they were not able to transform that alliance into a durable political influence at the time. During the early 1960s, the movement was able to gain a firm footing within the student movement which henceforth became their stronghold. By the mid-1960s, the movement emerged as a definite political party under the umbrella of the Islamic Charter Front (ICF). The same period witnessed the emergence of Hasan al-Turabi, the current leader, as the most influential figure in the movement.

Despite the increased politicisation of the Muslim Brothers, as indicated by their participation in two general elections during the 1960s (1965 and 1968), they stayed on the periphery of the political system and their influence remained confined mainly to the student sector. The period, however, was not without achievements as far as the *Ikhwan* strategy was concerned. They managed to mobilise the public in a highly emotive campaign that resulted in banning the Communist Party of Sudan (CPS) on charges of atheism (1965). Furthermore, and largely through their agitation, the call for an 'Islamic constitution' assumed centre stage and the mainstream parties – the Umma Party, and the Democratic Unionist Party (DUP) – were converted to it.

Internally, however, the movement was still ridden with factionalism and uncertainty. Towards the end of the 1960s differences crystallised around two tendencies. First, the 'political' school led by Hasan al-Turabi, which advocated that the movement should throw its lot in the political sphere with the purpose of influencing public affairs and eventually achieving power as a pre-requisite of Islamist transformation. The second tendency, the 'educationalist', was led by a number of the movement's pioneers, and emphasised indoctrination and society's reform as a priority, and that the movement should preserve its puritanical image and refrain from over-indulgence in politics. An extra-ordinary congress was held in April 1969 to resolve the differences – and al-Turabi's tendency prevailed.[5]

Nimeiri's *coup* of 25 May 1969 forced the *Ikhwan* underground and froze its effective split into two groups for a while. During the lengthy period of Nimeiri's rule (1969–85) the *Ikhwan* were subjected to varying situations and experiences and its fortunes underwent a radical transformation whereby it was converted from the tiny elitist group of the 1960s into a mass political movement by the mid-1980s.

As we have seen earlier, the *Ikhwan* had been in opposition to the Nimeiri regime since 1969. They were actively involved in all attempts to overthrow Nimeiri's regime staged by the right-wing National Front opposition coalition in 1970, 1973, 1975,1976.

The understanding of the *Ikhwan*, was that following the ousting of Nimeiri's regime, the parties of the National Front would share power on the basis of an Islamist programme. The *Ikhwan*, however, soon realised that once Nimeiri was out of the way, they would most likely be reduced to a negligible minority in any emergent power arrangement or even excluded altogether. Furthermore, with the failure of the numerous attempts to overthrow the regime by force, the *Ikhwan* became doubtful about the utility of the National Front as their main platform of political activity.[6]

For all these considerations, the leadership of the *Ikhwan* resolved to adopt a strategy for the movement to grow as an independent and influential political force competing for power in its own right. However, they also realised that such a policy may only be pursued under uninhibited conditions where the movement could operate normally. It needed peace with Nimeiri's regime. The chance presented itself when Nimeiri made his offer of 'national reconciliation' to the National Front opposition in 1977.

By the end of the Nimeiri era in 1985 the Islamist movement had actually grown into a formidable force with substantial influence and resources. The positions of power and influence accorded to the *Ikhwan* as a result of the national reconciliation had undoubtedly facilitated the implementation of their strategy of growth and expansion. It does not, however, fully explain the rapid growth of a mass movement from a tiny organisation. That is best done by investigating the social and economic dynamics, which transformed the Sudanese society during the 1970s and 1980s and created a conducive atmosphere for the implementation of the *Ikhwan*'s strategy.

THE IMPACT OF NIMEIRI'S POLICIES

As argued in the previous chapters, few changes occurred in the social and economic set-up of the Sudanese society throughout the post-independence era up to the rise of the Nimeiri regime. Nimeiri's era, however, witnessed or rather precipitated traumatic changes and transformations.

During its populist phase (1969–77), the Nimeiri regime introduced strategic structural changes and policies in the educational, administrative and economic fields in pursuit of modernisation and 'socialist' transformation of the Sudanese society.

In 1970, the regime declared a new policy that aimed at the reform and expansion of the educational system. The major impact of these reforms has been a radical expansion in the education system that in turn greatly increased the number of pupils, school leavers and students in higher education. Accordingly, the numbers of pupils attending schools witnessed a steady rise from 1970 onwards.[7]

With regard to administration, the regime also sought to reform the local government in both structural and functional terms. Thus, a Peoples' Local Government Act, replacing the colonial 'native administration system', was promulgated in 1971.[8]

In the field of development the regime worked out and sought to pursue a number of plans, such as the five-year plan of 1970/71–1974/75, the interim programme of Action of 1973/74–1976/77, and the six-year plan of 1977/78–1982/83.[9]

Things, however, did not go exactly as planned in all areas. One fundamental problem was the power struggle inside the regime's ruling circles. As we have seen, the leftist coalition that assumed power after the May coup had rapidly disintegrated under disagreements over policies, strategies and ideologies which culminated in the violent conflict of July 1971 between the Communists and other forces inside the regime. The disintegration of the leftist alliance meant, initially, a confused start for the ambitious 'revolutionary' programmes and schemes, and ultimately ended in a radical change of direction and strategies. Other problems of subjective or objective nature appeared in the process of implementation.[10]

The regime's conspicuous failure to 'revolutionise' the Sudanese society was clearly manifested in the field of socio-economic development. The gross failures in this field have rendered the reforms in education and local government largely irrelevant and ultimately problematic.

The aborted dreams of socio-economic development meant that few outlets of employment opportunities were opened to the ever increasing numbers of university and school graduates. Similarly, the new local government administrative reform resulted in the destruction of the traditional local institutions but failed to establish the required system of popular participation. Instead, the local government institutions became a mechanism of redistribution of wealth and power.

The combined mechanisms of educational expansion and experiments in development projects have accelerated the patterns of urbanisation. Modern economic ventures, whether successful or not were pursued at the expense of traditional economies of agriculture and pastoralism. In such a situation, it is unsurprising to note that all those who attained even the minimum level of education were not inclined to remain in a dying economy. They had to move to fend for themselves in the towns

The accelerated rural-urban migration, however, was not confined to the educated groups. With the rapid deterioration of the traditional economy an ever-increasing number of rural population were forced to make the move. By the early 1980s, the urban population had increased alarmingly.[11] In its turn, this process aggravated urban unemployment and put severe strains on the already precarious services and infrastructures of the urban centres, resulting in growing hardships for the majority of the country's population.

As mentioned earlier, people responded to these problems in different ways and forms. One of the most common responses was international migration, mainly to the oil-producing Arab countries, which was feverishly pursued by the Sudanese in the 1970s and 1980s.

THE MUGHTARBIN CLASS

The phenomena of out-migration (Arabic *ightrab*, people = *mughtarbin*) of Sudanese expatriates to the oil-producing Arab countries started in earnest with the oil crisis of the mid-1970s. It began as an attractive venture owing to the lucrative earnings of the migrants. However, by the late 1970s the phenomena had become fashionable as people from all walks of life and occupations were trying to cope. By the mid-1980s, and despite a decline in the prosperity of the Arab oil-producing countries, out-migration had become a necessity for the survival of most households in the country.

Although it has always been difficult to identify the exact number of Sudanese expatriates, extant specialised studies seem to agree that migrants have constituted a significant proportion of Sudan's active labour force. In 1979 the figures estimated suggest that migrants constituted 10% of the male population between the age of 20 and 34. In 1985, it was estimated that two-thirds of Sudan's professional and skilled workers were employed outside the country.[12]

Despite the negative implications of this haemorrhage of the Sudanese workforce on the country's economy and society, policy makers and advisors were hoping to find compensation through the injection of migrant's savings and remittances in the economy. Migrants' remittances and savings were expected to bail Sudan's economy out from its growing indebtedness and balance of payments deficits. Yet, throughout the years which followed the *mughtarbin* boom, to the fall of Nimeiri and after, the Sudanese governments conspicuously failed even to approximate this goal. Instead, the country's socio-economic situation continued to deteriorate from bad to worse.

That was not because there were no remittances, but rather because the expatriates tended to transfer them largely outside the official economic channels. Rather than contributing to a recovery of a rapidly deteriorating economy, remittances provided the key to the growth and expansion of what came to be known as the 'hidden economy' which 'refer to the structure of transactions generated by unrecorded capital flowing across national boundaries due to employment of nationals [abroad]'.[13]

The 'hidden economy' operates through the interaction of three interrelated mechanisms: international migration which generates remittances; the spread of an underground (black market) economy outside the state's control; and the capital flight.

A survey conducted in the year 1984/85 among a representative sample of Sudanese expatriates established that Sudanese migrants annually remit about US$3 billion.[14] Yet, there is no evidence in the formal economic indicators that such massive capital flows were actually taking place. This is because remittances were channelled almost exclusively through informal networks.

The problem started with the foreign exchange crisis that beset the Sudanese economy by 1978 owing to the rise of the import bill and the widening of the country's trade deficit, growth of foreign indebtedness, and the dying out of foreign capital and aid.[15] This foreign exchange crisis quickly led to a fall in the market value of the Sudanese pound. Yet, this effective devaluation of the pound was not recognised by the regulated exchange rates administered by the official monetary authorities. Consequently, holders of foreign currency, such as the rapidly expanding expatriate community, found it more lucrative to transfer their remittances away from the government regulated currency exchange.

Henceforth, and despite the series of devaluation's to which the Sudanese pound was subsequently subjected, the expatriates kept their remittances firmly within the informal channels, particularly as the exchange rates in the latter were consistently higher than the *devalued* official rates. In the course of time, the unofficial channels developed their own networks and structures with a chain of money dealers, intermediaries and entrepreneurs.

For its part, this remittances' mechanism tend to fuel and regenerate the growth of an underground economy, the second dimension of Sudan's 'hidden economy'. The expatriate remittances which were transferred home through informal channels, surfaced as demand for local currency. The networks of money dealers and entrepreneurs who supplied the required local currency gained access to the increasingly valuable foreign assets. On another level, added income in the hands of migrants and their families increased demand for consumer goods and services. Yet, the formal economy was not in position to meet this demand due to the decline of local production and its ever-deepening foreign exchange crisis. Hence, increased demand resulting from the inflow of migrants' remittances was confronted by severe shortages of supply of goods and services.

The growing scarcity of consumer goods, including many essentials, encouraged private currency dealers and entrepreneurs to invest a portion of their hard currency earnings in this sector through direct import of scarce commodities, and/or through sale of foreign currency to importers. Thus, like the migrants remittances themselves, provision of goods and services on demand by consumers were increasingly diverted from the formal to the informal economy, the underground economy which became the place where everything from sugar and petrol to licences and customs exemption could be bought and sold.

Yet, by its very illegal nature the underground economy was not capable of solving the supply problem. Therefore, a curious situation prevailed in which 'massive remittances co-existing with shortages of goods, [rising] inflation in the prices of importables and further erosion of the local currency'.[16] Such a situation suggests that most of the foreign currency obtained through informal channels was not used for purposes of supply of goods and services. Rather it was largely held, or sent, abroad as hard currency assets, a process generally known as capital flight.[17] During the the period 1978–87 – the *mughtarbin* boom decade – it has been suggested that a total estimate of US$21 billion had left the country as capital flight. This figure converts Sudan from a net debtor into a net exporter of capital.[18]

In its totality the hidden economy was essentially a non-productive economy. As such, its rapid growth at the expense of the formal economy was an assured recipe for disaster. Thus, under the weight of the hidden economy, most of the productive sectors entered into a state of terminal decline and decay. On the other hand, the operation of the hidden economy precipitated the emergence and reproduction of new economic and social imbalances.

THE DISINTEGRATION OF THE OLD ORDER

As the ill-fated modernising adventures of the May regime ended in the destruction of the traditional sector, the hidden economy of the *mughtarbin* boom resulted in the demise of the modern sector. This process led to the rapid disintegration of the old order that dominated the Sudanese society since the colonial era. Yet, as is clear from the preceding assessment, the old order was by no means replaced by a new one. The result was rather social dislocation on a massive scale as manifested in, and further precipitated by, internal and international migration.

The rural migrants who were driven *en masse* to the urban areas have lost the care and protection accorded to them by their traditional familial and/or tribal affinities without any compensation from alternative urban institutions. Help was not to be expected from a government that was, at least partially, responsible for the problem in the first place. On the other hand owing to the totalitarian nature of the Nimeiri regime, and the level of development of the Sudanese society there were no autonomous civic institutions which could accommodate the migrants, cater for them or merely articulate their demands. Therefore migrants were left to device their own techniques of survival and adaptation on individual or group level.[19]

On another level, apart from their inability to provide migrants with job opportunities, housing and other essentials, the towns were increasingly unable to offer the newcomers proper 'urban life' and culture. The impending crises of the 1970s and 1980s with its associate problems of infrastructure decay and industrial decline has robbed the cities from most of their glamour. At the same time, state's monopoly over organs of culture and communication coupled with its limited resources, have increasingly led to a 'cultural poverty' particularly in its literary and artistic forms (books, journals, papers, theatre, cinema, etc.). Nevertheless, these limitations notwithstanding, whatever was on offer from the town's culture was literally beyond the migrants' reach, as the latter were barely struggling for survival.

Thus, with the massive influx of the rural population in the cities, the decay of the latter's infrastructures, and an impoverished urban culture, the 'urbanisation' syndrome was reversed: the cities were ruralised – but a ruralised city is a deformed structure. It lacks the dynamism of a real city and the stability and tranquillity of a genuine village. It is governed by chaos and dominated by a 'pidgin' culture. That was greater Khartoum by the mid-1980s.

For its part, international migration triggered important social changes and implication both in connection with the pattern as a spatial move, as well as in relation to the economic dynamics activated by it.

In the first place, once started, out-migration soon became an important vehicle for upward mobility, rapidly replacing education in this respect, and even more so because migration requires just a trip across the Red Sea and a work contract, rather than the tedious and prolonged years of education. Out-migration therefore became the dream of particularly the male population across all professions and occupations.

Those who succeeded in their venture formed the *mughtarbin* class which rapidly grew in less than a decade. Members of this class were commonly identified by their foreign currency earnings, decent housing, cars and luxurious consumer materials. Yet, continued membership in this class was increasingly contingent on prolonged, or even permanent stay abroad as few, if any, among the *mughtarbin* were able to preserve their lucrative resource and luxurious lifestyle after returning home. In its turn, this situation made them extremely vulnerable to uncertainty on both fronts of job prospects or their post-migration future.

Those who fail to join the *mughtarbin* boat, that is, the majority of *ightrab* seekers, soon found themselves falling victims to the dictates of the 'hidden' economy generated and perpetuated by the migrants remittances. In other words the upward mobility of the *mughtarbin* seemed to have contributed to a downward mobility, particularly among the urban poor and medium stratas. At the same time, as we have seen earlier, the *mughtarbin* boom contributed to the growth and rapid enrichment of neo-business class (popularly known as the parasitic capitalism) from the entrepreneurs and brokers of the hidden economy, thereby enhancing the growing social cleavages.

On another level, the *ightrab* generated a set of social implications and changes, chief among which were the shifting pattern of relationships at the family, kinship and community levels.

In the first instance, as a result of their increased resource assets and financial contributions, the *mughtarbin* increasingly came to enjoy more power and prestige at the expense of the traditional patterns of authority at the levels of families and clans. At the same, time remittances 'made migrants more responsive to the more immediate family circle and weakened the sense of responsibility to the wider social group'. One consequence of such a process was the further weakening of the extended family, and the enhancement of inequalities among its members, such as between those who have a *mughtarib* and those who have not.[20]

One of the most important consequences of out-migration, however, was its contradictory impact on gender relations. On the one hand, the feverish pursuit of *ightrab* among the young generation of graduates and school leavers significantly contributed to a surge in girls' education at the secondary and higher levels. Similarly, the persistent drainage of graduates and employees created an increase of women officials at various levels of work. Thus, out-migration had indirectly contributed towards furthering the education of women and raised the degree of their participation in public affairs. Furthermore, due to the lengthy absence of their husbands, the *mughtarbin* wives were gradually assuming more control over the household and family affairs, thus increasing their independence (again *vis-à-vis* the extended family).

On the other hand, the *ightrab* seemed to have generated a setback in the women's role and participation. This happened particularly among the *mughtarbin* wives who joined their husbands abroad in the labour recipient countries. Most of them, including the highly educated and qualified, ended up as housewives with little if any, prospects of work or further training. Furthermore, though coming from a comparatively more liberal atmosphere, once in the Arab oil states, the Sudanese women were subjected to the conservative rules governing women in these societies, such as strict seclusion and confinement to household roles.

The setback of the women who follow their husbands could also serve as in indicator to the conservative influences to which a *mughtarib* was subjected in the new atmosphere and its potential implications.

To sum up, the dynamics set in motion under the Nimeiri regime had resulted in the destruction of the old order with far reaching consequences such as breakdown of the traditional institutions of socio-political and economic control, social dislocation at large-scale and growing hardships for the majority of the population. This process was accompanied by a redrawing of the social map as a result of the emergence of new forces and the decline of others.

Thus the era witnessed the rapid expansion of the urban poor, the rise of the *mughtarbin* class and the rise of the neo-business class. Although these groups grew alongside the old social groups, they were largely emerging at the expense of the latter. This was clearly noticeable in the cases of the traditional elite, *affendiyya*, and the merchants and industrialists who were experiencing a decline in fortunes and were losing ground to the neo-business and *mughtarbin* classes. The ranks of urban poor, on the other hand, were being primarily fed from the displaced farmers and herdsmen.

These changes generated various measures and responses ranging from resistance to attempts of adjustment and survival. It also produced new tensions particularly between the 'winners' and the 'losers' of the new status quo. All these changes and transformations were bound to leave an impact on the political and ideological situations and frameworks in the country. It has definitely provided the context and background for the genesis of the NIF ascent.

GRAND STRATEGY IN ACTION

Such were the brewing changes and transformation which accompanied the rise and growth of the *Ikhwan* into a mass movement throughout the 1970s and 1980s. The process was largely informed by the interaction between the *Ikhwan*'s strategy and the prevailing circumstances. In other words, the achievement of the *Ikhwan* in building and expanding their movement was primarily underlined by their ability to manipulate the changing circumstances to their own favour.

Implementation of the *Ikhwan*'s strategy may be assessed as a three- dimensional complex involving political, social and economic processes. As far as the political level is concerned the key to the whole process lies in the *Ikhwan*'s reconciliation with the Nimeiri regime as a result of which the movement enjoyed a considerable measure of freedom of action and a limited share in power. These advantages benefited the movement in a number of ways.

In the first place, the movement was able to expand its ranks through systematic recruitment facilitated by uninhibited propagation and discreet political activity. That has actually been the heart of the grand strategy adopted by the *Ikhwan* leaders on the eve of the national reconciliation. The exercise, however, was not without some complications such as the legal existence of the Muslim Brothers' organisation. As far as the 1973 constitution and the terms of the national reconciliation·are concerned, the *Ikhwan* could not operate publicly under their own name. Hence the leader of the organisation, Hasan al-Turabi, announced the dissolution of the Muslim Brotherhood, and declared that it would henceforth work from within the SSU. In reality, however, the *Ikhwan*'s organisation remained intact and flourishing. Necessary structural adjustments were, however, made to suit the new circumstances and facilitate the required expansion.[21]

In a way, the constraint on open political activity under their own name was even a blessing in disguise to the *Ikhwan* who sought to diversify their platforms and outlets of action. Thus they sought first to penetrate the official and popular structures of the state, such as the ruling political organisations – the SSU, the national and regional assemblies, and the youth and women organisations. However, knowing that these bodies were largely discredited in the eyes of the public, the *Ikhwan* launched their own mass organisations, particularly among youth and women (such as *shabab al-binna'*, and *raidat al-nahda'*) apparently with tacit approval of the government. Similarly, the *Ikhwan* were able to gain control of several of newly found Islamic missionary and relief organisations (such as the Islamic *da'wa* organisation, Islamic relief Agency) which were eventually deployed in the service of their strategy.[22]

On another level, participation of the *Ikhwan* leaders and cadres in the political system, such as ministers, MPs, and members of the leading structures of the ruling political organisation (Sudan Socialist Union, SSU), gave the movement a statesmanship experience and brought it closer to the realities of power. Moreover, by becoming recipients of government salaries as public officials, a nucleus of the *Ikhwan* leadership were able to devote time and energy to their organisation without straining its financial resources.[23] Such resources could now be channelled to other areas related to the movement's strategy and action.

By the same token, proximity to state power had enabled the *Ikhwan* to penetrate some of the most sensitive structures of the state, such as the army and security bodies. It was during this period that the *Ikhwan* established their first cell inside the army.[24]

Finally, the *Ikhwan*'s *rapprochement* with Nimeiri's regime coincided and was partially precipitated by the latter's gradual reliance on Islam as a source of ideology and inspiration. Such a tendency gave the *Ikhwan* sufficient grounds to campaign and mobilise for 'mandatory' Islamicisation of state and society – and enhanced their chances of recruitment, expansion, and making alliances. The peak moment in this process came in September 1983 when President Nimeiri decreed his *shari'a* laws. Nimeiri's *shari'a* experiment, as argued earlier, was partially designed to outmanoeuvre the *Ikhwan* and take the wind out of their sails. The *Ikhwan*, however, regarded such a move as a 'reward' and sought to make the best out of the experiment by throwing their weight behind it. In the process, the *Ikhwan* managed to forge a '*shari'a* coalition' transcending their own movement from individuals and groups, particularly the smaller *sufi* sects, who supported the experiment on religious or political grounds.[25]

At the social level the *Ikhwan*'s strategy seemed to have developed hand in hand with the social transformation that evolved during the period in question and the corresponding emergence of new social forces and groups.

From Campus to Community

Up to 1969, the *Ikhwan* movement was primarily a student-based organisation with pockets of sub-urban support in addition to the temporary influence cultivated via periodic alliances with other Islamist forces for particular objectives (such as the anti-communism campaign in the mid-1960s, and the campaigns for the Islamic constitution in the 1950s and 1960s). The student character of the movement was emphasised even more after the rise of the Nimeiri regime and the disintegration of the ICF. When most of their structures had all but crumpled, it was the student wing of the *Ikhwan*, the Islamic Direction, which was the most active during their opposition era to the May regime. Hence, the major preoccupation of the *Ikhwan* leadership after 1977 was how to transform an essentially student organisation into a mass movement capable of attaining power on its own right as their grand strategy had stipulated.

The starting point had to be the student constituency itself. By that time the *Ikhwan* were virtually in control of most of the students unions of higher educational institutions and secondary schools.

Up to the early 1970s, the influence over the student community was almost equally divided between the *Ikhwan* on the one hand, and the communists and other leftists on the other. By the mid-1970s, the balance started to tip in favour of the *Ikhwan*, who eventually assumed almost full control of the student bodies by the early 1980s. Reasons for this development may be attributed to a number of factors, chief among which was the weakening of the influence of the CPS after the events of July 1971, and the disintegration of the leftist coalition after the rise of the May regime. Apart from its direct implications on the campus politics, this development also allowed the *Ikhwan* to follow a systematic policy of recruitment at secondary and intermediate schools from an advantageous position. That policy was cultivated by the mid-1970s when *Ikhwan* members and sympathisers were increasingly admitted to the universities and higher institutes.

Furthermore, the years of anti-regime militancy which characterised the *Ikhwan* politics in the early 1970s, particularly those of their student wing, have accorded them with a reasonable political asset which they deployed in their attempts to control the student body. Therefore, the *Ikhwan* enjoyed continuous control of the student movement with very few interruptions throughout the 1970s down to the end of Nimeiri era in 1985. Gradually, this influence found its way and expression outside the campus and into the society at large. This happened basically, but not exclusively, through two mechanisms.

The continued control of the student movement by the *Ikhwan* enabled them to cultivate successive generations of student leaders and cadres whose experience and knowledge were put into the service of the organisation nationwide upon graduation. On the other hand, the persistent control of the student community by the *Ikhwan* has allowed them to expand their ranks in the student community and even to cultivate some ideological influence on the way as a result of their lengthy domination.

Apart from their contribution to their movements' routine activities, the cadres who emerged from the student movement were subsequently deployed by the *Ikhwan* to work in, or to lead mass, missionary or relief associations as well as other enterprises. Later, some of them appeared as parliamentarians, ministers, top officials, and media personnel.

As for the general political and ideological influence of the *Ikhwan* over the student community at large, it operated in a more complex way. The growth of the student and pupil population during the 1970s and 1980s meant an enlarged influence of the *Ikhwan* over the rapidly expanding educated groups throughout the country at large. That is to say, the ability of the *Ikhwan* to consolidate their political and ideological influence over the student community enabled them to transform that influence outside the campus and into the community at large.

The mechanism through which such a situation has come to prevail was the convergence of the *Ikhwan*'s strategy with the social transformation alluded to earlier. Apart from the students, the strategy of the *Ikhwan* seemed to have targeted three other groups: women, the urban poor and the *mughtarbin* class. Largely, through the efforts of their former student leaders and cadres, the *Ikhwan* were able to penetrate the three targeted forces. However, each of the three groups generated its own dynamics of grass-root expansion and support.

As pointed out above the *Ikhwan* student cadres were subsequently deployed to lead and run the newly founded mass, missionary and relief organisations. The work of these relief and missionary organisations was instrumental in allowing the *Ikhwan* a foothold among the urban poor. Being displaced from their home regions and lacking the protection of their traditional institutions the expanding communities of urban poor were disposed more to an ideology that promises solution to all problems of this world and salvation in the hereafter should the people return to Islam:

> for rural immigrants seeking security, employment, or wealth in the city, cut off from the ties of kinship or neighbourliness which made life in the village bearable, victims of urban processes they can neither understand nor control, and living in a society of which the external signs are strange to them – for these the religious community may provide the only kind of world to which they can belong. Its spokesmen use a language which is known and appeals to moral values deeply rooted in their hearts, its rituals and ceremonies are familiar.[26]

With regard to women, the genesis of the *Ikhwan*'s expansion among this group lies in their acknowledgement of the radical transformation women were undergoing and their ability to devise a relevant approach. The radical expansion of girls' education, the rise of women's participation in employment, the impact of out- migration, all meant an increased presence of women outside their traditional domestic boundaries and their growing participation in public affairs. This rapid change, however, was not accompanied by an equivalent growth in women's emancipation as a social and intellectual process.

Hitherto, women issues were virtually the domain of the left which had historically dominated the radical Sudanese Women Union (SWU). Yet, owing to the aforementioned disintegration of the leftist coalition during the first years of the May regime, the leftist leaders of the women's movement were also split. Whereas one group sided with the regime and helped found its official women organisation, another insisted on the preservation of the SWU which thenceforth continued clandestinely effectively becoming a branch of the CPS.

Between the discredited women organisation of the regime, and the over-politicised communist one, the radical transformation of women's situation was practically taking place in a vacuum. Both forces seemed incapable of becoming suitable platforms for the articulation and rationale of the new circumstances. It was this discrepancy that provided the *Ikhwan* with their chance of a breakthrough in this area.

Rather than fighting for *hijab*, or the re-domestication of women as is usually the case with Islamists agitation, the objective of the Sudanese *Ikhwan* was simply to rationalise the prevailing situation of women in an 'Islamic' garb. Their simplified formula in this respect

205

rested on an attempt of striking a balance between the dictates of a situation characterised by an increased presence of women outside household boundaries, and the requirements of the *shari'a*. Thus, the *Ikhwan* endorsed women's rights in education and work and its engagement or participation in any public activity provided that women abide with the *shari'a* regulations of modest dressing decent behaviour and a measure of religiosity in general.[27]

Within this formula, the *Ikhwan* sought to provide a new platform for women that was neither conservative nor liberal. Such was the ideology of the women organisation(s) set by the *Ikhwan* in the late 1970s. Judging by the rising popularity of the *Ikhwan* among the women sector during the 1980s, their formula seemed to have worked fairly well. The only women MPs to be elected after Nimeiri's fall were NIF members.[28]

As for the third category, the *mughtarbin* class it was a tale of considerable success for the *Ikhwan*'s strategy. One of the basic achievements of out-migration for the *Ikhwan* was that it has enabled them to reassert their influence among university and school graduates. Prior to the wave of migration, the *Ikhwan* were not in a position to sustain their ideological influence over former students owing to their negligible presence outside the campuses. Hence, upon graduation the student who confronted the society largely on his/her own would be forced to deal with the realities of a society that is largely dominated either by secular official institutions (e.g. civil and military services, various professions, business enterprises), or traditionalist ones (extended family, clan, sect). There seemed hardly any place for the *Ikhwan* and their Islamist version.

With out-migration the tables were somehow turned. By securing relative autonomy through lucrative income earned abroad the expatriate confronts the Sudanese society as a subject of change rather than an object of influence. At the same time, emphasis shifted from conformity with the dominant institutions of the Sudanese society to conformity with the traditions and requirements of the conservative societies of the Gulf.

The new situation benefited the *Ikhwan*'s strategy on a number of accounts. Politically, the *Ikhwan* enjoyed the sympathy of the regimes of Saudi Arabia and the Gulf, a factor which gave them an advantageous position in regard to job opportunities, and the ability to mediate between Sudanese migrants and the authorities of these countries. By the same token, the *Ikhwan* were the only Sudanese political force that enjoyed a measure of freedom in its activities among Sudanese expatriates. Consequently, the *Ikhwan* were able to re-establish contacts with former sympathies and members who had distanced themselves from the movement, to sustain their relationships with the graduate sympathisers, and even recruit new ones.

As members of the *Ikhwan* continued to flow to the Arab oil-producing countries they became the largest organised group there. Hence, they were able to consolidate their influence among the Sudanese communities even further and through various means ranging from direct political activity, to media and socialisation.[29] Moreover, apart from their immediate political input among the communities of Sudanese expatriates, the numerous *mughtarbin* from the *Ikhwan* membership were an important asset to their movement's economic expansion.

It was largely through the economic impact of the *mughtarbin* class that the *Ikhwan* made their biggest breakthrough at the economic, social, and eventually, political levels. This brings us to the economic dimension of the *Ikhwan's* strategy.

ISLAMINOMICS

It has now become commonplace that much of the *Ikhwan's* growth and influence is owed to their ability to achieve radical economic expansion during the period in question. It is also acknowledged that this economic power evolved largely through their control and manipulation of the Islamic banking and financial institutions which proliferated after 1978.

The growth of Islamic banking and similar institutions in the Sudan was the outcome of a combination of domestic and regional circumstances. At the domestic level the process coincided, economically, with the move to de-nationalise the banking system which began in the second half of the 1970s and resulted in the establishment of some private foreign banks in the country, and politically, with the post reconciliation process and the rise of Islamist rhetoric.[30]

On the other hand, the growth of Islamic banking in Sudan was also a reflection of a similar process generated primarily by the rising power of the petrodollar economies and the corresponding politico-ideological leverage accorded to Saudi Arabia and the Gulf states. The process started in 1975 by the inauguration of the International Islamic Development Bank as an intergovernmental institution by the Organisation of Islamic Conference (OIC). This was soon followed by the establishment of the first private Islamic bank in Dubai in the same year. Within the next three years (1975–78), private Islamic banks appeared in several Muslim countries, the most significant among which being the group of Faisal Islamic Banks founded by Prince Muhammad al-Faisal with contributions from leading Saudi business-men and shareholders from the respective countries. It was the Faisal Islamic bank (FIB) which initiated Islamic banking institutions in Sudan. By the early 1980s, the Islamic financial institutions were so well entrenched that they felt the need to expand their activities to the European markets as manifested by the foundation of the Geneva based *Dar al-Mal al-Islami* in 1981, and the London based *al-Baraka* Group in 1982.[31]

The basic idea behind Islamic banking is the categorical ban of usury *riba* dealings by the Islamic *shari'a* law. Accordingly, new types of operations were introduced as a replacement of interest-based transactions. The most widespread among these are: a) *mudarabah* which means that the bank supplies capital to an entrepreneur who uses it in an enterprise which he manages and controls. The profits are then divided between them on the basis of a predetermined ratio. b) *musharakah* which involves a more active partnership between agents who pool their capital and manage and control the enterprise together; profits and losses are divided according to a prearranged ratio. c) *murabahah* which operates on the basis of a 'mark up' sale in which the bank orders some goods for a firm which pays for them at a later date at cost plus an agreed profit element. d) *qard hasan* which means interest-free loans.[32]

As far as this study is concerned the significance of the growth of Islamic banks in Sudan lies less in the appearance of a *shari'a* compatible transactions, which is controversial, than in its role as agents of redistribution of wealth in Sudan. The Islamic financial institutions were literally the medium of the Sudanese *Ikhwan* to ascend to positions of economic prosperity and power. Again, this may be assessed at different levels.

First, in view of their religio-ideological stand and the sympathy accorded to them by the Gulf financiers at the time, the *Ikhwan* were well poised to assume control of the newly established Islamic banks as directors, administrators, employees and legal advisors. Conse-quently, the *Ikhwan* utilised their control over these banks to extend favourable credit facilities to their members. Accordingly, those who were already in business witnessed substantial boom, whereas others were able to enter the field and join the rapidly expanding and prospering Islamist business class:

The significance of the Islamic financial institutions is that they opened up avenues of economic mobility for many who would otherwise have been at the most high civil servants. In this the significance of the *Ikhwan* movement is that it became one of the important avenues of social, economic and political mobility on merit for young people who would have otherwise lacked the necessary connections.[33]

This development would not have been possible had it not been for the profitability of Islamic banks themselves. The secret of the Islamic banks' success lies partially in the concessions and privileges accorded to them by government (exemption from profit and income tax, no credit limitation, and free hand in hard currency dealings), and partially attributed to their unconventional commercial activities, particularly their over-indulgence in the lucrative *murabahah* transactions.[34] In their turn the prosperous Islamic banks became another source of power to the *Ikhwan*.

In view of the close association between the banks and the *Ikhwan* movement the former had effectively become an economic wing of the latter. As such they became an efficient tool for recruitment and growth especially among small businesses, and other sectors of the business community who saw the sudden growth of Islamist businessmen. Moreover, the Islamic banks were able to contribute to the *Ikhwan*'s strategy of growth and influence through their relief, donations and *Zakah* activities. Whether by design or not these activities helped to market the name of the Islamic banks and, by extension, the *Ikhwan*.

The most significant feature of 'Islaminomics', however, was perhaps its domination of the 'hidden economy' alluded to earlier. The Islamic banks, particularly the FIB, enjoyed free access, to and dealings in, hard currency as its foreign currency transactions were exempted from exchange control regulations. Such a concession allowed the Islamic banks an advantageous access to expatriates remittances (FIB and other Islamic Banks have offices in Jeddah, Saudi Arabia which accepts deposits from Saudi citizens and Sudanese expatriates in the Gulf). Thus, the Islamic banks enjoyed unmatched access to remittances of Sudanese expatriate community and other foreign currency resources. Foreign currency sources were further substantiated by the presence of a strong contingency of *al-Ikhwan al-mughtarbin* among the Sudanese expatriates.[35]

In its turn, this privileged access to hard currency enabled the

Islamic banks to engage in export /import industry, including the import of scarce commodities increasingly in demand by the public. The Islamic banks were well poised to play this active commercial role by the very nature of their transactions (such as *murabaha*, and *musharaka*) which involve substantial commercial dealings. Thus, the Islamic banks and their clients (mostly Islamist businessmen) gained access to both dimensions of the 'hidden economy': expatriate remittances and supply of scarce commodities. The 'hidden economy' transactions enhanced the profitability of the Islamic banks and Islamist businessmen and, by extension, the prosperity of the *Ikhwan* movement.

The growth and proliferation of 'Islaminomics' gave the *Ikhwan* access to substantial financial and economic resources, and gave birth to, and the rise of an Islamist business class. The process furthermore strengthened the movement by cementing the ties between the organisation and its individual members (graduates could now find employment in the Islamist institutions or private enterprises, while other members have access to credit and other banking facilities).

Such were the salient features of growth of the *Ikhwan* movement during the Nimeiri years along the lines of their grand strategy. Despite the belated clamp down on the *Ikhwan* movement and the leaders, Nimeiri's era may be regarded as the genesis of growth of the *Ikhwan*. The *Ikhwan*'s freedom of action and participation in power, combined with their enhanced financial resources, had enabled their movement to penetrate other sectors of society outside its traditional constituencies in the student campuses in the manner described above.

THE NATIONAL ISLAMIC FRONT (NIF)

Following the *Intifada* which ousted Nimeiri, the *Ikhwan* founded the National Islamic Front (NIF) in May 1985. The NIF was not just a new name for the *Ikhwan*. Rather it represented the movement that grew in breadth and strength during the Nimeiri years. The hard-core of this movement were the *Ikhwan*, but other factions included the '*shari'a* coalition' referred to above; some businessmen who were attracted to or seduced by the Islamists financial resources and credit facilities; and some groups and individuals who found themselves in a vulnerable position as a result of their close association with the Nimeiri regime (such as former security and army officers, SSU officials and ministers).

Because of their collision with Nimeiri on the eve of his departure, the *Ikhwan*, who became the NIF leaders, were able to diffuse the criticism levelled against them on account of their association with a corrupt and authoritarian regime. At the same time, due to this very association and the consequential advantages it incurred, the NIF did very well in the general elections of April 1986, coming next only to the mainstream parties, the Umma and the DUP. As both the Umma and the DUP joined together in a coalition government headed by al-Sadiq al-Mahdi, the head of the Umma Party, as Prime Minister, the NIF formed the official parliamentary opposition.

The main concern of the NIF leaders during the parliamentary period was how to secure the gains achieved during Nimeiri's years and expand the movement further. The endeavour exceeded all expectations. By its emergence as a legitimate party in the post-Nimeiri politics and its good performance in the 1986 elections, the NIF had both sustained and cultivated the results of its steady growth under the shadow of Nimeiri. The second step was to lead an assault on the Umma–DUP government with the aim of either inheriting their largely Muslim constituencies or forcing them into giving the NIF a share of power.

Towards this end the NIF launched a fierce and ruthless campaign against al-Mahdi's governments utilising the latter's internal differences, and its ineptness in the face of the country's immense problems. In its offensive the NIF, among other things, emphasised preservation of Nimeiri's *shari'a* laws, or their replacement with yet another 'Islamic alternative'; and advocated a tough militarist stand towards the civil war in the South. On both stands, the NIF aimed at discrediting the two mainstream parties and presented itself as the only authentic custodian of Arabo-Islamic culture in Sudan.

The offensive paid off. In early 1988, after barely two years in opposition, the NIF was called to join the Umma and the DUP in the government's coalition. The rest of the story has been told already.

The inclusion of the NIF in government demonstrated the formidable growth and expansion of the movement, and the extent to which it was effectively drawing the government's agenda even from the opposition benches. On the other hand, its exclusion from power in early 1989 as a result of extra-parliamentary pressure and the re-drawing of the government's priorities seemed to have prompted the NIF-led coup of June 1989.

The ability of the NIF to stage a military *coup* was a result of their long-term strategy to penetrate the army which began after their reconciliation with Nimeiri. Utilising their relative freedom of action

211

and the cover of religious missionary activities, the *Ikhwan* sought to penetrate the armed forces using various channels and techniques and the first cell of Islamist officers appeared around 1980/81.[36] Accordingly, the *Ikhwan* institutionalised their para-military organisation, usually called the 'Special Organisation', to include serving army officers, as well as trained civilian members. Between 1981 and 1985 the cells of Islamist officers grew considerably but not at the same pace as the Islamist movement at large.[37]

After the *Intifada*, the NIF intensified its efforts in this area utilising the relatively relaxed atmosphere of the parliamentary period and the growing politicisation of the army. It also utilised its close relations with the Transitional Military Council, its tough militarist stand in the civil war, and its huge financial resource, to enhance its infiltration of the armed forces. By early 1989 the NIF and its Special Organisation were ready for the *coup*.

II. IDEOLOGY AND PRAGMATISM

If the NIF's ascent to power may be regarded as a natural outcome of its political agenda and long-term strategy, it nevertheless questions the ideological credentials of the Islamist movement. That is, is it religiously or ideologically right to overthrow an elected government by force in order to establish the required Islamic order? On the other hand, the rise of the NIF to power, controversial means notwithstanding, focuses attention on this projected Islamic order.

On the first account, the choice of the NIF of the military *coup* as a means of its transition to power is a legitimate offspring of the movement's pragmatism. As we have seen earlier, the NIF leader Hasan al-Turabi deliberately refrained from specifying the means of transition to his projected 'Islamic' order. To reconcile the dominance of pragmatism with the essential tenets of Islamist ideology which emphasises morality over expediency it is necessary to review the ideological evolution of the Islamist movement through its various stages of development.[38] Such a review may also provide the necessary framework for a brief assessment of the ideological discourse of the present Islamist regime.

Ideological Adjustments

The development of the Sudanese Islamist movement included important ideological adjustments necessitated by the changing circumstances in which the movement operated or the changing emphasis and priorities of the movement itself. In view of the movement's history, one can discern three major phases of ideological adjustments. The first took place in the 1960s when the movement converted itself from a religious group into a political party with a religious agenda. The second phase facilitated the transition of the movement from a tiny political group into a mass movement during the 1970s and 1980s. Finally, the third adjustment came on the eve of the movement's taking control of political power in 1989.

In the beginning when the movement emerged as a political party in the 1960s the step did not entail any significant ideological innovation or adjustment. The transformation was rather of a political and organisational character. As for ideology, the Sudanese *Ikhwan* remained loyal to the basic ideas and teachings of Hasan al-Banna (and partially to Qutb), and as such remained ideologically dependent on the Egyptian Muslim Brotherhood despite their organisational independence from the latter.[39] Yet, the definite politicisation of the movement brought with it some necessary adjustments. As a puritanical movement, the Muslim Brotherhood was essentially anti-sufist and anti-sectarian. However, with their involvement in politics the Sudanese *Ikhwan* found it necessary to reconcile themselves to a Sudanese society dominated by traditions of popular Islam and sufism in order to get a foothold there. By the same token, they watered down their anti-sectarianist rhetoric and allied themselves with the mainstream parties the Umma and the DUP; first to combat communism and then to build a coalition for the enforcement of an 'Islamic constitution'.

The most important consequence of this process had been the development of an embryonic sense of pragmatism in the movement's discourse. From then on, the movement would pursue what it saw best for its political priorities at a given period rather than what was considered *right* from the viewpoint of its religious ideology. The second consequence was that by focusing its attention on the Sudanese political realities, the Sudanese *Ikhwan* enhanced their political and organisational independence from the Egyptian parent organisation (which was being severely suppressed at the time) and even sowed the seeds of ideological independence. This came in the second phase in the wake of the *Ikhwan*'s transformation into a mass movement.

Up to 1976, the movement was governed by a 'pressure group mentality', reminding leaders, other politicians and the public of the necessity of an Islamic constitution or legislation. However, when the movement reconciled itself with the Nimeiri government in 1977, it did so with a clearly defined strategy that emphasised building the movement in such a way that it would be capable of taking power in its own right. Yet, this strategy did not involve posing and settling essential questions such as the substance and form of the Islamic order, or the means of transition to it. Rather, the 'grand strategy' opened the door to pragmatism, which became the dominant feature of the movement's activism.

The first manifestation of pragmatism was the reconciliation deal itself, which involved the trading of ideology for the possibility of freedom of action and the opportunity to gain practical experience in the running of the state.[40] Secondly, rather than agitating for some lofty ideals, all the efforts of the Islamists were now geared towards the objective of strengthening their movement and expanding its ranks by any means. In its turn this involved reducing the level of ideological indoctrination required in the new members to facilitate the rapid growth of the movement in the shortest possible time.[41]

On another level, the movement's discourse as symbolised by al-Turabi's writings sought to address new areas and situations resulting from the movements expansion, its endeavour to accommodate new groups, and growing complexity of its activities. A case in point is the question of women, to which we have refered earlier. Another example is the attempt to formulate the ideological foundations for Islamic economics.[42]

In both areas practical experiment preceded the theoretical framework. This is of course an essential feature of al-Turabi's realism which appeared first when he reconciled his movement to the Sudanese society by tacitly endorsing popular Islam and sectarianism. Then he reconciled the movement to the state without any elaborate ideological conditions attached. Both steps were considered transitory, aimed at improving the movement's chances of growth and influence. Both, however, opened the door wide for pragmatism.

Although the dominance of pragmatism has essentially asserted itself in the sphere of practical politics, there are theoretical foundations for this pragmatic attitude in the discourse of the movement's leader and ideologue Hasan al-Turabi. Al-Turabi argued that Islamic thought and jurisprudence should rationalise practical actions and not the other way round.[43]

Al-Turabi's discourse, however, involved more than just the legitimation of pragmatism. His concepts of *Iman*, *tawhid*, and worship are capable of both idealist and pragmatic injunctions. It appears that in questions pertaining to the movements growth and partisan interests and political positions in general al-Turabi is likely to be guided by pragmatic considerations. His projection of an Islamic state or order is mostly clothed in an idealist garb.[44] Where pragmatism and idealism overlap the latter is mostly a window-dresser for the former. For example, although the 'national reconciliation' of 1977 had essentially been a deal between Nimeiri's regime and the opposition National Front, it was presented by the *Ikhwan* as a reconciliation between the state and Islam, 'the state repenting to Islam'. They maintained that such a situation enhances the potential of vigorous Islamicization wherein both state and society will succumb to the *shari'a* regulations. Within such a framework groups and individuals are assured that all problems will be solved under an Islamic state which has now become a close possibility. Meanwhile, should a crisis arise then this must be regarded as a test from Allah to the patience and sincerity of Muslims. The peak moment for this discourse was when Nimeiri enacted the *shari'a* laws in 1983. Then, despite their knowledge that Nimeiri issued the said laws chiefly for political expediency and partially to outmanoeuvre them, the *Ikhwan* pledged their full support to the experiment and even paid homage to Nimeiri when he declared himself an '*Imam*'.

NIF's Populism

The foundation of the National Islamic Front in 1985 signalled the third ideological adjustment of the Islamist movement. During this phase, pragmatism which appeared vividly in the post-reconciliation era asserted itself and became the dominant norm of the NIF. Furthermore, unlike the *Ikhwan* movement of the 1950s and even the 1960s, which was essentially a religious group with a political agenda, the NIF emerged as a political party with a rather fluid religious agenda. Both of these features may be explained by the very nature of the NIF which represented a broader coalition than its hard-core component, the *Ikhwan*, and as such represented a myriad of various groups and interests. It was also a movement whose target was primarily to control power as the most effective tool of Islamicisation rather than the indoctrination of the individual. In other words, politics rather than the *da'wa* was the main field of the movement.

As mentioned earlier, the NIF's agenda for the parliamentary period was basically to sustain its growth and ascent at the expense of the Traditionalist parties, Umma and the DUP. Competing with Umma and the DUP over the loyalty of the Muslim constituency had led the NIF to launch a ruthless offensive on these parties aimed at discrediting them and presenting the NIF as the only viable alternative. Towards this end the NIF adopted a discourse that was characterised by a strong populist tendency.

Essentially, the NIF's populism was deployed to ascertain the movement's transition from an elitist organisation run and supported by a faction of the educated minority into a mass movement capable of appealing to the public at large. It should be stressed, however, that the NIF's populism primarily operated at the level of rhetoric rather than a genuine adoption or articulation of popular grievances.

The first manifestation of the NIF's populist discourse was its assault on sectarianism. As we recall, anti-sectarianism was an essential feature of *Ikhwan*'s ideology during the 1950s and early 1960s. In those days, however, the *Ikhwan* were essentially posing as a revivalist movement concerned mainly with purification of religion from intermediate loyalties such as sufism and sectarianism. As for the NIF, its discourse emphasised the nature of sectarianism as an institution of socio-economic and political hegemony and its deplorable hereditary privileges and exploitative nature. The NIF went on to question the religious credentials of the sectarian leaders and to accuse them of manipulating the 'popular' call for the implementation of *shari'a* to sustain their own positions in power. The NIF's assault on sectarianism, therefore, is primarily deployed from a position of a political competitor rather than from a platform of religious reformism.

Furthermore, the anti-sectarianist discourse of the NIF emphasised the 'empowerment and liberation' of the people from the hereditary domination of sectarianism. In this regard, the NIF sought to draw an analogy between the 'anachronistic' and unjustly privileged institution of sectarianism and the 'modern Islamist movement' – the NIF – which sprang from among the people's ranks and as such have more claim and legitimacy to their representation.[45]

The willingness of the NIF to openly challenge sectarianism after more than a decade of co-operation (during the 1960s and 1970s) was motivated first by its rapid growth during previous years under the shadow of Nimeiri. Secondly, this challenge was facilitated by the structural and societal changes of the previous decade particularly the ruralisation of the city and its consequential implications, chief among which was the weakening of the traditional structures and institutions that enhanced sectarian loyalties and domination. By the same token, these changes improved the NIF chances of establishing direct contacts and links with the rural population, the stronghold of sectarianism.

The second manifestation of the NIF's populism was the call for *shari'a* itself. Although, the call for the application of the *shari'a* has all along being the *raison d'être* of the Islamist movement, it assumed some populist connotations during the third democratic episode. The NIF's discourse emphasised that the call for the *shari'a* is an articulation of the will of the Muslim majority and their interest to be ruled in accordance with the injunctions of their faith. The presentation of the *shari'a* 'cause' in a populist disguise was probably informed by the atmosphere of liberal pluralism which inadvertently accompanied the parliamentary experiment. In the circumstances, the *shari'a* slogan has been advanced as the will of the majority in the face of the sinister calls for a secular Sudan from the SPLA/M, other regional groups and the leftists in the north. Moreover, as noted earlier the call for the *shari'a* was directed against the sectarian leaders who commanded the loyalty of substantial sectors of this 'Muslim majority'. Accordingly, the NIF presented itself as the 'peoples' party' and the embodiment of their cultural authenticity, symbolised by the *shari'a*.

Finally, the NIF's populism revealed itself in questions of practical policies. In its offensive against the paralysis in al-Mahdi's successive governments, particularly in the economic field, the NIF advocated populist policies such as its opposition to a deal with the IMF which involved austerity measures, its critique of government's inability to curb inflation and the scarcity in necessities. By the same token, the NIF-led sectoral and mass organisations undertook a number of highly publicised initiatives such as the organisation of group marriages, harvest camps, and the ever-flourishing relief work for famine stricken and displaced squatters. All these activities appear to have been deployed for the purpose of cultivating for the NIF the image of the party that operates not only as an articulator of the people's will and interest but also as a force capable of alleviating the people's suffering and promotion of their welfare.[46]

The populist discourse of the Islamist movement continued after the *coup d'état* of June 1989, albeit in a reconstructed form to suit the new reality of power. Notwithstanding the multiple failure of the third parliamentary experiment and the dismay and cynicism associated with it, the new power holders knew that they had to face up the question of legitimacy sooner or later. A military regime which succeeds a pluralist democracy by nature suffers from a precarious legitimacy, particularly in its formative period before it lays claim to some 'achievements'. In the case of the NIF, it overthrew a system in which it enjoyed full freedom of operation and even a share of power at one point.

Consequently, the 1989 *coup* leaders deployed a populist discourse to shore up their regime's legitimacy. The new regime's populism may be viewed both as a continuation of the aforementioned NIF's populist discourse and a reflection of the 'authoritarian populism' associated with the secular military regimes. The Islamist regime, therefore, maintained the anti-sectarianist discourse of the NIF, albeit in a different form and context. Whereas the NIF *party* sought to present itself as a popular alternative to sectarianism during the parliamentary period, the NIF *regime* sought to legitimise itself by emphasising the sectarianist failure to run the country or solve any of its problems. Accordingly, the new power holders boasted that their regime is legitimate first by its success to topple the sectarian rule and second by solid commitment to the people and to endeavour to salvage the country.

As the NIF moved from a situation in which it was operating as one player among others to one where it was becoming the main player, its populist discourse assumed a strong authoritarian framework. This feature manifested itself clearly when the Islamist regime advocated and eventually implemented its version of 'grass roots democracy' as embodied in the 'congresses system' which curiously resembles those of the secular populist regimes in Africa and the Middle East in the 1960s and 1970s.

Similarly, the Islamist regime followed the same example of secular populist regimes in some of its policies, such as its radical expansion of educational institutions, its emphasis on the interest of the rural population as the focus of the state's economic policies, and its rhetoric on 'self-sufficiency'.[47] Likewise, the NIF's regime pursued a systematic policy of mass mobilisation and set up a number of 'popular' institutions, such as the Popular Defence Forces (PDF), the Popular Police Corps, and the Popular [Neighbourhood] Committees. This institutionalised mass mobilisation is supplemented by excessive public appearances and crowd gathering events (e.g. parades, public rallies, anniversaries) again a typical feature of populist regimes.

On another level, the Islamist regime adopted the same anti-imperialist anti-Western rhetoric which characterised the populist regimes. This discourse has become a dominant component of

Sudanese foreign policy, particularly since the second Gulf War of 1990/91. As in similar cases, the anti-imperialist rhetoric provided the Islamist regime with external enemy imagery with all its consequential injunctions of emphasising national unity and vigilance and the necessity of support to the government in the face of external conspiracies.

Where the Islamist regime parted company with the secular populist regimes was in its agenda of change. While the latter advocated national liberation, economic development and social progress, or socialism, the Islamists works for the Islamicisation of the state, society and the individual. This brings us to the substantive nature of the NIF's Islamist project.

Islamic Symbolism

In January 1991, Lt General Umar al-Bashir, then the RCC chairman, decreed the enactment of a new penal code based on the *shari'a*, the Criminal Act 1991 which repealed the Penal Code of 1983. The new code was effectively the Criminal Bill (CB) 1988, which was drafted by al-Turabi in his capacity as minister of justice and Attorney General during the *wifaq* government. As we know, the CB was frozen by the Constituent Assembly in 1989 to pave the way for the peace process with the SPLA/M. The controversy generated by the draft CB and September laws before that, reflected the wider controversy surrounding the relationship between Islam and politics in the Sudan.

Thus, the enactment of the new penal code, in spite of all the controversy around it, meant that the new regime has unilaterally passed a verdict on an issue cutting directly into the problem of consensus building and the nature of the required political system. Such a move was to be expected from the NIF-led *coup*, which was in itself a blow to the efforts of consensus building at the time as manifested in the Sudanese Peace Initiative and the programme of the UNF government. Furthermore, the enforcement of the *shari'a* law has all along been the *raison d'être* of the NIF's politico-ideological discourse and the most definite category in its rather elusive vision of an Islamic state.

By the enactment of the *shari'a* the emphasis shifted from the agitation/controversy around the *shari'a* to the implication of the enforced laws on the society and their potential for the Islamist regime. As mentioned above, the Criminal Act 1991 had primarily been the enactment of the CB 1988 which provided for application of all the *hudud* penalties in full, including apostasy and the stoning of the married adulterer.[48] As such the new code appeared to have the potential of subjecting the society to even harsher sanctions than the ones endured during Nimeiri's *shari'a* experiment, which generated a lot of resent.

From the start, however, the new legislators seemed rather keen to give an impression of moderate and considerate application as opposed to the cavalier deployment that characterised the 1983 experiment. Thus, the CA 1991 categorically stated that it had no retrospective effect, and went on to establish that 'in cases not dealt with, provision of this Act shall apply where they are beneficial to the accused'. Significantly, the CA stated that 'the non-execution of *hudud* punishments before the coming into force of this Act shall be a doubt (*shubha*) which omits the *hud* [sic] punishments and penalties'.[49] The main mandatory concession, however, has been the exemption of the 'Southern States' form the provisions of articles 78 (1), 79, 85, 126, 139 (1), 146 (1), (2), (3), 157,168, and 171, that is, all the *shari'a*-related legislation's.[50]

Exemption of non-Muslims has always been the *cause célèbre* of the NIF's legal projects during the controversy around the alternative laws after the *Intifada*. Under the CA 1991, however, even for the Muslims there was a noticeable concession in the way the new code was implemented. Ever since its coming to force in March 1991, there were hardly any reports of stoning, amputation or crucifixions. Flogging was widely practised, mostly for alcoholism, and other non-*hudud* (*ta'azir*) penalties were used sometimes deliberately for humiliating suspected opponents. However, cases were not widely publicised as was the case during Nimeiri's experiment.

This 'lenient' implementation generated a lot of curiosity, particularly in view of the NIF frenzied agitation for *shari'a* when it was in the opposition, and its heated denunciation of the *de facto* freeze of the *hudud* penalties after 1985. A possible explanation, and one likely to reflect the NIF's official stand, is that it is essential to enshrine the *shari'a* in the body of the law as a manifestation of commitment to the Divine will. Once this is done, then the authorities should emphasise the merciful nature of Islam by always looking for ways to avoid inflicting the *hudud* punishments as much as possible. This argument is in harmony with the history and tradition of classical Islam but it does not necessarily inform the NIF's position. As we recall, the leaders and lawyers of the NIF (*Ikhwan* at the time) not only put the seal of legitimacy on Nimeiri's experiment but were actively involved in its implementation, including some of the most draconian applications (such as the imposition of *hudud* on non-Muslims, excessive amputations, and the deliberate terrorisation of the populace, and significantly, the execution of a 76 year-old Islamist leader on charges of apostasy). Other opinions argue that the Islamist regime refrained from explicit infliction of the *hudud* sanctions because it was concerned with a possible backlash from the West. That could hardly be the case in view of the fact that relations between Khartoum and the Western governments are practically non-existent, and may not likely to improve by a more moderate application of the *shari'a*. Reasons behind this deterioration are not necessarily the *shari'a*. As we know, there are countries which apply *shari'a* – such as Saudi Arabia and the Gulf states – and enjoy very close relations with the West.

An alternative view is perhaps to place the *shari'a* issue in a wider context of the Islamists' strategy. Consonant with their ideological elasticity, the *shari'a* theme assumes different values at different times. When the Islamist movement was in the opposition or a junior partner (as during the post-reconciliation era with Nimeiri), the *shari'a* was a means of its empowerment. On the one hand, the influence of the Islamists rose whenever the issue of the *shari'a* became a major item in the country's political agenda. Such was the case during the debate around the 'Islamic' constitution in 1966/67, during the discussion on the revision of the laws to comply with the *shari'a* after 1978, during Nimeiri's *shari'a* experiment in 1983/84, and during the *shari'a* controversy after the *Intifada*. Apart from being actively involved in the drafting and discussion of Islamic legislation projects during all these experiences, the Islamists were actually the ones who set the scene of ideological discourse. Other forces, secularists included, discussed on their terms and mostly assumed defensive or apologetic postures. On the other hand, the Islamists used the issue of the *shari'a* to rework the country's agenda and its political map at a given period. This happened most conspicuously during the post-Nimeiri era when the NIF played the *shari'a* card to break and make alliances.

After the NIF's ascent to power, the *shari'a* has assumed a different value. As a law in the hands of an extremely authoritarian state, the *shari'a* sanctions definitely have the potential of a repressive tool which may be deployed against political opponent at will. Otherwise, the substantive nature of the laws is hardly the focus of the regime's propaganda in any significant way. Rather, what seems to be the focus of attention is the *symbolic* nature of *shari'a*. The *shari'a* symbolism manifests itself at various levels. In the first place, it is advanced to enhance the regime's precarious legitimacy. As the Islamists have always argued that the *shari'a* rule represents the will of the Muslim majority then the regime which enacts *shari'a* is by default an embodiment of this will and its legitimate representative. Secondly, the *shari'a*, which is often presented as beyond, or above, any negotiations, draws the boundaries within which the regime accommodates or excludes other political forces. Finally, the enforcement of the *shari'a* acts as a manifesto to the new regime, an expression of its unequivocal orientation, and sets the tone for further ideological injunctions and symbolism.

The most symbolic value of the *shari'a* is that it is portrayed as a manifestation of the intention of both rulers and subjects to submit their souls to the divine will of *Allah*. As such the enactment of the *shari'a* is the reconstruction of the harmony between faith, state and the individual Muslims; it is the resurrection of the 'cultural authenticity' of the *umma*.

As an embodiment of cultural authenticity the NIF regime today claims that only now has Sudan achieved its independence and true sovereignty. The claim to cultural authenticity ties rather neatly in with the anti-imperialist discourse of the regime. 'Sudan', it is often argued by president al-Bashir and other officials, 'is targeted and singled out by the United States and the West simply because of its *al-mashru' al-hadari* [literally civilizational scheme, but may also be translated as cultural authenticity] . . . because it has chosen to live by the rule of the *shari'a*'.[51]

As the enactment of the *shari'a* served as the manifesto of *al-mashru al-hadari*, it also set the scene of a more comprehensive Islamicisation of society. Steps in this direction included:

(1) Islamisation of the economy through generalisation of 'usury-free' finance and banking, introduction of 'Islamic formulas' in other economic dealings, and expansion and institutionalisation of 'Zaka fund'. (2) Organs of media and education have been reconstructed to serve as mediums of indoctrination of the public in Islamic teachings and values. (3) Women implored, occasionally coerced, to wear *hejab* (i.e. revealing only the face and the hands but not *niqab* which covers the face as well) and not to mix with 'foreign' men unless it is a necessity. (4) A new ministry, the Ministry of Social Planning has been established in 1993 to oversee the implementation of the Islamicisation programme.[52]

The most significant injunction, however, is the deployment and feverish pursuit of an ideology of *jihad*. *Jihad* has always been an important component of Islamist ideology and regarded as an essential method in the achievement and implementation of the Islamic order. Yet, various movements accord various meanings and interpretations to the concept of *jihad*, ranging from the exertion of all necessary effort to the actual use of force. Various definitions notwithstanding, the concept of *jihad* invariably involves a degree legitimation of violence. Yet, there are important differences between a *jihad* which is deployed as a means of transition to power and its deployment from a position of power. In the first instance, an Islamist movement uses the method and concept of *jihad* in its fight for power or resistance to oppression. In the second instance, an Islamist regime confers a religious dimension on an existing or emerging conflict. For the Sudanese Islamist regime the context of its *jihad* policy has been the ever-escalating civil war in the South.

Consonant with its tough militarist stand on the civil war, once in power, the NIF vowed to 'eliminate' the SPLA/M rebels or at least force them to accept a peace deal on the government's terms. Towards that end the Islamist regime mobilised huge material and human resources and launched one offensive after another against the SPLA/M strongholds. In this regard the recruitment and expansion of the Popular Defence Forces (PDF) constituted an essential element in the regime's military strategy.

With the growing military operations and rising casualties, the civil war has been increasingly portrayed as a *jihad*, the PDF as *mujahidin*, and those lost in battle as martyrs. Themes of *jihad* and martyrdom have become an essential feature of the official discourse, particularly in mass media organs. Images from the 'glorious' Islamic past have become regularly invoked to give the current civil war, which the government insists has nothing to do with religion, an air of divinity. 'We are living in the time of *sahabah* (the Prophets Companions)', said Umar al-Bashir in an address to a gathering of '*mujahidin*', 'these difficulties and tests will only enhance our faith and (vigilance) . . . we are living today the time of the battle of *Khandaq* when the Prophet Muhammad confronted [and prevailed over] scores of enemies . . . .'.[53] Martyrs and martyrdom are excessively celeberated and commemorated with various events (e.g. the Day of *al-shahid*, martyer's day, mother of *al-shahid*, the *al-shahid* foundation) and numerous public gatherings. In 1995 the regime staged a heavily publicised mobilisation under the theme '*zad al-mujahid*' (the *mujahid*'s provisions) where the public were asked to donate all they could to prepare the convoys of *mujahidin* and contribute to their sacred battles.

The exercise has sometimes been accompanied by bizarre tales of miracles which grasped the attention of even a foreign observer:

> Radio and television . . . talk of miraculous rains, of monkeys voluntarily embarking on mine-clearing operations, of martyrs who smell of musk and whose blood never clots . . . armies transforming themselves into white horses, woods where trees whisper 'Allah'.[54]

A civil war which has been almost a constant component of Sudan's post-independence history suddenly becomes a source of all unusual occurences and the shortest path to paradise.

If the enforcement of *shari'a* has set the scene for further injunctions of Islamic symbolism then the *jihad* and its associated imagery represents the most vivid manifestations of this symbolism.

III. CONCLUSION

The rise of the NIF to power may be taken to represent the culmination of the process of attempted or actual Islamicisation of laws, politics and state which characterised Sudanese post-independence affairs as manifested in the calls for an Islamic constitution in the 1950s and 1960s, Nimeiri's *shari'a* experiment in the early 1980s, and the attempts of *shari'a* legislation after the *Intifada*. The NIF and its forerunners were indeed at the heart of this process. Consequently, the NIF's ascent to power seemed to carry the potential for triggering a radical process of Islamicisation of state and society. Yet, as we have seen, the NIF regime seemed to have deployed Islamic injunctions primarily for symbolic purposes rather than being engaged in the construction of a new system that is both different from and superior to the secular ones. A comprehensive assessment of the present regime lies beyond the scope of this book, but certain observations may be made.

As pointed out above, the Islamist movement's leader and ideologue, Hasan al-Turabi, has been decidedly ambiguous regarding both the substance of his projected Islamic state and the manner of transition to it. Accordingly, the movement finds it fairly legitimate to gain access to power through a military *coup d'etat*. On the other hand, al-Turabi's discourse gradually shifted the emphasis from the *umma* as the main source of legitimation (under the *shari'a* of course), to the Islamist movement, which appropriated for itself the right of representing the *umma* and the articulator of its will.

Although transition to power has been brushed aside by al-Turabi as unimportant, it indeed affects the way power is structured and exercised. Therefore, the NIF regime which was installed via a military *coup* and without an explicit mandate from the people, lacks either a political or a religious consensus. Despite, their claim that they represent the embodiment of the will of the Muslim majority, the Islamists have not allowed the free expression of this will in any recognisable form. Likewise, they have blocked all avenues of institutionalised criticism and the expression of alternative views and visions.

Having set the boundaries and conditions for political participation and accommodation, the Islamist regime sought to legitimise its own rule itself (as in the case of the elections of March 1996), establish a mechanism which ensures the continuity and reproduction of its control over power, and enforce its will and hegemony over the society.

In the absence of a clear-cut blueprint of an Islamic state the movement seemed to have unilaterally appropriated for itself the right of deciding what is Islamic and what is not on behalf of the entire community. Yet, in so doing the Islamist regime risks widening opposition to its rule to include certain religious groups who were not known for their direct political activism, such as the orthodox *Ansar al-sunna al-Muhammadiyya* (supporters of Prophet Muhammad's Tradition), some smaller *sufi* orders, and perhaps the *'ulama'* associations. These groups are generally supportive of *shari'a* rule and have been, in various degrees, part of the *shari'a* lobby which the NIF helped to create and duly exploited at crucial times. Consequently, they would have expected at least a share of power in an Islamic state if not a full partnership. But then why should the NIF, which has worked so tirelessly for the control of power, agree to share it with some 'ineffective' and 'old fashioned' religious traditionalists?

Here perhaps lies the heart of the matter for the NIF and its conduct of political affairs. In its eagerness to lay its hands on power, the Sudanese Islamist movement seems to have endorsed and legitimised the game of politics with all its cynicism and shameless pursuit of partisan interests at the expense of religious morality and principles. In other words in its endeavour to re-invoke the religious ideal through its control of state power, the NIF appears to have alienated itself by itself from this very religious ideal. Accordingly, once in power the movement seems to have been left with merely religious symbolism and imagery.

Notes

1 BACKGROUND: THE IMPACT OF THE CONDOMINIUM

1 For the Condominium period see:
   - Abbas, Mekki, *the Sudan Question: Dispute Over the Anglo-Egyptian Sudan 1884–1951*, London, Faber and Faber, 1952;
   - Abdel Rahim, Muddathir, *Imperialism and nationalisn in the Sudan: A Study in Constitutional and Political Development 1899–1956*, Oxford, Oxford University Press, 1969;
   - Beshir, M.O., *Revolution and Nationalism in the Sudan*, London, Rex Collings, 1974;
   - Daly, M.W., *Empire on the Nile: The Anglo-Egyptian Sudan 1898–1934*, Cambridge, Cambridge University Press, 1986;
   - Daly, M.W. *Imperial Sudan: The Anglo-Egyptian Condominium 1934–1956*, Cambridge, Cambridge University Press, 1991;
   - Woodward, Peter, *Condominium and Sudanese Nationalism*, London, Rex Collings, 1979.
2 Kirk-Greene, A.H.M., *The Sudan Political Service: A Preliminary Profile*, Oxford, Parchment (Oxford) Ltd, 1982.
3 Daly, *Empire On the Nile*, pp 420ff; Jal, Gabriel Giet, *The Sudan Question in the Anglo-Egyptian Treaty of 1936*, Juba, Sudan, Juba University Press, 1989: pp 50ff.
4 Beshir, M.O, *Educational Development in the Sudan: 1898–1956*, London, Clarendon Press, 1969.
5 El-Mahdi, Saeed M.A., A Guide to Land Settlement and registration, Khartoum, Khartoum University Press (KUP), 1971.
6 Gaitskell, Arthur, *Gezira Scheme: A Story of Development in the Sudan*, London, Faber & Faber, 1959.
7 Daly, *Empire*, pp 379 ff.
8 Bakheit, G.M.A., British Administration and Sudanese nationalism in the Sudan, 1919–1939, Cambridge, Cambridge University (unpublished PhD thesis, 1965). Arabic Translation Published under '*al-idara al-biritaniyya wa'l-haraka al-wataniyya fi'l-Sudan*' Beirut-Khartoum Dar al-thaqafa, 1972. (Citations here are from the arabic version.)

227

Politics and Islam in Contemporary Sudan

9 Mahmud, F.B. *The Sudanese Bourgouisie: Vanguard of Development?*, Khartoum and London, Khartoum University Press, Zed Press, 1984.
10 Beshir, M.O., *The Southern Sudan: Background to Conflict*, London, C. Hurst & Co. 1968: pp 59ff; Bakheit, *British Administration*, pp 208ff; Abdel Rahim, *Imperialism*, pp 66ff.
11 Bakheit, *British Administration*.
12 Daly, *Empire*, p 194.
13 Niblock, Tim, *Class and Popwer in the Sudan: Dynamics of Sudanese Politics 1898–1985*, London & New York, Macmillan, 1987: p 99.
14 Ibid: pp 47 ff.
15 Beshir, *Revolution*, p 47 ff.
16 Abdin, Hasan, *Early Sudanese Nationalism 1919–1925*, Khartoum, Khartoum University Press, Sudanese Library Series (14), 1985: pp 32 ff; Beshir, *Revolution*, pp 81ff; Daly, *Empire*, pp 291 ff.
17 Beshir, *Revolution*, pp 88–90.
18 *Note on the Graduates Congress*, 5 July 1938 [FO371/21999]; *The Times* 29 July 1938; Beshir, *Revolution*, pp 153ff; Abu Hasabu, Afaf Abdel Majid, *Factional Conflict in the Sudanese Nationalist Movement 1918–1948*, Khartoum, Khartoum University Press, Graduate College Publications No.12, 1985: pp72ff.
19 *Collins Cobuild English Language Dictionary*, London, Collins, 1988: p 1306.
20 Kitchner's Memorandum to Mudirs, Enclosure In Cromer to Salisbury, 17th March 1899 [FO/78/5022].
21 Bakheit, *British Administration*, p 38; Abdel Rahim, *Imperialism*, p 89; Abdin, *Early Nationalism*, p 27.
22 Bakheit, *British Administration*, p 86/87.
23 Warburg, Gabriel, *Islam, Nationalism and Communism in a Traditional Society: the Case of Sudan*, London, Frank Cass, 1978: pp 28–43.
24 Ibid; Niblock, *Class*, pp 51 ff.
25 Momorandum on Mahdism [FO371/20870]; Beshir, *Revolution*, pp 139ff.
26 Holt, P.M, *The Mahdist State in the Sudan: 1881–1898*, Oxford, Oxford University Press, 1958.
27 The power struggle for the control of the Mahdist state also reflected a wider friction between the Western tribes who supported al-Khalifa 'Abdullahi, and the riverian tribes who opposed him. See Holt, P.M. *The Mahdist State in the Sudan 1881–1898*, Oxford, Oxford University Press, 1958.
28 Voll, J., *The Khatmiyya Tariqa, Phd Thesis*, Michigan Unniversity, 1971: p 115.
29 Ibid.
30 Ibid: pp 274–277.
31 Beshir, *Revolution*.
32 Beshir, M.O., *Educational Development*, pp 131ff.
33 Ibid: tables XVII, XVIII pp 211/ 212.
34 Niblock, *Class*, pp 99ff.
35 For a discussion of these slogans see: Warburg, G., *Historical Discord in the Nile Valley*, London, Hurst & Co., 1992: pp 62–120.
36 Vatikiotis, P.J. *The History of Egypt: From Muhammad Ali to Sadat*, london, Weidenfeld & Nicolson, 1980: pp 215ff.

228

37 Abu Hassabu, *Factional Conflict*, pp 52ff; Al-Kid, Khalid Hussain A.Osman, 'The *Effendia* and Concepts of Nationalism in the Sudan', unpublished PhD Thesis, Reading (UK) University of Reading, 1987: pp 112 ff.

38 Ibid: pp 122, 132.

39 al-Fajr, 1 March 1937, quoted in Ibid: p 142.

40 Ibid: pp 157 ff.

41 Beshir, *Revolution*, pp 160/161; Abu Hassabu, *Factional Conflicts*, pp 160/161.

42 Henderson, K.D.D. (ed): *The Making of Modern Sudan: The Life and Letters of Douglas Newbald, K.B.E*, London, 1953: p xxii.

43 Abu Hassabu, *Factional Conflict*, pp 109ff, al-Kid, *The Effendia*: pp 190 ff.

44 Ibid.

45 Abu Hassabu, *Factional Conflicts*, p 54.

46 Constitution of the Umma Party [FO/371/45984].

47 The Socialist Republican Party contested the 1953 separately and returned three candidates who subsequently joined either the Umma or NUP, and the SRP thence disappeared from political life. See Abdel Rahim, *Imperialism*; Daly, Imperial Sudan: pp 287/8.

48 Mahgoub, M.A. *Democracy on Trial: Reflections on Arab and African Politics*, André Deutsch, London, 1974; al-Azhari, Isma'il, *al-tariq 'ila al-barlaman* (Way to to the Parliament), Beirut-Khartoum, 1965.

49 The Communist Party of Sudan, *lamahat min tarikh al-hizb al-shuyu'i al-sudani* (Aspects from the History of the Communist Party), Khartoum, Dar al-Wasila, 1986; Sulayman, Muhammad, *al-ysar al-sudani fi 'asharah a'wam*, (Sudanese Left in Ten Years), Wad Madani, Al-Fajr, 1970.

50 Sudan Workers Trade Unnion Federation (SWFTU) was founded in 1951; Gezira Tenant Farmers founded in 1952, Niblock, *Class:* pp107ff.

51 Communist Party of Sudan, *al-markisiyya wa qadhayya al-thawra al-sudaniyya* (Marxism and Problems of Sudanese Revolution), Khartoum, Dar al-wasila, 1986.

52 Mekki, Hasan, *Harakat al-'ikhwan al-muslimin fi al-sudan: 1944–1969* (Movement of Muslim Brotherhood in the Sudan), Khartoum, Afro Asian Studies, University of Khartoum, Seires No. 16, 1982; El-Affendi, Abdel Wahab *Turabi's Revolution*, London, Grey Seal, 1991.

53 See *mithaq al-hizb al-ishtraki al-Islami* (Charter Islamic Socialist Party), Khartoum, 1966. The party championed the idea of *Islamic socialism*.

54 Taha, Mahmud Muhammad, *The Second Message of Islam.*, Translanated by 'Abdalla A. An-Na'im, Syracuse University Press, 1987. Arabic *'al-risala al-thaniyya min al-islam'*.

2 THE SECULAR FACE OF SECTARIANISM

1 On constitutional Developments, See:
  – Abdel Rahim, Muddathir, *Imperialism and nationalism in the Sudan*, Oxford, Oxford University Press, 1969;
  – Fabunmi, L.A. *The Sudan In Anglo-Egyptian Relations*, New York, Longmans, 1960;

- Sinada, Mamoun, 'Constitutional Development in the Sudan 1944–1956', Oxford, Oxford University, 1972 (unpublished PhD thesis).
2 Mahmud, *Bourgouisie*, pp 33ff, and pp 80/81; Niblock, *Class*: pp 99ff.
3 First, Ruth, *The Barrel of a Gun: Political Power in Africa and the Coup d'etat*, London, Allen Lane, 1970: p. 153.
4 Abdel Rahim, *Imperialism*, pp 180 ff.
5 Beshir, M.O., *The Southern Sudan: Background to the Conflict*, London, C.Hurst & Co., 1968: p 73; See also *Report of the Commission of Enquiry into the Disturbances in the Southern Sudan During August 1955*, Ministry of Interior, Khartoum, MacCorquodale & Co. Ltd.
6 Deng, Francis, *Dynamics of Identification, A Basis for National Integration in the Sudan*, Khartoum, Khartoum University Press, 1973: p 37.
7 Niblock, T., *Class*: p 299: note 32.
8 *Proceedings of the Administrative Conference*, Khartoum, 1947.
9 *Juba Conference Proceedings* Appendix No.9 in Beshir, *Background to Conflict*; Deng, *Dynamics*, p 44. (Most Southern Intellectuals believe that the Juba Conference, apart from being unrepresentative of Southern view did not actually endorse unity with the north.)
10 The South's only economic venture was the Azande scheme which was implemented in the 1940s. See: Niblock, T., *Class*: pp 29 ff.
11 Beshir, *Background*, p 72; Wai, Dunstan, *The African-Arab Conflict in the Sudan*, New York, Africana Publishing Co, 1980.
12 Declaration of Independence, *Transcripts of the House of Representatives*, 23 December 1955 (the Session was a joint one between the house of Representatives and Senate).
13 *Report of the Sudan Electoral Commission*, Khartoum, December 1953.
14 Al-Tom, Amin, *Zikriyyat wa mawaqif fi tariq al-haraka al-wataniyya 1914–1969 (memoirs)*, Khartoum, KUP, 1987: pp 108/109.
15 Nugdalla, S. 'The Sudanese Political Leadership', PhD thesis, Manchester, Manchester University: p 146.
16 See: The Court of Criminal Appeal: Abdalla Abdel Rahman Nugdalla vs Sudan Government, Case Ref. HC/Maj. Ct./14/1954, *Law Reports Journal*, Khartoum, 1954/55: pp 61–80.
17 Al-Mahdi, al-Sadiq (ed) *jihad fi sabil al-istiqlal* (Struggle for Independence): p 137.
18 Al-Mahdi, *Jihad*, pp 141/151.
19 Ibid: pp 143 ff.
20 Holt, P.M., *Modern History of the Sudan: From the Funj Sultanate to the Present Day*, Weidenfeld & Nicolson, London, 1961: p 176; Sulayman, M., *al-yasar*, p 196.
21 *Al-Ayam Daily*, No. 827, 28 June 1956.
22 Al-Mahdi, *Jihad*: p 165.
23 Mahgoub, M., *Democracy*; First, R., *Barrel*; Nugdalla, S., *Political Leadership*.
24 Riadh, Henry, *mugaz tarikh al-sulta al-tashri'iyya fi'l-Sudan* (A Concise History of the Legislative Authority in the Sudan).
25 Haj Musa, Ibrahim, *al-tajruba al-Demoqratiyya wa tatwur nuzm al-hukm fi al-Sudan* (The Democratic Experiment and Development of Govern-

ment in the Sudan), Cairo 1970; Awad, M.H. *al-istighlal wa fasad al-hukm fi al-Sudan* (Exploitation and Corruption of Government in Sudan), Khartoum, 1970.

26 *Elections' Law 1957, Khartoum*, Government press; Holt, *History*: p 179; Niblock, *Class*, p 211.

27 *Elections Commissions Report 1958*, Khartoum, Government Press, Henderson, K.D.D, *The Sudan Republic*, London, Ernest Benn Ltd, 1965: pp 108 ff.

28 Nugdalla, *Political Leadership*: p 246.

29 In 1957, Egypt stated its intention to claim all the territories north of 22nd parallel which were administered by Sudan since the time of conquest. Halayib is a small village in the north-east across the Sudanese-Egyptian border. See Henderson, Republic, pp 109 ff, Holt, *History*, pp. 176–177.

30 Holt, P.M., *History*, pp 182–183; First, Ruth, *Barrel*; Sulayman, M., *al-yasar*, pp 322 ff.

31 *Parliament Transcripts* 3 July 1958; some 107 deputies voted for the Aid Bill, 57 against, Sulayman, M. al-yasar: p 327.

32 Holt, P.M., *History*: pp; First, Ruth, *Barrel*.

33 First, R.: p 138; emphasis added.

34 *Report of the Technical Committee for the Constitution* (Arabic), Khartoum, Governement press, January 1957.

35 Hasan Muddathir, *muzakkira l wad' dastur mustamud min mabadi' al-shari'a al-Islamiyya* (A Memorandum for the Enactment of a Sudan Constitution Devised from the Principles of Islam), Khartoum, no publisher, 1956.

36 *Proccedings of the National Committee of the Constitution* (Arabic), Khartoum, Government Press, 6th Session.

37 *Translation of the Meanings of the Glorious Qur'an*, by Pickthall, Muhammad Marmaduke Tripoli, The Islamic Call Society, pp 107, 110.

38 *Proceedings of the National Committee of the Constitution*, 6th, 7th, and 8th Sessions.

39 Ibid, 8th session.

40 *Al-Saraha* Daily, 9 February 1957.

41 Mekki, *harakat al-Ikhwan*: pp 44 ff.

42 Statements by Babilker Karar, representative of *al-Jama'a al-Islamiyya* in the National Committee of the Constitution, '*Proceedings*' 10th Session.

43 Ibid: 13th Session.

44 Awad, Ahmad Safyy al-Din, *ma'alim al-dastur al-Islami* (Features of the Islamic Constitution: A Collection of Articles), n.d. n.pl.

45 Judging by the composition of the Technical Committee and the Content of its draft Contitution, one may infer that it was the work of secularists. The report touches on the question of religion only in relation to whether the constitution should specify an official religion for the state or not. *Technical Committee Report*, February 1957.

46 Henderson, K., *Sudan Republic*: p 108.

47 Ibid: p 108.

48 One of the most notorious events in this process of clamp down were the events of Goda in February 1956, just after independence. Goda was a private agricultural scheme of 5150 feddans on the White Nile. As a result

of the tenants' refusal to deliver the cotton crop, the tenants leaders were arrested. Demonstrations followed in which 24 tenants were killed, many injured, and more than 200 arrested. Of those arrested 197 died of suffocation as they were detained in a tighly closed ward. See: Sulayman, M. al-yasar, pp 205–209.

3 GENERALS, MILITANTS AND POLITICIANS

1 Report of the Judicial Inquiry in the Causes of the 17 November Coup (Arabic), Ministry of Justice, Khartoum, Government Press, 1965; First, R.: p 230; See also: al-A'zami, Walid M.S., *al-Sudan fi'l wathiq al-biritaniyya: inqliab al-fariq Ibrahim 'Abbud* (Being a Study in the British Foreign Office Documents which became accessable on 1/1/1989), Baghdad, n.pub. 1990.
2 *Legislative Supplement to the Sudan Gazette, 6th and 10th of December 1958,* Khartoum, Government Press.
3 Ibid, Riyadh, Henry, *mujaz:* pp 82–85.
4 *Legislative Supplement, 1958.*
5 Muhammad Abu Ranat, *Report of the Constitutional Developments Committee* (Arabic), Khartoum, Government Press, 1962.
6 Holt, P.M., & Daly, M.W., *A History of the Sudan from the Coming of Islam to the Present Day* (4th ed.), London, Longman, 1988: p 177; Sudan Almanac, 1964, The Republic of the Sudan, Khartoum, Government Press, 1964: pp 116ff.
7 Holt, P.M. & Daly, M.W.: p 180.
8 Sanderson, L.P, & Sanderson, N., *Education, Religion, and Politics in Southern Sudan 1899–1964,* London and Khartoum, Ithaca Press & KUP, 1981: pp 357/8.
9 Ibid: pp 361 ff.
10 Beshir, *Background to Conflict,* p 81; Deng, *Dynamics,* pp 30–39.
11 Malwal, Bona, *People and Power in the Sudan: the struggle for national stability,* Reading (UK), Ithaca Press, 1981: pp 61 ff; Akol Ruay, Deng D. *The politics of Two Sudans the south and the north: 1821–1969,* Uppsala, The Scandinavian Institute of African Studies, 1994: pp 103/104.
12 Texts of the support declarations of the two Sayyids reproduced in al-A'zami, W, *al-Sudan,* pp 36–38 [Foreign Office Doc. No.FO 371/131712].
13 First, R., *Barrel:* pp 238–239.
14 Haj Musa, Ibrahim, *al-tajruba al-demoqratiyya:* pp 262–265.
15 *thawrat sha'b* (A People's Revolution) Complied by the Communist Party of Sudan, Cairo, Akhbar al-Yum Corp., 1965.
16 Khalid, Mansour, *The Government They Deserve: The Role of the Elite in Sudan's Political Evolution,* London & New York, Kegan Paul Internationa, 1990: pp 199 ff.
17 *Mideast Mirror,* 5 December 1964.
18 First, R., *Barrel:* p 259.
19 Riadh, *mujaz,* pp 108/109; Haj Musa, *al-tajrubah al-demoqratiyya,* p 300; First, R. *Barrel:* pp 262 ff.
20 *Al-Ayam Daily,* No.432332, 27 January 1965.
21 Nugdalla, S., 'The Sudanese Leadership', pp 304/305.

22 *Mideast Mirror*, 27 February 1965.

23 *A Special Supplement to the Republic of Sudan Gazette*, December, 1964.

24 *Mideast Mirror*, 20 February 1964; *al-Rai al-Amm Daily*, No. 6226, 19 February 1965.

25 *Al-Ayam Daily*, No. 4335, 16 February 1965.

26 *Al-Ayam Daily*, No. 4313, 15 January 1965.

27 Alier, *Southern Sudan*: pp 24/25.

28 O'Ballance, Edgar, *The Secret War in the Sudan 1955–1972*, London, Faber & Faber, 1977: p 59; Anya Nya means snake poison in the language of the southern Sudanese tribes of Madi, Moru and Latuka.

29 Malwal, B., *People*: p 77.

30 On Sunday 6th December 1964, southerners, residents of Khartoum, converged on Khartoum Airport to receive Interior Minister Clement Mboro who was scheduoled to return from a tour of the south. When his plane unexpectedly delayed rumours circulated that Mboro and his team had been arrested in the south. In disappointment southerners went on a rampage in the airport and downtown. The response of northern residents was anger and severe retaliation. Seven southerners lost their lives and many were wounded in what has become a wild racial confrontation. See Alier, *Southern Sudan*, p. 27, Malwal, people, pp. 85–87.

31 Alier, *Southern Sudan*: p 27; Malwal, *People*: p 76.

32 Alier, *Southern Sudan*, p 31; Beshir, *Background*, Appendix 16: pp 174–178.

33 Ibid, p 96.

34 Beshir, M.O., The Southern Sudan: *From Conflict to Peace*, London, C. Hurst & Co., 1975: pp. 13–23.

35 Malwal, *People*: p 72.

36 Mekki, H. *harakat al-ikhwan*: pp 67 ff; al-Affendi, *Turabi*.

37 A new programme was issued by the Umma party after the uprising titled: *islah wa tajdid* (Reform and Renovation), Khartoum, 1965.

38 First, R., *Barrel*: p 266.

39 *Elections Commission Report*, 1965.

40 *National Charter of the Coalition*, al-Rai al-Amm Daily; al-Ayam Daily, 25.6.1965.

41 Sulayman, Muhammad, *muzikerat na'ib sudani* (Memoirs of a Sudanese MP), Beirut, Dar al-Thaqafa, 1970: pp 41ff.

42 Transcripts of the Constituent Assembly, Session No. 20, 15 November, 1965.

43 *Transcripts of the Constituent Assembly*, Sessions No. 20–24, and 39, November, December 1965.

44 *Al-Ayam Daily*, No. 4520, 20 November 1965.

45 *Al-Ayam Daily*, No.4523, 23 November 1965.

46 *The Economist*, December 1965.

47 *Al-Ayam Daily*, No. 4529, 29 November, 1965.

48 *Transcripts of the Constituent Assembly*, Session No. 24.

49 Warburg, G., *Islam*; p 117. As quoted in Warburg. The full statement does not make much sense. This is a shortened quotation.

4 THE MAKING OF AN ISLAMIC CONSTITUTION

1 Joseph A. Garang vs. The supreme Commission and Others (Case No.HC/ CS/93/1965), *The Sudan Law Journal and Reports*, 1968, Khartoum, The Judiciary, 1968.

2 *salafiyya* (Arabic) is derived from *salaf* = ancester, and is used to denote the tradition of past generations of Muslims, particularly in matters of jurisprudence and theology. *Neo-salafiyya* are those Islamist movements which adhere to the past and aim at reviving the 'golden age of Islam while utilising modern methods of organisation and politics. Such has been the main contribution of Hasan al-Banna the founder of the Muslim Brotherhood movement.

3 Sharabi, Hisham, 'The Transformation of ideology in the Arab World', *Middle East Journal*, vol.19 (1965), No.4.

4 Mazru'i, 'Ali, 'The Mutiple Marginality of the Sudan'; Abd al-Rahim, Muddathir, 'Arabism, Africanism and Self-Identification in the Sudan', *in* Hasan, Yusuf Fadl (ed.) *Sudan In Africa*, khartoum, KUP, 1971: pp 228–229; and p 240ff.

5 El-Tayeb, Salah al-Din al-Zein, *KUSU*, Khartoum, KUP.

6 The official publication of the ICF *al-mithaq*, devoted a great deal to anti-communist campaign during 1965–67.

7 Haj Hamad, Muhammad Abul Qasim, *al-Sudan: al-ma'zaq al-tarikhi wa 'afaaq al-mustqbal* (The Sudan: Historical Crisis and Future prospects), Beirut, Dar al-Fiker, 1980: pp 240ff.

8 *Constitution of the Communist Party of Sudan*, Khartoum, Dar al-Fiker al-Ishteraki, 1967; CPS, *al-marksiyya*: pp168–170.

9 The 44–man committee was composed of 7 representatives each for Umma, NUP, and PDP, 5 ICF, 9 representatives for the Southern parties and 9 independents. However, the committee was boycotted by PDP, SANU and the Southern Front.

10 *Technical Committee Memorandum*, Khartoum, Government Press, 1968.

11 *Proceedings of the National Committee for the Constitution*, Session No. 9, pamphlet No. 1, Khartoum, Government Press.

12 Haj Musa, Ibrahim, *al-tajruba al-demoqratiyya*: pp 307/309.

13 *Draft Constitution, 1968*, Khartoum, Government Press.

14 *National Committee proceedings*, pamphlet No.8.

15 Ibid: pp 1202–1230, 1231ff.

16 Ibid: p 1245.

17 *Technical Committee Reports*, Khartoum, Government press, 1968.

18 Awad, Ahmad Safyy al-Din, *ma'alim al-dastur al-islami*.

19 Ibid, emphasis added.

20 *Procceedings*, pamphlet No. 1.

21 Mahmud Mauhammad Taha, *usus dastur al-Sudan li-qiyam hakumah jamhuriyya fedraliyya demoqratiyya ishtrakiyya*, Umdurman, 1968. (Basis of a Sudanese Constitution for the establishment of a Federal Republican Democratic Socialist Government), Umdurman, 1968.

22 *Technical Committee Memorandum, Khartoum*, Government Press; Wenin,

Notes

Deng A., Southern *Sudan and the Making of a Permanent Constitution in the Sudan*, Khartoum, University of Juba Publications, 1987.

23 *Akhbar al-Isbou'* Weekly, 1967.
24 Sulayman, M. *Memoirs:* pp 183 ff.
25 The Bourbon dynasty were the monarchs of France who, after being ousted by the French Revolution of 1789, returned to power after the defeat of Napolean I with the same aristocratic arrogance. The quotation here is taken from Mansour Khalid, *Nimeiri*: p 5.
26 A seat came up through the resignation of an Umma MP in the White Nile region, a stronghold of the Umma party.
27 Mahgoub, M.A., *Democracy:* pp 200/201.
28 *Elections' Commission Report* 1968, Haj Musa, I. *al-tajruba al-demoqratiyya*: p 448.
29 Mahgoub, M.A., *Democracy*: p 202.
30 First, R. *Barrel*: p 264.
31 Holt & Daly, *History*: p 194.

5 FROM A POPULIST LEADER TO AN 'IMAM

1 For a more informed outlook in this era, see Khalid, Mansour, *Nimeiri and the Revolution of Dismay*, London, KPI Ltd, 1985.
2 *mithaq al-quwa al-ishterakiyya* (Charter of Socialist Forces), Khartoum, Dar al-Fiker al-ishteraki, 1968.
3 Statement No. 1 by Major-General Ja'far Muhammad Nimeiri, President of the RCC of 25 May 1969, in Conte, Carmelo, *The Sudan as a Nation*, [translated by Richard Hill], Giuffre Editore, 1976: pp 191–199.
4 'Self-Government Regional Act for Southern Provinces', *Democratic Republic of the Sudan* Gazette, Khartoum, March 1972.
5 'Permanent Constitution of the Democratic Republic of the Sudan', *Democratic Republic of the Sudan Gazette*, Khartoum, May, 1973.
6 Ibid.
7 Khalid, M., *Nimeiri*: p 44.
8 *Permanent Constitution.*
9 Holt, P.M. & Daly, M.W.; Mekki, Babiker H., *al-Nimieiri al-imam wa'l rawlate* (Nimeiri: The Imam and Gambler), Cairo, 1987: pp 99 ff.
10 Hamid, M. Beshir, *The Politics of National Reconciliation in the Sudan: The Nimeiri Regime and National Front Opposition*, Washington, Centre for Contemporary Arab Studies, Georgetown University.
11 Khalid, M., *Nimeiri*: pp 12–13.
12 Haj Hamad, Abul Qasim, *al-Sudan*: p 444.
13 Khalid, M., p 71, 202.
14 Ibid, p 77.
15 qouted in Khalid, M., *Nimeiri*: p 61.
16 Ibid, p 84.
17 *Presidential Order No. 236*, 23 May 1977, Khartoum.
18 Interview with Dr. Hasan al-Turabi, Sudanow, Vol. 6 No. 2 February, 1981; Khalid, M., *Al-fajr al-kazib: Nimeiri wa tahrif al-shari'a* (Niemeiri and Falsification of the *shari'a*), Cairo, Dar al-Hilal, 1985: pp 32–36.

19 Elfatih Shaaeldin & Richard Brown, 'Towards an Understanding of Islamic Banking in Sudan: The Case of Faisal Islamic Bank' *in* Barnett, Tony & Abdel Karim, Abbas, *Sudan: State, Capital and Transformation*, London, Croom Helm, 1988: pp 121–140.

20 Nimeiri, J.M. *al-nahjj al-islami limatha?*, Cairo, al-Maktab al-Masri al-Hadith, 1980.

21 Khalid, M., *Nimeiri* pp 259; Mekki, B., *al-rawlate*: pp 64 ff.

22 Taha, Mahmud, M., *Second Message of Islam.*

23 Interview with Sadiq al-Mahdi, *Arabia, The Islamic World Review*, No. 15, November 1982: pp 30–31.

24 Nimeiri, *al-nahjj.*

25 *Sudanow*, Vol. 4, No. 11, November 1979; Abd al-Rahim, Muddathir & Zein al-Abddin, al-Tayeb (ed.) *al-islam fi'l -Sudan* (Islam in the Sudan), Khartoum, Dar al-Fiker, 1987.

26 al-Sadiq al-Mahdi, *Arabia*, 15 November, 1982.

27 al-Sadiq al-Mahdi, *Sudanow*, Vol. 6, No. 4, May 1981.

28 al-Sadiq al-Mahdi, *Arabia*, 15 November, 1982.

29 al-Sadiq al-Mahdi, *'mustaqbal al-islam fi'l-Sudan'*, *in* Abd al-Rahim, M., & Zein al-Abddin, A., al-Islam: pp 426–445.

30 al-Sadiq al-Mahdi, *Sudanow*, Vol. 4, No. 11, November 1979.

31 Al-Turabi, Hasan, *al-'iman: atharhu fi hayat al-insan* (Religious Belief: Its Effect on the Life of the Individual), (no place of publication), Manshurat al-'asr al-Hadith, 1984.

32 Ibid: pp 97, 234/235.

33 Al-Turabi, Hasan, *tajdid al-fiker al-Islami* (Renovation of Islamic Thought), Al-Rabat (Morocco), Dar-al-Qarafi l'l-Nashr wa'l-tawzi', 1993. This volume is an unedited collection of individual pamphlets and lectures by al-Turabi.)

34 Al-Turabi, *tajdid usul al-fiqh al-islami* (Renovation of the Mythodolgy of Islamic Jurisprudence), Khartoum, Dar al-Fiker, 1980: pp 14–15.

35 Ibid: pp 28 ff.

36 al-'Awa, Salim & al-Turabi, Hasan, *min ma'alim al-nizam al-islami* (Some Features of the Islamic System), Khartoum, Jama'at al-Fiker wa'l Da'wa al-Islamiyya, occasional papers No. 1, n.d.

37 Ibid; cf: al-Turabi, Hasan, 'The Islamic State', *in* Esposito, John, *Voices of Resurgent Islam*, Oxford, Oxford University Press, 1983: pp 241–251.

38 al-'Awa & al-Turabi, *ma'alim*: p 49.

39 Ibid: p 56.

40 El-Affendi, Abdel Wahab, *Turabi's Revolution: Islam and Power in Sudan*, London, Grey Seal Books, 1991; Mekki, Hasan, *al-haraka al-islamiyya fi'l-Sudan 1969–1985: tarikha wa khitabha al-siyyasi* (The Islamic Movement in the Sudan), Khartoum, ma'had al-buhuth wal dirasat al-ijtima'iyya, 1990: pp 90/91.

41 Al-Turabi, Hasan, (*al-haraka al-islamiyya fi'l-Sudan* (The Islamic Movement in the Sudan), Cairo, Dar al-Qari' al-'Arabi, 1990: p 195.

42 *Al-Ayam Daily*, 23 March 1979.

43 *Sudanow*, Vol. 8, No. 11, November 1983.

44 Mekki, H., *al-haraka al-islamiyya*, p 82 ff, 128/129.
45 Safwat, Safia M., 'Offences and Penalties in Islamic Law', *Islamic Quarterly*, Vol. 26 (1982): pp 149–181.
46 *Supplements to the Democratic Republic of the Sudan Gazette*, 1983.
47 *Sudanow*, Vol. 8, No.11 November 1983.
48 There are differences regarding the number and categories of *hudud* offences. See Safwat, Safia, 'Offences and Penalties'.
49 *Penal Code, 1983*; Amin, S.H., Middle East Legal Systems, Glasgow, Royston Ltd, 1985 (The Legal System of the Sudan): pp 328–351.
50 Chief Justice Dafa'alla al-Hajj Yusuf, *Sudanow*, Vol. 8, No. 11 November 1983.
51 See for example:
   – Khalid, M., al-Fajr al-kazib;
   – Gordon, Carey N. 'The Islamic Legal Revolution: The Case of Sudan', *The International Lawyer*, Vol. 19, No. 3 (1985): pp 793–815;
   – Fluer-Lobban, Carplyn, 'Islamization in Sudan: A Critical Asessment' *in* Voll, J. *Sudan: A State and Society in Crisis*, Washington, 1990;
   – Safwat, Safia, 'Human Rights Violations in Sudan', n.pl., Amensty Sudan, n.d.
52 *Sudanow*, Vol. 8, No.11, November, 1983.
53 This is '*qanun usul al-ahkam al-qada'iyya*' (The Judgement Law, 1984).
54 Khalid, *Nimeiri*: pp 257–258.
55 For the resumption of conflict see: Prunier, Gerard, 'From Peace to War in Southern Sudan: 1972–1984', Hull, University of Hull, Department of Sociology and Social Anthropology, occasional papers, No. 3, 1986.
56 Holt, P.M. & Daly, M.W.: p 212.
57 Khalid, M., *Nimeiri*: pp 243 ff.
58 Khalid, M., *al-fajr al-kazib*: pp 84–86.
59 For details of these cases see al-Kabbashi, al-Mukashfi Taha, *tatbiq al-shari'a al-islamiyya bayn al-haqiqa wa'l ithara* (Application of the Islamic shari'a between Fact and Fiction), Cairo, Dar al-Zahra', 1986. The author headed the court of Appeal which confirmed the execution verdict of Mahmud M.Taha.
60 The text of *bay'ah* is as follows:

> I swear allegiance to obey you in easy and difficult matters, save what God hath forbidden; I solemnly swear to render counsel to you and to struggle in God's name under your leadership; I swear allegiance to you to uphold the faith, follow the *shura* and justice and work for the interests of the Umma; I pay allegiance to you as God is my witness.

61 Text of Memorandum by Abel Alier and Joseph Lagu, 1984 reproduced in Mekki, Babiker H., *Nimeiri al-imam*.
62 Khalid, M., *Nimeiri*: pp 275 ff.
63 Al-Sadiq al-Mahdi, *al-'uqubat al-shar'iyya wa mawqi'ha min al-nizam al-ijtima'i al-islami* (shari'a Penalties and its Position in the Islamic Social System), Cairo, Dar al-Zahara', 1987.
64 *Sudanow*, Vol. 5, No. 2 February 1980.
65 *Sudanow*, Vol. 8, No. 11 November 1983.

66 Mekki, Hasan, *al-haraka al-islamiyya*, pp 106/107; Mekki, Babiker, *al-rawlate*: p 126.
67 Khalid, M., *al-fajr al-kazib*: pp 378 ff.

6 THE POST-NIMEIRI SUDAN

1 By the end of Nimeiri's period Sudan's accumulated arrears to the IMF alone amounted to about US$130–150 million. Its total foreign debts stood at about US$ 13bn.
2 On the IMF's stabilisation programme see: Barnett, Tony & Abd al-Karim, Abbas, *Sudan: State, Capital and Transformation*, London, Croom Helm, 1988.
3 El-Ghonemy, M. Riad, *Land, Food and Rural Development in North Africa*, Boulder, Westview Press, 1993: pp 104 ff; Hulme, Mike & Trisbach 'Rainfall Trends and Rural Changes in Sudan since Nimeiri: Some thoughts on the relationship between environmental and political control' *in* Woodward, P., *Sudan after Nimeiri*, London & New York, Routledge, 1991: pp 1–17.
4 *BBC Summary of World Broadcasts (Middle East and Africa)* ME/7919/A-ME/7922A, 6–11 April 1985 (hereafter BBC SWB).
5 The intention of the *Intifada* forces was to deny the NIF the right of political activity on grounds of the *ikhwan*'s collaboration with Nimeiri. The TMC, however, affirmed that 'the question of excluding certain political parties which had cooperated with the former regime was ruled out', Suwar al-Dhahab in a press conference (Khartoum), 15 April 1985, *BBC ME/7928/A/i*.
6 El-Affendi, Abdel Wahab, *Turabi's Revolution*: p 138.
7 *Intifada Charter*, Khartoum, 6 April 1985.
8 It was later revealed that Juzuli Dafa'alla, the Prime Minister, and Husayn Abu Salih, minister of health, were both connected with the *Ikhwan*; Suwar al-Dhahab himself had a relationship with the *Ikhwan* in the 1950s. Both the prime minister and TMC chairman were given jobs in *Ikhwan*-run relief organisations after the transitional period.
9 Elections Commission Report, 1986.
10 *Economist Country Reports*, Sudan, Economist Intelligence Unit, London, No. 1, 1987, p. 4.
11 Al-Mahdi in a statement to Radio Juba (Sudan), 11 May 1986.
12 Text of Sudanese Peace Initiative *BBC SWB ME/0314 A/5,6* 21 November 1988; cf: Muhammad al-Hasan, Muhammad Sa'id, *al-salam al-mumkin wa al-mutahil: waqai' akhtar mubadarah sudaniyya* (The possible and impossible peace) being a documentary of the Sudanese peace initiative, n.pl., n.pub., n.d.
13 *BBC SWB ME/0345 i* 29 December 1988.
14 Text of Amed Forces Memorandum, *BBC SWB ME/0396 A/6,7,8*, 28 February 1989.
15 Press statements by NIF leader Hasan al-Turabi, *BBC SWB ME/0403 A/8*, 8 March 1989.
16 *BBC SWB ME/0401 i – A/7,8* 6 March 1989.

17 The Rural Forces Solidarity Movement appeared during the elections of 1986 from the regional organisations of the Beja Congress, the Nuba Mountains Union (which became the Sudan National Party), and Darfur Development Front. Of these groups only the Sudan national party succeeded in returning candidates to the Constituent Assembly.

18 A series of agreements has been signed between USAP and SPLA/M in Addis Ababa, Kampala, and Nairobi during 1987. See: Ahmad, Abdel Ghaffar M. & Sorbo, Gunnar M., *Management of the Crisis in the Sudan: Proceedings of the Bergen Forum 23-24 February 1989*, Bergen, Centre of Development Studies, University of Bergen, 1989: Annexes 4,5,6: pp 145–150.

19 Alier, A., *Southern Sudan*: pp 240 ff; Johnson, D.H. & Prunier, Gerard, 'The Foundation and Expansion of the Sudan people's Liberation Army', *in* Daly, M.W. & Sikainga, A.A. *The Civil War in the Sudan*, London and New York, 1993: pp 117–141.

20 Johnson, D. and Prunier, G., 'Foundation'.

21 Garang, John, *The Call for Democracy in Sudan*, edited with an introduction by Mansour Khalid, London, KPI, 1992.

22 De Wal, Alex, *War in Sudan: An analysis of a conflict*, London, Peace in Sudan Group, 1990.

23 Ibid: p 20.

24 Ibid:p 19; Alier, A., *Southern Sudan*: p 283.

25 De Wal, Alex, 'On Militias' *in* Daly & Sikainga, *The Civil War*: pp 142 ff.

26 Alier, A., *Southern Sudan*: pp 284/5.

27 BBC SWB ME/8064/A/10 24 September 1985.

28 For texts of various agreements see: Ahmad, A. & Sorbo, G. *Management of the Crisis*, Annexes.

29 Ibid: pp 130–132.

30 Ibid: pp 169–170.

31 Alier, A., *Southern Sudan*: p 273; Garang, J., *Democracy*: pp 77–84.

32 SPLM/SPLA Deparment of Information, 'On the New Sudan', *in* Ahmad, A. & Sorbo, G., *Management of the Crisis*: pp 83–90.

33 The National Islamic Front: 'The Sudan Charter' *in* Ibid: pp 133–144; emphasis added.

34 Article 5 of the Universal Declaration of Human Rights states: 'No one shall be subjected to torture or to cruel, inhuman or degrading treatment or punishment.' This principle is reflected in article 29 of Sudan's Transitional Constitution, 1985 which provided for the protection of the accused persons from torture and cruel, inhuman or degrading punishment. Whereas article 18 of Sudan's Transitional Constitution states: 'All persons shall enjoy the freedom of belief and the right to practise religious rites within the limits of morality public order and health as may be required by law.' See also Kok, Peter N. 'Conflict over the laws in the Sudan from Pluralism to Monolithism' *in* Bleuchot, H., Delmot, C. & Hopwood, D., *Sudan, History, Identity and Ideology*, Reading, Ithaca Press.

35 *BBC SWB ME/8136/A/6*, 17 December 1985.

36 Alier, A., *Southern Sudan*: pp 273/4.

37 al-Sadiq al-Mahdi, *al-dimoqratiyya fi'l-Sudan 'aidah wa rajihah* (Democracy in Sudan will Return and prevail), n.pl., edited and published by the Umma Party, n.d.: pp 102–104.

38 The Criminal Bill, 1988; Kok, Peter, 'Conflict'.
39 al-Sadiq al-Mahdi, *al-'uqubat al-shar'iyya wa mawqi'ha min al-nizam al-ijtima'i al-Islami* (Islamic penalties and its position in Islamic social system), al-Zahra', Cairo, 1987, pp 177 ff.
40 El-Affendi, A. *Turabi's Revolution*: p 164.
41 CPS, *al-mu'tamar al-dasturi* (On the Constitutional Conference), Khartoum, Dar al-Wasila, 1988.
42 Neither did the founding SPLA/M manifesto tackle the issue of democracy, nor did its entire discourse during the period in question seem to endorse the system of parliamentary democracy.

7 PAXA ISLAMICA

1 Republic of the Sudan Gazette, Khartoum, Attorney General's Chamber, n.d; BBC, SWB ME/0497/A/1,1 July 1989.
2 Constitutional Decree No. 13 which was said to effect the transition from 'revolutionary to constitutional legitimacy', has nevertheless preserved the Constitutional Decree No. 2 with its state of emergency and categorical ban on freedoms of expressions and organisation.
3 *'al-Sudan wa thawrat al-inqaz'*, A special issue of *Qadaiyya Dwaliyya* (political Weekly Report), Vol. 4, No. 187, 2 August 1993.
4 BBC SWB ME/ 0499/A/1,2, 4 July 1989.
5 El-Affendi, A. *Turabi's Revolution*, Mekki, H. *harakat al-ikhwan*.
6 Mekki, H. *al-haraka al-islamiyya*: pp 55–73, and pp 230 ff.
7 The numbers of pupils at primary schools increased from 800,000 in 1969/70, to 1,207,661 in 1976/77 to 1,332,015 in 1981/82; while the numbers of pupils at intermediate schools increased from 147,427 in 1976/77, to 261,343 in 1981/82. See *Sudan Yearbook 1983*, Khartoum, Sudanow, 1983: pp 33–34.
8 Act No. 84, 1971, *Democratic Republic of the Sudan Gazette*.
9 Mahmud, Abd al-Rahim al-Rayah, 'The Machinery of Economic Management', *in* Abdel Rahim, M., Badal, R., Hardlo, A., & Woodward, P., *Sudan Since Independence: Studies of the Political Development since 1956*, London, Gower, 1986: pp. 96–107.
10 For a critical assessment of Nimeiri's economic policies, see for example: Brown, Richard, *Public Debt and Private Wealth*, London, Macmillan, 1992; Gurdon, Charles, *Sudan at the Crossroads*, Middle East and North African Press Ltd, 1984.
11 In 1956, Khartoum received a net of inflow of 58,000 migrants; this figure became 192,000 in 1973 and reached 511,000 in 1983. See Abdalla, El-Tom Hassan 'Migration in Sudan'; and Omar El Tay & Sultan Hashmi 'A Quarter Century of Population Change in the Sudan' *both in* Ertur, Omar S & House William J., *Population and Human Resources Development in the Sudan*, Iowa, Iowa State University Press, 1994: pp 126–139 & 35–47 respectively.
12 Galal al-Din, Mohamed el-Awad, 'Sudanese Migration to the Oil Producing Arab Countries', in O'Neill, N & O'Brien, J. (ed), *Economy*

and Class in Sudan, London, 1988: pp 291–305; Brown, Richard, Public Debt and Private Wealth, London, Macmillan, 1992: p 211.

13 Choucri, Nazli, 'The Hidden Economy: A New View of Remittances in the Arab World', *in World Development,* Vol. 14, No.6, Washington, DC, 1986: pp 697–712.

14 Ibid.

15 Gurdon, Charles, *Sudan at the Cross Roads*: pp 56 ff.

16 Choucri, N. 'The Hidden Economy'.

17 Brown, R., *Public Debt*: pp 211 ff.

18 Ibid.

19 The phenomena is, of course, common in Africa as a whole. A World Bank Report published in 1989 warned that rural Africa is disappearing: 'In 30 years, at the current urbanisation rates, most Africans will be living in massive urban slums. Governments will find it increasingly difficult to feed, clothe and shelter these people, let alone find work and provide social care for them.', *South,* February 1989: pp 22–27 (contains highlights of the report).

20 Russell, Sharon S., 'Remittances from International Migration: A Review in Perspective', *in World Development,* Vol. 14, No. 6: pp 677–696.

21 The movement drafted and adopted a new constitution in 1982, Mekki,H., *al-haraka al-islamiyya*: pp 120–123 and 369 (the text of the constitution).

22 Ibid: pp 123 ff.

23 El-Affendi, A. *Turabi's Revolution*: pp 113 ff.

24 Taha, Hayder, *al-Ikhwan wa'l-'asker: qisat al-jabha al-islamiyya wa'l sulta fi'l-Sudan,* (Muslim Brothers and the Military: The Story of the NIF and Power in the Sudan), Cairo, Markaz al-hadhara al-'Arabiyya, 1993: p 74.

25 El-Affendi, A. *Turabi's Revolution*: pp 136 ff.

26 Bannerman, Patrick, ·*Islam in Perspective: A guide to Islamic society, Politics and Law,* London, Routledge for the Royal Institute of International Affairs, 1988: pp 168–169.

27 Al-Turabi, H., *risala fi al-mar'ah* (A Thesis on Woman), n.p, n.publ., n.d.

28 Report of 1986 Elections.

29 Mekki, H., *al-haraka al-islamiyya*, p 130.

30 Shaaeldin, E. & Brown, R. 'Faisal Islamic Bank'; Gurdon, R. *Sudan at the Crossroads*: pp 69 ff.

31 Ayubi, Nazih N. *Political Islam: Religion and Politics in the Arab World,* London, Routledge, 1991.

32 See Amin, S H., *Islamic Law: Introduction, Glossary and Bibliography,* Glssgow, Royston, 1984: section on Islamic Banking and Finance.

33 El-Affendi, A., *Turabi's Revolution,* pp 117–118.

34 Mahmud, Abd al-Rahim, A. 'Machinery of Economic Management': pp 96 ff.

35 Ibid: pp 104–105.

36 Taha, Hayder, *al-ikhwan wa'l-'asker*: pp 62, 74, 130.

37 On the Special Organisation, see Mekki, Hasan, *al-haraka al-islamiyya*: p117; Taha, H.*al-ikhwan wa'l-'asker*: p 274.

38 For a critique of the NIF's discourse see Ali, Hayder Ibrahim, *azmat al-*

islam al-siyyassi: al-jabha al-islamiyya al-qawmiyya fi'l-Sudan namuzajan (Crisis of Political Islam: National Islamic Front in the Sudan as a model), Casablanka, Sudanese Studies Centre, 1991 (2nd edn): pp 143 ff.

39 Mekki, Hasan, *harakat al-Ikhwan*: pp 100–108.
40 El-Affendi, *Turabi's Revolution*: p 166.
41 Mekki, Hasan, *al-haraka al-islamiyya*: pp 125/126.
42 Mekki, Hasan, *al-haraka al-islamiyya*: pp 138–149; al-Turabi, H. *al-haraka al-islamiyya*: pp 171–176.
43 See for example al-Turabi, H., *tajdid al-fiker al-islami*: p 11; *al-haraka al-islamiyya*: pp 212 ff; see also Ali, Hayder I. *azmat al-islam al-siyassi*, for a discussion of this theme.
44 An example of this is his project of an 'Islamic state' *in* Esposito, John L. (edn), *Voices of Resurgent Islam*, Oxford & New York, Oxford University Press, 1983: pp. 241–251.
45 NIF media during the parliamentary period; cf Warburg, G. 'Islamism and Mahdism in the Sudan', *International Journal of Middle Eastern Studies*, vol 27, No 2 (1995) pp 219–136.
46 For example in 1987 the NIF staged anti-governement demonstrations in protest of a deal with the IMF which implied austerity measures.
47 One of the famous slogans of the Islamist regime in 1990/91 was self reliance 'we eat from our harvest, dress from our manufacture'.
48 *Republic of the Sudan Gazette*, March 1991, An English Translation is published in the Arab Law Quarterly, Vol. 9, Part 1, 1994: pp 32–80.
49 Criminal Act, Chapter Two, Ibid: p 35.
50 Ibid.
51 President Umar al-Basher in an interview to *Qadaya Dawliyya*, Vol. 4, No. 187: pp 39.
52 Uthman, 'Abd al-Rahman A., *'al-mashru' al-islami fi'l-Sudan: juzurahu, tatwurahu, wa 'aqbatahu*' (The Islamic Project in the Sudan: Its Roots, Development and Obstacles) *in* Ibid: pp 10–12.
53 Quoted in *al-Ray Alakher*, Vol. 2, No. 4, January 1996.
54 Mitchison, Amanda, 'All the Conspirators?', *The Independent Magazine*, 9 October 1993: p 31.

Index